Globalization in Southeast Asia

Asian Anthropologies
General Editors:
Shinji YAMASHITA, The University of Tokyo,
and
J.S. EADES, Ritsumeikan Asia Pacific University

GLOBALIZATION IN SOUTHEAST ASIA

LOCAL, NATIONAL AND TRANSNATIONAL PERSPECTIVES

Edited by

Shinji YAMASHITA

and

J.S. EADES

Berghahn Books
New York • Oxford

First published in 2003 by
Berghahn Books
www.berghahnbooks.com
© 2003 Shinji Yamashita and J.S. Eades

Library of Congress Cataloging-in-Publication Data

Globalization in Southeast Asia: local, national and transnational perspectives
/ Edited by Shinji Yamashita and J.S. Eades
p. cm. -- (Asian Anthropologies)
Includes bibliographical references and index.
ISBN 1-57181-255-5 (cl. : alk. paper) -- ISBN 1-57181-256-3 (pb. : alk. paper)
1. Asia, Southeastern -- Civilization. 2. Globalization -- Asia, Southeastern. I.Yamashita, Shinji.
II. Eades, J.S. (Jeremy Seymour), 1945- III. Series.

DS523.2.G56 2001
959--dc21   2001037816

British Library Cataloguing in Publication Data
A catalogue record for this book is available from the British Library

Contents

Preface

This is the first volume in a series devoted to making available some of the best of the anthropological research being carried out by scholars based in Asia to the wider international scholarly community. As such, it represents one of a series of initiatives over the last decade by Asian scholars to develop links within Asia and channels for sharing the results of their research. Others in which we ourselves have been involved include the launching by the Japanese Society of Ethnology of an English language journal, the *Japanese Review of Cultural Anthropology*, growing links between the Japanese Society of Ethnology and other anthropological associations, a series of panels organized by Asian scholars at the annual meetings of the American Anthropology Association, and a number of workshops and symposia within Asia itself supported by the Japanese Ministry of Education, Science, and Technology (Monbukagakushô) and major research foundations. Asian scholars were also well represented at the International Congress of Anthropological and Ethological Sciences held at Williamsburg, Virginia, in the summer of 1998, and it was there that the original idea for this series arose over a lunch with Marion Berghahn. The third volume in the series will consist of a survey of the development of anthropology in Asia, arising out of two of the Williamsburg sessions chaired by Shinji Yamashita and Joseph Bosco.

The roots of this particular book lie in an earlier research project entitled "The Dynamics of Ethnic Culture in Insular Southeast Asia: The Interplay of Local, National and Global Perspectives," organized by Shinji Yamashita from 1994 to 1996, and a Japan-Southeast Forum organized at the International House of Japan with the support of the Toyota Foundation, which provided an open platform for the exchange of ideas between Japan and Southeast Asia. These in turn gave rise to a Japan-Southeast Asia workshop held in Tokyo in the autumn of 1996, which discussed the dynamism of local and national culture in Southeast Asia, and globalization and culture in Southeast Asia today. The authors represented here were participants in that workshop, with the exception of Eades whose paper on Taiwan arose out of his presentation at Williamsburg.

The themes dealt with in this volume, the local, regional and national impact of the forces of globalization, are among the most important problems currently being explored by Asian anthropologists, against the background of high-speed economic growth followed by economic crisis and growing opposition to the process of globalization. For this reason, the papers presented here provide an overview of, and introduction to, many of the major issues to be dealt with in later volumes in the series.

We would like to thank the Japanese Ministry of Education, the Toyota Foundation, and Tatsuya Tanami, formerly of the International House of Japan, and his staff for helping to make these earlier initiatives possible. We would also like to thank Marion Berghahn for agreeing to publish the series as a whole, and Vivian Berghahn for guiding this first volume through the press.

Shinji Yamashita and Jerry Eades

July 2002

A Note on Names and Transliteration

Name order is a recurring problem in expressing the names of Asian scholars in English. In Japan and China the normal order is family name first, followed by personal name(s), though this is often reversed in Western publications. For the names of authors in this book we have followed the authors' preferred order when writing in English. Family names have been indicated with small capitals in the table of contents, chapter headings and headers to make this clear.

In the main text, the Japanese name order has been retained, with the exception of names of writers, where the Western order is used.

In Thailand, the usual order of bibliographical entries is by authors in alphabetical order, arranged by the first rather than the family name. This convention has been followed where appropriate here.

In the text and bibliographies, words in standard Japanese have been transliterated using the Hepburn system, with circumflexes used to denote long "o" and "u," except in the case of personal names and common place names such as "Tokyo." Translations of titles of important Japanese sources have also been added.

Contributors

Bachtiar ALAM, Director, Center for Japanese Studies, University of Indonesia, Kampus UI Depok, Indonesia.

Eriko AOKI, Faculty of Sociology, Ryukoku University, Otsu 520, Japan.

J.S. EADES, Ritsumeikan Asia Pacific University, 1-1 Jumonjibaru, Beppu, Oita 874, Japan.

Shota FUKUOKA, National Museum of Ethnology. 10-1 Senri Expo Park, Suita, Osaka 565, Japan.

Anan GANJANAPAN, Department of Sociology and Anthropology, Faculty of Social Science, Chiang Mai University, Chiang Mai 50200, Thailand.

Wayan I GERIYA, Juruan Antropologi, Fakultas Satra, Universitas Udayana, Jl. Nias No. 13, Denpasar, Bali, Indonesia.

Haruya KAGAMI, Kanazawa University, Kakuma-machi, Kanazawa, Ishikawa 920, Japan.

LIAN Kwen Fee, Department of Sociology, National University of Singapore Kent Ridge, Singapore 0511.

Teruo SEKIMOTO, Institute of Oriental Culture, The University of Tokyo, 7-3-1 Hongo, Bunkyo-ku, Tokyo 113, Japan.

Hiromu SHIMIZU, Dept. of Cultural Anthroplogy, Kyushu University, 4-2-1 Ropponmatsu, Chuo-ku, Fukuoka 810, Japan.

Ikuya TOKORO, Research Institute of Languages and Cultures of Asia and Africa (ILCAA), Tokyo University of Foreign Studies, 4-51-21 Nishigahara, Kita-ku, Tokyo 114, Japan.

TONG Chee Kiong, Department of Sociology, National University of Singapore, Kent Ridge, Singapore 0511.

Shinji YAMASHITA, Department of Cultural Anthropology, The University of Tokyo, 3-8-1 Komaba, Meguro-ku, Tokyo 153, Japan.

Fernando N. ZIALCITA, Department of Sociology and Anthropology, Ateneo de Manila University, P.O.Box 154, 1099 Manila, Philippines.

Chapter 1

Introduction: "Glocalizing" Southeast Asia

Shinji YAMASHITA

Southeast Asia in Motion

Until the onset of the financial crisis at the end of 1997, the Southeast Asian countries had experienced several years of critical change due to rapid economic growth. In Indonesia during the three decades from 1961 to 1990, for instance, the agricultural sector of the work force decreased from 71.9 percent to 55.9 percent in numerical terms, and from 52.2 percent to 19.6 percent in terms of Gross Domestic Product, while the urban population increased from 14.8 percent to 30.9 percent of the total population. In 1991 the industrial sector (19.9 percent) overtook the agricultural sector (18.5 percent) in terms of GDP. Indonesia was therefore transforming itself from an agrarian to an industrial society. As an example of this new industrial strength, on the occasion of the celebration of the fiftieth anniversary of Indonesian independence, in August 1995, a new Indonesian-made aircraft called the N250 was officially announced by B.Y. Habibie, at that time Minister of Science and Technology, and was displayed to the media and the public.

The Indonesian case was only one example of rapid development in Southeast Asia. Malaysia, Singapore and Thailand developed even faster, helping make the Southeast Asian region one of the most rapidly developing and industrializing areas of the world during the 1990s. In the latter half of 1997, beginning with a serious currency crisis, this economic growth came to a sudden halt. Some countries of the region were hit worse than others, and were able to recover relatively quickly, though Indonesia itself remained dogged by political and economic problems. But what the crisis showed, paradoxically, was just how strongly Southeast Asia had become connected with the rest of the contemporary world system.

1

Despite the boom-and-bust cycles of the capitalist world economy, the Southeast Asian countries during recent decades have generally experienced massive inflows of goods, money, information and people. Metropolitan centers such as Manila, Jakarta, Singapore, Kuala Lumpur and Bangkok were flooded with imports from elsewhere in the global economy, with people busily coming and going between the newly constructed skyscrapers. As Richard Robison and David Goodman (1996: 1) have neatly described it, we have now become familiar with "images of frustrated commuters in Bangkok and Hong Kong traffic jams, Chinese and Indonesian capitalist entrepreneurs signing deals with Western companies; white-coated Malaysian or Taiwanese computer programmers and other technical experts at work in electronics plants; and, above all, crowds of Asian consumers at McDonalds or with the ubiquitous mobile phone in hand." These new images of Southeast Asia remain in spite of the 1997 crisis, for Southeast Asia cannot revert to its position before the economic takeoff.

Furthermore, thanks to parabolic antennas, television programs from around the world are now enjoyed not only in the big cities of Southeast Asia but also in remote villages such as those in the Tana Toraja region of the Sulawesi Highlands with which I have been familiar for more than twenty years. When asked his opinion on whether the tourism introduced to Tana Toraja in the early 1970s had been a major agent of cultural change, a Toraja man answered, "tourism is not important in our lives – we see the world on television every night" (Smith 1989: 9).

The people themselves also move, not only from villages to cities within national boundaries but also across national boundaries. In 1995 I was surprised to find a great number of Toraja migrant workers living in Tawau, a town located on the border between Sabah, Malaysia and East Kalimantan, Indonesia. In terms of mobility, the Filipino people are perhaps the most active in the region: over four million of them, or approximately 7 percent of the national population, are abroad, whether in Japan, Hong Kong, the Pacific region, the Middle East, or the United States. In Japan, *Japayuki* migrants from the Philippines, many of them women working in the entertainment sector, became a conspicuous phenomenon in the 1980s.

In 1991 Kuwahara noted that there were between twenty-five and thirty million guest workers and eighteen million refugees worldwide (Kuwahara 1991: 15–16). In 1995, there were over five hundred million international travelers worldwide, of which approximately one tenth, or fifty million, were guest workers or refugees. By 2000, these figures had risen to 750 million and seventy-five million respectively. Within this context of global migration, Asians – not only the Overseas Chinese, of whom there are about twenty million, but also the Southeast Asians – are now emerging as among the most active migrants in the contemporary world. It has become part of everyday reality for contemporary Asians to leave their places of origin for urban centers, or to move on further across national boundaries in order to be able to pursue better lives. Southeast Asia is thus in a new age of motion, and this trend may even be accelerated by economic crises such as the recent one, as could be seen for instance in the increasing number of illegal Indonesian migrants in Malaysia after the collapse of the Indonesian rupiah.

The Transnational Anthropology of Southeast Asia

In a related development in anthropological theory, Arjun Appadurai has described the global movement of people using the concept of "global ethnoscape." He writes that "the landscape of persons who make up shifting worlds in which we live: tourists, immigrants, refugees, exiles, guest-workers, and other moving groups and persons constitute an essential feature of the world and appear to affect the politics of and between nations to a hitherto unprecedented degree" (Appadurai 1991: 192).

The "global ethnoscape" is one of five dimensions of the "global cultural flow." Appadurai argues that the new global cultural economy has to be understood as a complex, overlapping, disjunctive order. It cannot any longer be understood in terms of existing center-periphery models, or simple models of push and pull, surpluses and deficits, or consumers and producers. Within this "global cultural flow" he looks at the relationship between five separate dimensions which he calls (a) ethnoscapes, (b) mediascapes, (c) technoscapes, (d) financescapes, and (e) ideoscapes (Appadurai 1990: 296).

If we accept Appadurai's observations on contemporary people and culture in motion, then it is not possible to maintain the conventional aim of ethnography which is "to record coherent, patterned cultural worlds enclosed within discrete territories, languages, and customs" (Rosaldo 1989: 201). In other words, within the landscape of the global cultural flow, it is apparently no longer possible to study culture as a discrete closed system. In my previous work (Yamashita 1988), I suggested the need for a "dynamic ethnography" to examine the cultural dynamism of the Toraja people of Sulawesi in relation to the Indonesian nation-state. However, if we consider that a great number of the Toraja people are now guest workers in Sabah, Malaysia, we have to widen the scope of "dynamic ethnography" to include observation of transnational human and cultural movements.

We therefore need, as Appadurai has proposed, a "macroethnography" or "transnational anthropology" which can respond to the transnational age (Appadurai 1991: 197). In macroethnography, culture does not constitute either a coherent or a homogeneous system as the classic functionalist eth-

3

nographers assumed. Instead, we have to see culture as a "global ecumene" within which people, goods and information all flow (cf. Hannerz 1992: 217–67).

It is this kind of cultural dynamism that this book attempts to examine, focusing on Southeast Asia. In doing so, we hope to shed new light both on the interface between new and traditional cultures in the region, and to contribute to a new anthropological theory of culture in an age of globalization.

Globalization and Two Conceptions of Culture

Like other popular catchwords, the meaning of the term "globalization" is vague and elusive. I follow Roland Robertson (1992: 8) who defines it as a "compression of the world" due to increased global (international/interregional) interdependence. Since the mid-1980s, the term has been used to describe current ongoing changes in this direction, even though, according to Robertson, the origins of these processes can be traced back a long way, to a period even before the modern expansion of Europe.

So far there have been many discussions of the phenomena of globalization in the fields of economics and politics, but rather fewer examinations of the outcomes of globalization in the field of culture. Taking cases from the Southeast Asian region, this book investigates these ongoing cultural processes in relation to economic and political globalization. As agents of cultural production, national, ethnic, or subregional communities have long been the most important factors in cultural change. They are, however, no longer the same entities that they were. As the boundaries of those communities have become more fluid owing to the process of globalization, the cultural homogeneity within each community has been called into question. Cultural identities are being contested everywhere, as multinational agencies, states and governments, different social classes, and groups based on gender, ethnicity and locality attempt to redefine and assert new cultural forms. As a result, the voices we are hearing are increasingly culturally diverse.

The rise of new lifestyles among the urban middle classes is a particularly striking feature of Southeast Asia today. Young, well-educated middle-class city dwellers, who only a few decades ago firmly believed that they belonged to national and local communities, now perceive that they may have more in common with the middle classes in the older industrialized countries than with their own fellow countrymen on the periphery. This gives rise to a number of questions: Is global culture prevailing over local and national cultures? What is going on on the peripheries of states? What are the roles of nation-states in these changing circumstances? And what other cultural agencies are gaining in importance?

It is helpful in this regard to consider the distinction between the concepts of "territorial culture" and "translocal culture" proposed by the Dutch sociologist, Jan Nederveen Pieterse (1995). "Territorial culture" refers to situations where culture is seen as being essentially territorially based and is assumed to stem from a learning process that is localized. The implication is that cultures can be distinguished from each other, such as a Japanese culture, a Balinese culture, or whatever. This notion goes back to the nineteenth-century German romanticism of J. D. Herder, but it was later elaborated in twentieth-century anthropology, particularly in relation to cultural relativism, through the work of Franz Boas, the German scholar who became a founding father of American anthropology. "Translocal culture," on the other hand, refers to culture as a general form of human behavioral "software" which is acquired during a translocal learning process. This notion of culture has been implicit in theories of evolution and diffusion through translocal learning.

In the present era of globalization we observe that translocal phenomena have been developing in almost every dimension of our lives and have resulted in the "creolization" or "hybridization" of culture. Pieterse mentions examples of the "global mélange" such as Thai boxing by Moroccan girls in Amsterdam, Asian rap music in London, and a Shakespeare play performed in Japanese kabuki style for a Paris audience at the Theatre Soleil. Less conspicuous expressions of the "global mélange" can be observed everywhere in our lives today: Japanese wear shirts made in China, eat shrimp imported from Indonesia, and live in houses built in a mixture of Japanese and Western styles. American children play Nintendo games, London businessmen listen to Sony Walkman tape and disc players, and Indonesian children watch Doraemon on television.

During my stay in Jakarta in 1994 I was very much impressed by the sight of Indonesian children reading Japanese comics in Indonesian translation at bookstores, from Doraemon to Dragon Ball Z, and from Candy-Candy to Sailor-Moon (cf. Shiraishi 1997). These characters appear on television as well. A Javanese newspaper reported that Javanese children today are crazy about Doraemon and Ksatria Baja Hitam ("Iron Soldier"), but are not interested in the *wayang* puppet theater (Sekimoto 1995). Even in *ketoprak*, a form of Javanese popular theater, Ksatria Baja Hitam appears instead of Javanese princes. These foreign-made programs, therefore, can have a great influence on children who come from a different cultural background.

We can observe examples of translocal culture in Southeast Asia today just as we can anywhere else in the contemporary world. However, it must be noted, as Pieterse points out, that translocal culture cannot exist without a place – indeed, there is no culture without place. Culture has to be localized. Therefore, just as Japanese baseball, which is American in origin, has become "Japanese" for the Japanese, Nintendo games have become "American" for American children, and Doraemon has become "Indonesian" for children in Indonesia. It is therefore one of the basic tasks of contemporary anthropology to study such processes as the translocalization and relocalization of culture within the global cultural flows.

"Glocalization"

It is useful to refer to the notion of "glocalization" discussed by Roland Robertson (1995). The word is a combination of "globalization" and "localization" which appeared in the 1991 edition of the Oxford *Dictionary to New Words* (Tulloch 1991). Here the term "glocal" and the related processual noun "glocalization" are defined as being "formed by telescoping global and local to make a blend." According to the dictionary, the notion is modeled on the Japanese concept of *dochakuka*, "becoming autochthonous," derived from *dochaku*, meaning "aboriginal," or "living on one's own land." This was originally used to refer to the agricultural principle of adapting one's farming techniques to local conditions, but it was also adopted in Japanese business as a term to refer to "global localization," which means a global outlook adapted to local conditions.

The thinking behind the word "glocalization" is quite interesting, because it presupposes not the opposition of globalization and localization but their simultaneous occurrence. In this perspective, globalization is not a unidirectional homogenizing process, but a dual process of hybridization. Conversely, localization is viewed as a process which is caused by globalization. Likewise, but from a slightly different angle, Marshall Sahlins has discussed the "indigenization of modernity." He writes: "the very ways societies change have their own authenticities, so that global modernity is often reproduced as local diversity" (Sahlins 1994: 377).

Let me cite examples of glocalization in Southeast Asia. The first example is taken from contemporary Indonesian music: *dangdut*. This is a form of Indonesian popular music developed by Rhoma Irama ("the king of *dangdut*") who established it as a distinct musical style by the mid-1970s (Frederic 1982). It is a hybrid of Malay, Indian and Western popular music. At first it had low status as a musical genre, but it has since developed into a form of Indonesian national music, and it plays an important role at Indonesian national ceremonies, as was seen on the occasion of the 1995 celebration of the fiftieth anniversary of Indonesian independence.

The second example is taken also from Indonesia, and is that of Bali in the 1930s. Following Robertson, globalization is not necessarily a recent phenomenon of the "postmodern" era, but may go back to an earlier period of modern history. In this sense colonialism was also a form of globalization. As I have discussed in detail elsewhere (Yamashita 1995, 1999), Balinese art forms which are now famous, such as the *kecak*, *kris* (sword), or *barong* (lion) dances, were "invented" during the colonial period under the influence of Western artists, scholars and tourists. A major figure in this development was Walter Spies, a German artist who settled in Bali at that time. His circle came to include people such as: Miguel Covarrubias, a New York artist of Mexican origin, who wrote the now classic book, *The Island of Bali* (1937); Colin McPhee, a New York musicologist; Jane Belo, McPhee's then wife and an anthropologist who wrote *Trance in Bali* (1960); Margaret Mead, the famous American anthropologist, who carried out research with her then husband Gregory Bateson, following earlier work in Samoa and New Guinea; and Reloi Goris, a Dutch archeologist. These people contributed not only to the introduction of Balinese culture to the West, but also helped "invent" it by studying and staging it. In other words, Balinese arts and dances emerged as an outcome of Bali's encounter with the West (Yamashita 1999: 37–65).

If we also look at history in this way, the history of Southeast Asia itself can be seen to be a good example of glocalization. Early Indian and Chinese influences, followed by the introduction of Islam and European colonialism, blended with indigenous elements to create the contemporary culture of the region. Malaysia itself is a particularly interesting case in point. It can be said to be the product of various glocalization processes since 1511, the year in which the Portuguese destroyed the powerful Islamic Sultanate of Malacca. Between the sixteenth century and the nineteenth century, the Netherlands and Britain succeeded Spain and Portugal as the main European colonial powers, and in 1819, the British established Singapore as their colonial base in the Malay Peninsula. In the latter half of the nineteenth century, as tin mining was exploited and rubber plantations were established, a mass of Chinese and Indians migrated into British Malaya as workers. This caused a radical change in the composition of the Malayan population: in 1830 it had consisted of 88 percent Malays, 8 percent Chinese and 4 percent Indians. In 1930 it consisted of 45 percent Malays, 40 percent Chinese and 15 percent Indians.

Tsuyoshi Kato (1990), following Charles Hirschman (1987), has examined this shift in more detail by focusing on the politics of the census. In British Malaya the first census was carried out in 1871, and in it the population was classified into categories based loosely on "nationality," which included "European," "British Military," "Armenian," "Jewish," "Eurasian," "Chinese," "African," "Annanese," "Arab," "Bengali," "Malay," "Achenese,"

"Bugis," "Javanese," and so on. But in 1891, new racial categories were adopted, and the population was categorized into "European," "Chinese," "Malay and Other Indigenous People," "Tamils and Other Indians," and "Others." After 1911, only four racial categories, "European," "Malay," "Chinese" and "Indian," were recognized. Needless to say, this paralleled the development of the anthropological theory of races.

What is of particular importance in this historical process is the birth of the category "Malay" within these colonial census categories. The Achenese, Minangkabau, Javanese, and Bugis were merged together as the indigenous peoples of Malaya. Before the British colonial censuses, the concept of "Malay" had been more loosely defined, as we know also from the phenomenon of *masuk Melayu* or "becoming Malay" through which Dayak people could become Malay by converting to Islam. The category of "Malay" is itself a product of historical glocalization processes, including those of Islamization and colonization.

Southeast Asia in Globalizing Perspectives

With this "glocal" history of Southeast Asia in mind, we turn to the papers in this volume, which is divided into three parts. In Part One, "Southeast Asia in Globalizing Perspectives," Fernando N. Zialcita, Tong Chee Kiong and Lian Kwen Fee discuss the region as a whole in relation to globalization. As we mentioned earlier, the term globalization here refers not only to recent phenomena but also to processes in earlier periods.

Zialcita emphasizes the point that Southeast Asia includes not only Indianized or Islamized countries such as Thailand, Burma, Malaysia or Indonesia, as has often been noted, but also Hispanicized, Christianized and Sinicized countries, such as the Philippines and Vietnam. In relation to whether Southeast Asia is best seen as a jigsaw puzzle or a collage, he examines the region as an ecumene of world civilizations – India, China, Islam and the West – as the result of its history. At the same time he tries to identify the qualities of "Southeast Asia-ness" which link the region together in various aspects of culture such as costume, food and housing styles.

Importantly, Zialcita argues that the concept of "Southeast Asia" is still evolving. For centuries the Chinese referred to the region as "Nanyang" and the Japanese (using the same Chinese characters) as "Nanyô," the "South Seas," while the Indians saw it as "Further India." "Southeast Asia" was a twentieth-century term invented in the West which became popular at the end of World War II when the Allies organized the Southeast Asian Command. The Southeast Asians themselves, however, had no common term for the region, but Zialcita concludes that the birth of ASEAN (the Association of Southeast Asian Nations) and closer exchanges between the Southeast Asian countries have made the question "What is Southeast Asia?" important for Southeast Asians themselves.

As to whether Vietnam belongs to Southeast Asia or to the Far East, and whether the Philippines belong to Southeast Asia or to the Hispanic world, Zialcita makes a counterproposal: why cannot they belong to two or more worlds? He then asserts that Malaysia and Indonesia belong to both Southeast Asia and the Islamic world, while cultural expressions such as the traditional shop houses in Singapore with Chinese roofs, Corinthian pillars and Portuguese tiles obviously combine several traditions. It is natural for Southeast Asians to have plural identities rather than a single identity.

In passing we may note that the imperative for Southeast Asian countries after their independence has been to build the nation state. What, then, is the relation between nation building and the current process of globalization? Comparing Singapore, Malaysia and Indonesia, Tong Chee Kiong and Lian Kwen Fee give an excellent overview of the state of cultural globalization in contemporary Southeast Asia. They examine "the limits of globalization" from the point of view of the nation-state, which, they point out, is the site in which the universalizing tendencies of globalization are articulated.

According to Chun (1996: 70) quoted by Tong and Lian, the imperatives of nation building require the state to essentialize and totalize. They argue that, "To essentialize means to reduce something to its supposed pure form and to treat it as if it exists in reality. For example, states in Southeast Asia often essentialize ethnicity by assuming that ethnic groups possess inherently different cultural or behavioral characteristics; these are then used to distinguish them for the purpose of government ... To totalize is to apply the classification to as many of the inhabitants as possible in order to facilitate government. In this way, the nation-state homogenizes, categorizes, and absorbs in order to eliminate ambiguity."

These imperatives of nation building are understandable, particularly in the case of Indonesia which is discussed in several papers in this volume. Since the day of independence, the main task for Indonesia as a nation has been to attempt to create national unity and a national culture. However, in the era of global cultural flows and transnationalization, this process has entered a new phase in which the role of the nation-state itself is called into question. Tong and Lian have discussed the contradictory roles of nation-states facing globalization by examining Indonesia and Malaysia. The recent Southeast Asian economic crisis has also presented new challenges to the nations of the region in an age of transnationalization.

9

The Local, the National, and the Transnational

The papers in Part Two examine the dynamics of the local, the national, and the transnational in Southeast Asia by focusing mainly on Indonesia, so I will first summarize the Indonesian context. As I have mentioned, one of the most important tasks for the Indonesian government has been to build a national culture (*kebudayaan nasional* or *kebudayaan bangsa*). An "annotation" (*penjelasan*) to the 1945 Constitution states that the Indonesian government will create a "national culture" (Article 32), which will consist of the highest achievements or "summits" (*puncak-puncak*) of the ancient indigenous local cultures created by the Indonesian people. It also states that Indonesia will attempt to promote its history, culture, and national integration, without rejecting those foreign elements which enrich and advance the culture of the Indonesian people.

This is the fundamental idea of Indonesian cultural policy. We see culture involved at three levels here: at the local/regional level, the national level, and the transnational level. "National culture" develops as a result of the interaction of these three levels. In other words, Indonesian national culture is constructed out of the "summits" of local cultures within the Indonesian nation and the "positive elements" of foreign or international cultures. The cultural "summits" include items which are now also seen as prominent examples of Indonesian national culture, such as the Javanese *wayang* or puppet drama, Balinese dances, and Toraja or Batak houses. It is noteworthy that they include art forms such as theatrical performances, dances, dress, architecture and so on.

To achieve this aim, the Directorate General of Culture (Direktorat Jenderal Kebudayaan) has been taking a central role. Since the end of the 1970s, it has attempted to investigate, record, and preserve the cultural heritage so as to create an Indonesian national culture. What is remarkable in these attempts is that the cultures of ethnic groups in Indonesia are regarded primarily not as examples of "ethnic culture" but rather of "regional/local" culture (*kebudayaan daerah*). From this viewpoint, Toraja culture is seen as the culture of the province of South Sulawesi, and Balinese culture is seen as the culture of the province of Bali (Picard 1993). In this way Indonesia is attempting to "domesticate" local/ethnic cultures within a national framework, as is excellently illustrated in the open air museum at the Miniature Park of Beautiful Indonesia (Taman Mini Indonesia Indah) located in Jakarta.

In this volume, Haruya Kagami examines the issue of the formation of the regional culture of Bali under the cultural policy of the Suharto New Order Government. He pays special attention to Pesta Kesenian Bali or the

Balinese Arts Festival which was introduced in 1979 by Ida Bagus Mantra, at that time Governor of Bali province, in order to call the attention of the Balinese people to their own cultural tradition. Since then, the festival has been held every year to promote Balinese culture, ranging from traditional dances to offerings to the gods made out of palm leaves. The festival has become an active agent in the creation of contemporary Balinese local culture. In addition, he examines the question of *adat* or local custom. In the 1980s the local government introduced the concept of *lomba*, or "contest" in various forms, such as the *lomba desa adat* (customary village contest), *lomba subak* (irrigation society contest), *lomba subak abian* (dry field society contest), and *lomba seka terna* (village youth association contest). Through these devices Balinese custom has been not only preserved but also remade in response to the current situations. Balinese local culture is fabricated in this process with the help of the state.

Wayan I Geriya focuses on Balinese culture in relation to Balinese tourism which until the start of the 1997–98 economic and political crisis was a major industry with over a million overseas tourists annually. He examines both the positive and negative impact of tourism on Balinese society and culture. Using the examples of the three villages of Sangeh, Ubud, and Tenganan, he draws attention to village tourism as a new strategy of tourist development. The Balinese people in this way have discovered the value of "culture" as a form of symbolic capital of their own (Picard 1995: 60).

If these papers on Bali examine the dynamics of local culture within the national and transnational context in Indonesia, the two papers that follow deal with Java. Shota Fukuoka, an ethnomusicologist, deals with the *degung*, a form of Sundanese traditional music in West Java which was previously the music of the Sundanese aristocracy. With the decline of the aristocracy, it lost its socioeconomic basis. The *degung* tradition, however, has persisted by adapting itself to new circumstances. Tracing the development of *degung* music since the 1920s, Fukuoka examines the historical process though which the reevaluation and recontextualization of this tradition have been achieved. In so doing, Sundanese musicians have not only maintained the tradition but have also created a new repertoire for a new audience. For instance, through the introduction of female singers they have created a new kind of *degung, degung kawih,* which has popularized *degung* music in general.

Interestingly, modern technology such as radio broadcasting has played an important role in preserving the *degung* tradition. In the 1950s, the Bandung branch of RRI (Radio Republik Indonesia) regularly broadcast *degung* music played by musicians affiliated with the office of the regent. Furthermore the introduction of commercial cassette recordings in the 1970s gave the musicians further opportunities to demonstrate their creativity. This may differ from the situation elsewhere in Java, where cassette tapes have led to the homogenization of gamelan traditions (Sutton 1985).

In his paper, Teruo Sekimoto discusses the two aspects of the use of batik cloth: as a commodity and as a cultural symbol. As a commodity it is in everyday use, both in Indonesia, where it is used for loincloths (*sarong*), and in other parts of Southeast Asia where imported Indonesian batik is seen as a cheap and durable consumer item. On the other hand, it is also a cultural symbol through which the Indonesian people express their pride. Batik is seen by most Javanese not as a commodity but as a cultural symbol which reminds them of Indonesia. Examining the history of batik production, Sekimoto demonstrates how a contemporary tradition based on a rich history extending back to premodern times has emerged within the constraints imposed by modernity.

Tradition, then, does not belong to the past but to our contemporary experience. Sekimoto points out the mistake in setting up a rigid dichotomy between the old and the new, or between tradition and modernity. Criticizing the conventional view of tradition as being opposed to modernity, he explores the way in which it is established under modern social conditions. Only in this way, he argues, does tradition become meaningful as part of our living experience.

In the final chapter of Part Two, the Thai case is examined by Anan Ganjanapan who investigates the dynamics of culture in the context of the rising middle class. He argues that globalization does not entirely imply the hegemony of Western modernity. Rather, in Thailand he observes the revitalization of religion in the form of the emergence among the urban middle class of new types of Buddhist sects such as Thammakai and Santi Asok, and cults of the supernatural such as Sadet Pho Ro Ha and Chao Mae Kuan Im. These phenomena indicate both the dynamics and the contradictions of culture as it undergoes change in the context of continuing globalization, the construction of contradictory values and the commodification of self-identity.

Furthermore, he discusses the struggles for collective rights over common village property in the villages in northern Thailand. Interestingly, even though these villages are seen as marginal, they nevertheless have a variety of useful networks, and have allied themselves with local NGOs (non-governmental organizations) and urban intellectuals to advocate community rights over resources. In these processes, Anan concludes that local knowledge seems to be a dynamic form of local culture which is most frequently revitalized by those in the new urban environment as they adjust to such global values as individualism, consumerism, and materialism.

The Periphery of Nation-States

Part Three examines the question of what is going on the periphery of the nation-states in Southeast Asia. Here there exist less domesticated forms of society and culture. In Indonesia, for instance, the category of *masyarakat terasing* or "alien society" includes people such as the forest or sea peoples in Sumatra, Kalimantan or West Papua (formerly Irian Jaya). There was also the critical issue of East Timor with its violent confrontations between the local people and the Indonesian army, preceding and surrounding the transition to independence. On the southern periphery of the Philippines, there is the MNLF (Moro National Liberation Front), a Muslim force which rejects integration into Christian Filipino society. Even in the "homogeneous" nation-state of Japan, the Ainu in Hokkaido on the northern periphery and the people of Okinawa on the southern periphery have cultural traditions which are markedly different from those of the main part of the country.

Eriko Aoki analyzes the historiography of Flores, on the eastern periphery of Indonesia, by examining the center/periphery opposition at the local, national, and transnational levels. Interestingly, according to the historical perceptions of the people of Flores, "Indonesians" are often equated with "Javanese," and are regarded as just the latest in a line of foreign invaders which has included the Portuguese, the Dutch and the Japanese. In other words, "Indonesia" still appears to the local residents in peripheral areas like Flores as external and alien, a perception of the Indonesian nation-state which also helps shed light on the problem of the independence of East Timor (Anderson 1993).

Ikuya Tokoro examines the transformation of shamanistic rituals among the Sama-speaking people in Tabawan, in the Tawi Tawi Province of the Sulu Archipelago in the Southern Philippines. Shamanism in Tabawan is now in crisis due to the Islamic resurgence in the region. He examines the case in which a shaman made a critical speech in front of the villagers criticizing the *ustadz*, the teachers at Muslim religious schools, who usually criticize shamanistic practices as being against Islam. Wearing the robes a pious Muslim uses for praying in the mosque and imitating the style of the *ustadz*, the shaman justified shamanistic practice as conforming to Islam. Following Michael Taussig's concept of "mimesis" (Taussig 1993), Tokoro points out that the shaman in this way tried to derive his own power and authenticity from Islam. This is a complicated process of religious transformation, involving what Tokoro calls the "politics of meaning." Tokoro also emphasizes that the fundamental agent of religious transformation in the southern Philippines is not the nation-state, as is the case with Indonesia, but rather the transnational Islamic network.

Hiromu Shimizu is concerned with the emergence of ethnic awareness among the Pinatubo Ayta people of Luzon in their struggles for survival after the 1991 Mt. Pinatubo eruption. Before the eruption, the Ayta people subsisted by hunting and gathering in relative isolation at the foot of the mountain. With the eruption, these people suddenly lost their homeland and experienced the bitterness of diaspora – exodus, suffering, and rehabilitation in new locations. Some were forced to come to Manila and earn their living by begging in the streets. In these processes, as Shimizu points out, the Pinatubo Ayta became conscious of their own ethnic identity and their distinctive cultural heritage, especially through being exposed to contact with lowland communities and through negotiations with journalists, government officials and transnational NGO workers. In other words, "Aytaness" was awakened when the Ayta became a diaspora community, transplanted from their homeland to contemporary metropolitan Manila where they were forced to think about their own ethnic identity in order to survive.

In the penultimate chapter, Bachtiar Alam examines the case of the island of Okinawa, the largest of the Ryukyu Islands in the extreme southwest of Japan. Japan is often considered a homogeneous nation, but the presence of ethnic and other marginal groups, such as the Ainu, the *burakumin*, the Koreans, and the Okinawans, has posed complex problems, both conceptually and politically. Being culturally distinct from the rest of Japan, Okinawa and the rest of the Ryukyus captured the imagination of early observers. The pioneer of Japanese folklore studies, Kunio Yanagita, for instance, thought that the Japanese had originated in the south and made their way north through the Ryukyu Islands. His celebrated disciple, Shinobu Orikuchi, proposed that the original form of Shintoism could be found in Okinawa. However this early fascination with Okinawa's distinctive cultural background, based as it was on various Orientalist assumptions – either that the islands were radically different from the rest of Japan, or that they provided an archetype for the rest of Japan – no longer survives today. In his paper in this volume, Alam locates Okinawa within the Southeast Asian mosaic and sheds new light on the dynamics of religious change in the region by examining Christianity in a village in the northern part of the island.

Finally, Jerry Eades examines the case of the aborigines of Taiwan, and the various images of them presented by outsiders during successive waves of occupation and colonialism, from the seventeenth century to the present day. The history of these peoples, who originally spoke Austronesian languages related to Malay rather than Chinese, is a complex one. Their earliest contacts with Europe were with Spain and Portugal, but it was the Dutch who established the most complete control over the island in the early seventeenth century, converting part of the indigenous population to Christianity. They in turn were displaced by Chinese from the mainland in the mid-seventeenth century and the island was gradually transformed into a province of the Chinese empire. The Chinese settled mainly in the west of the island, absorbing and assimilating many of the aboriginal ethnic groups, but they never gained complete control over the mountain areas to the east, in which aboriginal enclaves survived. Japanese colonial rule followed, from 1895 to 1945, bringing the aboriginal populations into greater contact with the rest of Taiwanese society, and Japanese became a local lingua franca for many of these groups. Finally, the reestablishment of Chinese control under the Kuomintang regime in 1945 led to a new phase of Sinicization of aboriginal culture. Aboriginal languages have survived where there is a critical mass of speakers, or where they are shared by members of different generations, though their long term future may be in doubt because of the impact of Chinese in education and the mass media. Ethnic identities also survive, along with distinctive "aboriginal cultures," even though these are in large part invented traditions created under the gaze of the regional tourist industry. As a final development, elements of these are being appropriated and reworked by Taiwanese politicians in the debate over the island's future, and by the global media.

Conclusion

It is clear now that globalization does not necessarily involve cultural homogenization throughout the world, nor is it opposed to localization. Rather, globalization results in hybridization and the localization of culture. The history of Southeast Asia demonstrates the reality of glocalizing processes. By focusing on these processes, this volume aims to contribute to an understanding of their role in contemporary Southeast Asian culture, as well as to the construction of a perspective in which culture is viewed as constantly emerging.

The American cultural theorist, James Clifford, has pointed out that modern ethnography has oscillated between various "meta-narratives of culture," describing it in terms of homogenization and loss on the one hand, and of emergence and invention on the other (Clifford 1988: 19). We do not intend to reduce cultural realities to mere narratives. However, narratives of emergence enable us to observe culture in the glocalizing world from a dynamic perspective. This volume is then an attempt to apply this approach to the analysis of the contemporary emergence of Southeast Asian culture within the context of globalization.

References

Anderson, Benedict. 1993. "Features: Imaging East Timor," *Arena Magazine* 4.

Appadurai, Arjun. 1990. "Disjuncture and difference in the global cultural economy," pp. 295–310 in *Global Culture: Nationalism, Globalization and Modernity*, ed. Mike Featherstone. London: Sage Publications.

Appadurai, Arjun. 1991. "Global ethnoscapes: notes and queries for a transnational anthropology," pp. 191–210 in *Recapturing Anthropology*, ed. Richard Fox. Santa Fe: School of American Research Press.

Belo, Jane. 1960. *Trance in Bali*. New York: Columbia University Press.

Chun, A. 1996. "Discourse of identity in the changing spaces of public culture in Taiwan, Hong Kong and Singapore," *Theory, Culture and Society*, 13 (1): 51–75.

Clifford, James. 1988. *The Predicament of Culture: Twentieth-Century Ethnography, Literature, and Art*. Cambridge and London: Harvard University Press.

Covarrubias, Miguel. 1937. *Island of Bali*. London: Cassell.

Frederic, William. 1982. "Rhoma Irama and the *dangdut* style: aspects of contemporary Indonesian popular culture," *Indonesia* 34: 103–30.

Hannerz, Ulf. 1992. *Cultural Complexity*. New York: Columbia University Press.

Hirschman, Charles. 1987. "The meaning and measurement of ethnicity in Malaysia: an analysis of census classification," *Journal of Asian Studies*, 46 (3): 555–82.

Kato, Tsuyoshi. 1990. "Esunishiti gainen no rekishiteki tenkai" [The historical development of the concept of ethnicity], pp. 215–45 in *Tônanajia no shakai* [Southeast Asian society], ed. Yasuhiro Tsubouchi. Tokyo: Kôbundô.

Kuwahara, Yasuo. 1991. *Kokkyô o koeru rôdôsha* [Transnational laborers]. Tokyo: Iwanami.

Picard, Michel. 1993. "Cultural tourism in Bali: national integration and regional differentiation," pp. 71–98 in *Tourism in South-East Asia*, eds. M. Hitchcock, V. King and M. Parnwell. London and New York: Routledge.

Picard, Michel. 1995. "Cultural heritage and tourist capital: cultural tourism in Bali," pp. 44–66 in *International Tourism: Identity and Change*, eds. Marie-Françoise Lanfant, John B. Allcock and Edward M. Bruner. London: Sage Publications.

Pieterse, Jan Nederveen. 1995. "Globalization as hybridization," pp. 45–

68 in *Global Modernities*, eds. M. Featherstone *et al.* London: Sage Publications.

Robison, Richard and David S. G. Goodman eds. 1996. *The New Rich in Asia*. London and New York: Routledge.

Robertson, Roland. 1992. *Globalization: Social Theory and Global Culture*. London: Sage Publications.

Robertson, Roland. 1995. "Glocalization: time-space and homogeneity-heterogeneity," pp. 25–44 in *Global Modernities*, eds. M. Featherstone et al. London: Sage Publications.

Rosaldo, Renato. 1989. *Culture and Truth: The Remaking of Social Analysis*. Boston: Beacon Press.

Sahlins, Marshall. 1994. "Good-bye to tristes tropes: ethnography in the context of modern world history," pp. 377–95 in *Assessing Cultural Anthropology*, ed. R. Borofsky. New York: McGraw-Hill.

Sekimoto, Teruo. 1995. "Indoneshia no Doraemon to 'minzokubunka'" [Doraemon in Indonesia and 'ethnic culture'], *Minpakutsûshin* 68. Osaka: National Museum of Ethnology.

Shiraishi, Saya S. 1997. "Japan's soft power: Doraemon goes overseas," pp. 234–72 in *Network Power: Japan and Asia*, eds. Peter J. Katzenstein and Takashi Shiraishi. Ithaca: Cornell University Press.

Smith, Valene ed. 1989. *Hosts and Guests: The Anthropology of Tourism* (2nd edition). Philadelphia: University of Pennsylvania Press.

Sutton, R. Anderson. 1985. "Commercial cassette recordings of traditional music in Java: implications for performers and scholars," *The World of Music*, 27(3): 23–46.

Tulloch, Sara ed. 1991. *The Oxford Dictionary to New Words*. New York: Oxford University Press.

Yamashita, Shinji. 1988. *Girei no seijigaku: Indoneshia Toraja no dôtaiteki minzokushi* [The politics of ritual: a dynamic ethnography of the Toraja of Indonesia]. Tokyo: Kôbundô.

Yamashita, Shinji. 1995. "Culture in the contexts of tourism: the interplay of national, regional and global perspectives," pp. 105–14 in *Regional Cooperation and Culture in Asia-Pacific*, eds. Khien Theeravit and Grant B. Stillman. Tokyo: United Nations University, pp. 105–14.

Yamashita, Shinji. 1999. *Bari: Kankô jinruigaku no ressun* [Bali: what can we learn from the anthropology of tourism?]. Tokyo: Tokyo Daigaku Shuppankai. (English version forthcoming as *Bali and Beyond: Explorations in the Anthropology of Tourism*. Oxford and New York: Berghahn.)

Part I

Southeast Asia in Globalizing Perspectives

Chapter 2

Is Southeast Asia a Jigsaw Puzzle or a Collage?

Fernando N. ZIALCITA

A sixteenth century Moslem could leave the Straits of Gibraltar, travel through the Middle East and northern India, cross over to the Malay Peninsula, go down to northern Sumatra and journey upwards along the west coast of Borneo to Sulu without leaving the familiar world he cherished. This was a world defined by the mosque and the minaret, the Sacred Book and its commentaries, a legal tradition based on Roman law and the Sacred Book, a philosophical system that drew inspiration from Aristotle, and an art that sought inspiration in abstractions and Arabic script. Though modern Islam never was a political unity and today in fact covers many independent nation-states, nonetheless it constitutes a felt unity. During the civil war in Bosnia in the 1990s, Malaysians (brown-skinned and speaking an Austronesian tongue) offered asylum to Bosnians (white-skinned and speaking an Indo-European tongue) because they were fellow Moslems.

Emotive, meaningful symbols that are shared create an ecumene, a moral and aesthetic community that embraces diverse cultures and races. Islam is an ecumene. So obviously is the West which began as the western half of a Christendom that had split along the fault lines of a collapsed Roman empire. Though the West expanded overseas to include new cultures, it continues to constitute a world with shared symbols: Christianity, whether Catholic or Protestant; the philosophical, political, and legal heritage of the Greeks and Romans; and art styles from Gothic down to Modernism. Do Chinese-influenced countries constitute an ecumene? To an outsider like me, it seems that they do. Despite bloody conflicts in the past, there is a community of symbols that they share: Confucian ethics, Taoist metaphysics, Mahayana

Buddhist soteriology, Chinese script, roofs with high ridges and upturned corner eaves, noodles and chopsticks. I find it easy to understand why in Hawaii, far from their ancient rivalries in Asia, Chinese, Japanese and Koreans prefer each other's company to that of other Asians.

Has Southeast Asia become an ecumene? What communalities link Southeast Asians together? What place does the Westernized Philippines have in this emerging community? The questions are not of mere passing interest. Since World War II, there has been a continuing attempt to create a political and economic community in Southeast Asia with the European Union as the model. Inevitably, questions about cultural communalities shared by the entire region arise. There are also questions about the "Southeast Asianness" of the Christian Filipino. It is often pointed out that whereas both the aboriginal culture of the uplands and the Islamized culture of Sulu and Mindanao have obvious links with the rest of the region, the majority culture, Hispanicized in many ways, has little. Indeed up till the 1960s, scholars hesitated to include the Philippines in cultural studies on Southeast Asia (McCloud 1986: 5; Osborne 1983: 12).

In addressing these questions, we should note two things. First, the concept, "Southeast Asia" has been constantly evolving. In centuries past, the Chinese referred to the "Region of the Southern Seas" as "Nanyang," the Japanese referred to it as "Nanyô," and the Indians called it "Further India" (Fifield 1958: 2; Osborne 1983: 12). But Southeast Asians themselves seem not to have had a common term for the region. "Southeast Asia" is a term coined by Westerners during the twentieth century, and it became popular at the close of World War II when the Allies organized a Southeast Asian Command (Tilman 1987: 16).

When George Coedès' book on the region first came out in 1944, the original title was *Histoire Ancienne des Etats Hindouisés d'Extrême-Orient* (Ancient History of the Indianized States of the Far East). The third edition in 1964 was called *Les Etats Hindouisés d'Indochine et d'Indonésie* (The Indianized States of Indochina and Indonesia). However, when it was translated and published in 1968, its title had become *The Indianized States of Southeast Asia*.

Second, we should make a distinction that is often overlooked when discussing "the unity of Southeast Asia." There are different ways of clustering cultures together. The communalities that link Southeast Asians together at present are not of the same order as those linking Europeans together. Despite internecine wars, Europeans share an ecumene defined by powerful, emotion-charged symbols. It is doubtful whether such a universe exists in Southeast Asia at present. Thus, on one of the anniversaries marking the end of World War II, the French government asked that a Beethoven symphony be played in Paris. As is well known, Beethoven was German. Yet, Europeans in general, and not only the French, regard the music of Beethoven and, for that matter, of Bach, Haydn, and Mozart, as belonging to all of them. It is significant that the European Union has chosen the "Ode to Joy" from Beethoven's Ninth Symphony as its anthem. Are there similar symbols that appeal to all Southeast Asians? At this point in time, I would say no. The *Ramayana* does indeed appeal to Indianized Southeast Asians but not yet to the northern Vietnamese or to Christian Filipinos. Nonetheless, there are communalities that do link most Southeast Asians together because there are other ways in which they form a culture area. The communalities may not be as powerful as the symbols of an ecumene, but they could well be in the future.

The other point I wish to make is that significant aspects of Hispanicized Filipino culture in fact link it to other cultures in the region. Indigenous elements survive, even in artifacts and institutions that seem to be Hispanic, because of outside influences. I will establish this by examining the Filipinos' basic food habits, their national costume, their supposedly "Spanish" houses, and the Good Friday procession to show how indigenous elements link them with the rest of the region.

Ways of Grouping Cultures

Cultures can be grouped in different ways. To illustrate each of these, I will give first mainly non-Southeast Asian examples, followed by a discussion of Southeast Asia in relation to each type of grouping.

A family of languages

Over time, societies originally sharing a common language may differentiate from each other in terms of social structure in response to political, economic, and ecological factors. They may share common myths because they originally shared a similar livelihood and social organization when they first appeared as a small group. Thus there is an Indo-European family of languages which includes Celtic, Germanic, Latin, Hellenic, Slavic, Iranian and Indian languages. Within these languages, myths centering on the sky gods and on cattle rituals are important (Lincoln 1987), for the Indo-Europeans began as cattle herders. However for the average speaker of those languages today this linguistic and mythological unity that scholars have unearthed has little relevance.

Responses to a common ecosystem

Societies which are faced with similar challenges from their particular ecosystem tend to respond similarly, according to cultural ecologists, because
their basic options are limited by the climate, topography, and resources
surrounding them. There is a Mediterranean environment characterized by
extended summer droughts, mild rainy winters, a relatively uniform tem-
perature, and "a close interdigitation of mountain, valley and sea" (Pitkin
1963 cited by Gilmore 1982: 77). In terms of settlement patterns, therefore,
a common response throughout the Maghreb, southern Spain and France,
Italy, coastal Croatia, and Greece has been to form compact, isolated towns
located near sources of water. To this I would add the preference for stone
houses with flat, rather than steeply pitched, tile roofs.

Again it is doubtful whether the similarities of these responses would
have meant much to ordinary Mediterranean residents. Historically, they
have been divided into three ecumenes: the Eastern or Orthodox Christian,
the Western Christian, and the Islamic. Though Western Christianity and
Orthodox Christianity have drawn closer to each other recently, ancient sus-
picions and hatreds still divide them at times, as can be seen in the former
Yugoslavia where Catholic Croats and Orthodox Serbs have fought bitterly,
despite a common language. (The main difference is that Croats use the
Roman script, and Serbs the Cyrillic script, similar to Russian.)

An ecumene united by a shared Great Tradition

As explained above, cultures in an ecumene are wedded together by a vision
of the world that is reinforced by communalities in ethics, law, politics, or
art.[1] According to the anthropologist Robert Redfield, the cultural tradition
in preindustrial states and cities has a dual character (Redfield 1956). The
literati and the powerful in urban centers have the resources to commission
the best talents to work for them; moreover, they specialize in mental work.
They thus develop a tradition which is more intellectual, more sophisticated, and more refined than that of the peasants and urban laborers. The
latter groups have little time for speculation, for they are immersed in poorly
compensated manual work. Besides in pre-nineteenth century societies, there
was no obligatory universal education from which they could have benefited. Temples, churches, and palaces embody the Great Tradition; wayside
shrines and huts manifest the Little Tradition. The Great Tradition defines
the ideals for the Little Tradition, but fashions and forms from the Little
Tradition may also enter the Great Tradition and transform it.

Most Great Traditions have been influenced by even older and more prestigious Great Traditions. For this reason a common universe of discourse tends to unite clusters of Great Traditions. Morocco, Egypt, Iran, and Aceh in Sumatra each have their own distinctive Great Tradition, thanks in part to the influence of the Little Tradition in each place. But there are communalities that unite them because of Islam which originated in Arabia. Similarly the Great Traditions of Italy, Spain, France, England, Germany, though different from each other, share communalities because they all partake of that fusion of Greco-Roman law and philosophy, Christian ethics, and Germanic customs that is commonly called "Western."

Communalities created by a shared Great Tradition are highly meaningful to those who share them, for, at the deepest level, they refer to the "basic and indubitable" in the realm of religion, ethics, philosophy, and the arts. Like everything human, however, this sense of the "basic and indubitable" is in fact culturally constructed. The myths created by a Great Tradition have this advantage over those created by a family of languages: they are propagated by highly organized institutions that enjoy legitimacy: the state, religious organizations, and schools. Moreover, their symbols are highly visible: the crescent and star for Moslems, the Latin cross for Western Christians. They give those who share the Great Tradition a sense of fellowship vis-à-vis those who do not. Nonetheless, these communalities have not prevented bitter wars among peoples who share a Great Tradition because the desire for dominance does upset these relations. Thus we have witnessed the wars among Western European countries, or the wars of liberation by the Arabs against the Turks, their fellow Moslems.

These are but some of the ways to classify cultures according to their communalities.[2] The boundaries of these types of classifications do not coincide with each other. Thus a country or a culture may well participate in one type of culture area but not necessarily in another. For instance southern Italy has communalities with India in language and myth, for both areas belong to the Indo-European family of languages. However, if responses to a particular ecosystem be the criteria, then this region shares communalities only with countries within the Mediterranean zone, be they Western Christian, Orthodox Christian, or Islamic. Finally, in terms of a shared "great tradition," the communalities most meaningful to southern Italians would not be any of the above but those linking them to the rest of the Christian world, including Catholic countries in the Americas and Asia.

The question is, therefore, which of these ways of grouping cultures applies to Southeast Asia?

Southeast Asia as a Unity

Many languages of Southeast Asia, like Malay, Sundanese, Javanese, Taosug, Cebuano, and Tagalog, belong to what is called the Western subgroup of Austronesian languages. But this grouping within Austronesian does not coincide with the geographical boundaries of Southeast Asia. Because of ancient migrations, peoples in Madagascar and in Micronesia also speak Western Austronesian languages. Other languages on the mainland, like Mon (Burma), Khmer (Cambodia), and possibly Vietnamese, belong to the Austroasiatic family (Bellwood 1985: 125). The Austronesian and Austroasiatic language families share similar myths and motifs: a dualism that emphasizes oppositions between female and male creators or between forces of the mountain and forces of the sea; and a tree of life from which male and female sprang (Keyes 1987; Fox 1987; Taylor 1983: 8). The hornbill bird and the crocodile have sacred status in both mythologies.

Then there is a third cluster of languages, the Tibeto-Burmese family of languages, including Lao, Thai and Burmese. It also includes Chinese, and seems very different because of the use of tones. However, the linguistic expert Paul Benedict posits that Thai and other Tai languages were originally related to both Austroasiatic and Austronesian (Bellwood 1985).

Southeast Asia can also be conceived of as sharing communalities because of ecology. Mountains predominate; flat lands are confined largely to "intermountain river basins, valleys, coastal fringes, and river deltas" (Winzeler 1976: 625). An extensive tropical rain forest covers many areas. Temperatures are high and the air humid throughout the year (Hutterer 1976: 224). In addition, E.L. Jones proposes that, compared with early Japan and Europe, there may be higher rates of disaster such as famines, floods, wars, and the spread of diseases such as malaria (1991).

Because of this common environment, certain forms of behavior are found throughout the region. Since waterways are more efficient avenues of transport and since bodies of water rich in marine life are present, many settlements are located beside them. As a protection against the humid ground and frequent floods, wooden houses built on stilts were once prevalent throughout the region. Even in Vietnam, there used to be houses on stilts, as shown by bas-reliefs on the drums of Dongson dating back to the fifth century B.C. However, because Chinese influence from the first century A.D. onwards emphasized building houses on raised platforms, the style is now found only in a few riverside settlements and in the village communal hall: the *dinh*. With respect to food, ordinary Southeast Asian food is flavored with fermented shrimp paste and fish sauce. Basic flavors therefore taste of marine life.

We come to the question: does Southeast Asia form a single ecumene with a shared Great Tradition? To answer this, qualifications need to be made.

Indian influence appears to have come in via traders and priests starting with the first century A.D. and to have spread from Funan (southern Vietnam) to Java, Sumatra, the Malay Peninsula, and to the region which now consists of Cambodia, Thailand, Laos, and Burma. It played a crucial role in the formation of the newly emerging kingly states and urban centers in the region, for it provided organizational and ideological models for organizing monarchies and their sacred cities. Indian culture preached that the king was an incarnation of a divinity, Shiva, or Vishnu, or had attained Buddhahood, and was therefore worthy to be revered by all, including rebellious nobles. Its other effects were the construction of buildings of stone and metal, with stupas guarding Buddhist relics and "mountain towers of stone" at Brahmanic temples; the popularization of the *Mahabharata*, the *Ramayana* and an aristocratic literature that glorified and justified the exploits of warriors and kings; and the adoption of new dance gestures and a style of dressing that wrapped cloth of varying sizes and shapes around the body. The ideology was provided by various forms of Brahmanism and Mahayana Buddhism. Centuries later another less esoteric form of Buddhism, Theravada, entered Laos, Cambodia, Thailand and Burma, and replaced Mahayana Buddhism (Coedès 1964: 2, 453 ff.; Harrison 1968: 18; Wolters 1968:10–11).

However, even then, from the fifth to the fifteenth centuries, large areas of what is now Southeast Asia were left out of this sphere of Indian influence: northern Vietnam, Borneo, the Moluccas, and the Philippines. True, Mahayana Buddhism found favor in the Vietnamese court. But, as in other Chinese-influenced cultures, this coexisted with Confucian ethics. Eventually the court preferred the latter because it provided a vision and framework for managing the state (Ho Tai 1985: 28). Moreover, the script, literature, music, architecture, costume, and etiquette of China rather than those of India became the models of the Vietnamese (Woodside 1971).

In the case of the Philippines, Indian influences entered Mindanao and Western Visayas, most likely through the agency of traders from either Sumatra or Java, rather than through visiting Indian traders and priests. The Philippines were too far to the north away from the spice route and too far to the west away from the main trade route between India and China (Francisco 1985: 50–51). But some of the influences can be seen, albeit in diluted form. Thus the notion that the universe is made up of layers above the earth and layers below found currency in Mindanao and Western Visayas. Traditional Bukidnons of the Mindanao highlands believe that there are

seven layers ascending skywards, and seven layers descending to the under-
world (Unabia 1986). Most likely, this is their interpretation of the Hindu-
Buddhist notion that the soul must undergo several cycles of purification,
seven heavens and seven hells, before attaining union with the One. In the
Visayas which are further to the north, ordinary people, now Christians,
believe that the entire universe has only seven layers (Magos 1986). But this
diffusion of Indian influence was not accompanied by the formation of monarchies whose king incarnated Vishnu or Shiva, nor by the erection of mon-
asteries where the Vedic or Buddhist texts were studied.[3]

Around the fourteenth century, Islam entered Southeast Asia, again via
Indian traders, and slowly gained adherents in the Malay Peninsula, the
Indonesian Archipelago (even in Sumatra and Java) and the southern Philippines. In the following century, Christianity came in with the Portuguese,
followed by the Spaniards in the sixteenth and gained a foothold in Malacca, Flores, the Moluccas and in much of the Philippines. Then came the
Dutch, the British, the French, and the Americans to trade and to colonize.
Between the seventeenth and nineteenth centuries, the Chinese migrated
southwards, not merely as traders but as migrants. They brought with them
their world view, their ethics, and their arts; and they established enclaves
that persist to this day.

There is thus not one Great Tradition that covers all of Southeast Asia
today, but four: the Chinese (Vietnam, Singapore), the Indian (Laos, Cambodia, Thailand, Burma, Bali, and, to a continuing extent, the aristocracy of
central Java);[4] the Islamic (Sulu, parts of Mindanao, Malaysia, most of Indonesia); and the Western (Singapore,[5] the Philippines, Flores, East Timor).
True, there are communalities in myth and behavior because of the related
languages (Austroasiatic and Austronesian); there are also communalities
created by a similar physical environment. But there are no highly charged
symbols that are universal throughout the region. This is not to say that no
such symbols will appear in the future.

There are laudable efforts to create a Southeast Asian consciousness on
the basis of similarities in art form. In general there are these noticeable
tendencies:

1. There is an emphasis on communalities shared by aboriginal art forms
in the region. Thus the jewelry and the sculpture of the peoples of the
Cordillera who have hitherto been animists can be shown to have continuities with those of animists in other parts of the region. The same can
be shown for their weaving.

2. There is an emphasis on communalities given by two Great Traditions: the Indian and the Islamic. The *Ramayana* epic has been drama-

tized throughout the Indianized lands through puppets and courtiers' dances. A *Ramayana* festival involving the participation of those countries has been organized. With regard to Islamic traditions, close contacts between Moslems take place through schools and exchanges.

3. On the other hand, there is a deemphasis of art shaped by the two other Great Traditions: the Chinese and the Western. Courses on "Southeast Asian theatre" or on "Southeast Asian architecture" at the University of Hawaii, during my stay from 1981 to 1987, ignored northern Vietnam and the Philippines. The focus was on the Indian cultures, with nothing either on Islamic influence on architecture. However, during my final year, I was asked to give a talk on Philippine theatre. In entries on Southeast Asian arts in the *Encyclopedia of Asian History* (Wicks 1988, O'Connor 1988) the emphasis is on Indian-inspired art. The Chinese-inspired temples and palaces of central and northern Vietnam were not mentioned. I find this strange. As stated above, the Chinese presence in northern Vietnam goes back to the first century B.C., and is thus older than Indian influence on other countries of the region. Little or no mention is made either of Islamic influence. This did arrive later, around the thirteenth century, but it has since altered the landscape of Malaysia, Indonesia, and the Philippines. As may be expected, there is complete silence about Filipino stone churches and their statuary from the seventeenth to the nineteenth centuries.

To conceive of Southeast Asia purely in terms of Pagan, Sukhotai, Angkor, and Prambanan is to close doors rather than to open them. The prevailing tendency is to imagine Southeast Asia as a piece of a larger jigsaw, that is, as a bounded cultural unity with definable boundaries that neatly set it apart from other cultural unities in the world jigsaw puzzle. It may be better to imagine it as a collage whose different materials cluster and overlap with each other, while extending at the same time into the surrounding space.

Bridges between Worlds

Many foreigners and even educated Filipinos imagine that the Philippines' artistic links to the rest of Southeast Asia are constituted by the art of aboriginal groups in the uplands of Luzon and Mindanao or the art of Islamized societies in the South. The art of the Hispanicized Filipinos is deemed "out of place" in "Southeast Asia." So likewise is the art of the Sinicized Vietnamese. What is forgotten is that both Islamic and Indic influences were also intrusive centuries earlier, but these eventually fused with indigenous traditions. The same thing has happened with regard to Hispanic influence in the Philippines and Chinese influence in Vietnam.

Cooking

Allegedly what defines the Southeast Asian flavor in cooking is the heavy use of chili pepper. Thus northern Vietnamese and Filipino food, with the exception of Christian Bicolano and the Moslem Taosug cooking, seem out of place and are likely to disappoint outsiders who have an a priori notion that authentic Southeast Asian cooking ought to be "spicy." In Amsterdam, a Filipino restaurant has had to introduce large amounts of chili to cater to this preconceived notion of Dutch customers.

However, what is forgotten is the fact that the chili pepper was domesticated in Mexico centuries before the Europeans came and may have first entered Southeast Asia via the Manila Galleon! The chili pepper (*Capsicum annuum L.; Capsicum frutescens L.)* was thus itself intrusive once upon a time. If communalities in taste must be sought, the communalities should be sought on an even more basic level: the frequent use of shrimp paste and fish sauce, and the fondness for rice and aquatic food. These are universal in both northern Vietnamese and Filipino food. In the case of the latter, marine-derived condiments acquire new dimensions because they are mixed in with another cooking tradition. Filipinos love to sauté fish or meat in garlic, onions and tomatoes, as in the Mediterranean. Sometimes they flavor this with fish sauce to create a bouquet, or they sauté the shrimp paste itself in the classic trio.

Costume

When people think of linkages between the Philippines and the rest of Southeast Asia in terms of costume, they think of either tribal costumes or the costumes of the Moslem ethnic groups. The costume of Hispanicized Filipinos supposedly does not fit in. Thus in a standard book on world costumes (Kennett 1994: 129), the section on the Philippines, classified under "Southeast Asia" featured the costume of the Ifugao but not that of the lowland majority. Nor was there mention either of Vietnamese costume under "Southeast Asia" and the (Sinicized) "Far East."

In fact the costumes of the Hispanicized majority do fit in. The *barong tagalog* is a loose shirt worn by men over long pants. It has a collar and long sleeves ending in cuffs; its unique translucence comes from its materials, either pineapple fibers (*piña*) or silk and pineapple fibers (*jusi*); and it has resplendent embroidery, often in traceried cutwork. Filipino writers of the past fifty years have claimed that it originated as part of a policy of racial discrimination by the Spaniards. Wanting to humiliate the natives, the Spaniards obliged them to wear their shirttails out. However, no law by the Spaniards to that effect has yet been found (de la Torre 1986: 14). Besides, wealthy Manilenos of Spanish descent were described by a French traveler of the early nineteenth century as wearing their shirts over their pants (La Gironiere 1962 [1853]: 16). Paintings of Manilenos of a similar status by Damian Domingo in the 1800s confirm this picture.

The origins of this shirt should be sought rather in the shirt (*kurta*) popularized by Indians, whether Moslem or Hindu, all over Southeast Asia. This is even looser in shape, is worn over the pants, and has buttons and collars but no cuffs. It is made of cotton rather than of the gauzy materials Filipinos love, and may be either plain or embroidered. Even when embroidered, it has no cutwork (Bhusan 1958: 36 ff.). Indonesians and Malaysians too wear their national costume, their batik shirts out. It is notable though, as Teruo Sekimoto (personal communication) points out, that these first appeared only during the 1960s. Before that the educated urbanites wore Western style trousers, jackets, shirts and ties. On the other side of the ocean, Mexicans and Central Americans wear their cotton shirt (*guayabera*) out. Collared, long-sleeved and cuffed, its distinctive characteristic is that it has a column of vertical pleats running down the front with occasional embroidery on both sides of the buttons, with no cutwork. Some Mexicans say that their shirt may have been influenced by the Filipino shirt which came in via the yearly Manila Galleon, which in turn may have been influenced by the Indian.

It is unfortunate that in two other books on textiles in Southeast Asia, there were no colored photos of the *piña* in all its embroidered finery. Instead the visuals of the Philippine section focused on textiles by either Moslems or hitherto tribal peoples (Fraser-Lu 1988; Maxwell 1990). The unstated assumption seems to have been that the *piña* with its dainty, monochromatic, cutwork embroidery does not fit into their preconceived notion of what Southeast Asian textiles should look like, namely rainbow-colored and non-Western. (Interestingly enough, neither were there photos of Vietnamese textiles, perhaps because they look too Chinese?) But the *piña* was invented by Filipino artisans in Southeast Asia and not outside the region, even though the pineapple fruit did indeed come from the Americas. We must be careful of preconceived notions about what Southeast Asia is supposed to be.

Fernando N. ZIALCITA

Houses

Filipinos and some foreigners think of either tribal houses or houses of Moslem communities as the bridges to Southeast Asia. The traditional houses of wood and stone that developed from the seventeenth to the early twentieth centuries in Luzon and the Visayas are regarded as "Spanish houses." And yet the curious thing is that visiting Spanish and Mexican architect friends keep asking: "Why are they called Spanish?" There was also a student of mine, Budhi Gunawan, a Sundanese anthropologist, whose instant reaction to one of them was, "It looks like a Bornean longhouse!"

The indigenous house at the time of Spanish contact had a steep roof that rested on posts, rather than on the walls. Floors were raised above the ground as a precaution against floods and insects. Like their peers elsewhere in the region, Filipinos love living by, or over, bodies of water. The house of the Visayan chief was a longhouse with walls of timber that was ornamented with carvings and had a thatch roof. His followers' houses were smaller and lower huts of either hardwood or bamboo with roofs of thatch (Alcina n.d., 1–IV: 33, 36).

Initially, after the foundation of Spanish Manila in 1571, the Spanish settlers constructed dwellings in the native manner but these were consumed by a fire in 1583. They then constructed tall palaces in cut stone with roofs of tile, following their accustomed style in Mexico and southern Spain (Rios de Coronel 1903–09: 286). But two earthquakes in the seventeenth century led to the collapse of these palaces. The fleeing residents saw the native frame houses still standing (Fayol 1903–09: 220–21, 225). A synthesis of two building traditions thus developed. The heavy roof was supported by wooden posts buried deep into the ground. These could sway freely during a tremor, whereas stone walls could not. The resulting house is thus low by Spanish and Mexican standards, for it has only two stories. The upper story has wooden walls; the ground story stone walls. Both are mere curtains. Often the great posts are exposed within the house or are made so that they stand freely beside the stone walls. In comparison with Mexico, Spain, and the rest of Southeast Asia, these traditional houses have long windows that extend almost from post to post with an additional small window (*ventanilla*) between the window sill and the floor sill (see Zialcita and Tinio 1980).

Budhi Gunawan was thus correct in likening the wood-and-stone house (*bahay na bato at kahoy*) to a longhouse. The construction system of much of the house, except for the stone walls, has continuities with the rest of the region. Its closest cousin is the *rumah gedung* of southern Sumatra which has a conventional hip roof over a wooden upper story and ground floor constructed out of stone.

This building style also has continuities with the Sinicized world. In contrast to the rest of Southeast Asia and to Mexico and Spain, it has long, continuous windows. Moreover, these are closed with wooden latticework panels that are made of translucent materials that are not glass. Traditionally in Spain and Spanish America, windows were French doors opening onto a projecting balcony. Up until the present in Thailand, Malaysia and southern Sumatra, windows are likewise full-length doors whose two wooden leaves are pushed out to extend over the facade. A wooden railing with balusters on the same plane as the wall keeps the insider from falling out of the window. In contrast China, Korea and Japan have latticework panels with thick rice paper pasted onto one side and which therefore allow light to filter through. In the Philippines flat capiz shells (*Placuna placenta*) serve as panes. Unlike Chinese windows, but like Japanese ones, the panels do not push out but slide in grooves on a sill. Chinese artisans migrated to the Philippines from the opening of Spanish rule down to the present. The Japanese, on the other hand, came during the early seventeenth century as merchants and refugees from religious persecution – in 1603, there were 1,500 Japanese in the Manila suburb of Dilao (Delacour 1994). They returned, as migrants, from the 1880s to the early 1900s.

During the nineteenth century Chinese artisans appear to have popularized wooden panels decorated with cutout and carved flowers and birds throughout Southeast Asia. So did Japanese artisans in the Philippines. Indeed, according to oral tradition, a master craftsman who carved some of the best traceries at Silay, Negros Occidental in the 1900s was called Kitai. This seems to me to have been a Japanese family name. These traceried panels have a functional purpose in the Filipino wood-and-stone style. Situated between ceiling and interior walls, they help wind and light circulate.

Given these various characteristics, it is illogical to continue insisting that the wood-and-stone Filipino houses are "Spanish" copies and have nothing to do with either Southeast Asia or Asia in general.

Indeed in comparison to Java and northern Vietnam, the millennial tradition of building on stilts has persisted longer in Filipino cities and villages, partly because of the wood-and-stone style. As a Filipino, I am always struck by the fact that many Javanese houses, whether in the city or the countryside, are single-storied and are of brick with a stucco finish rather than being frame houses on stilts. And yet in earlier centuries, central Javanese houses were built on stilts, as suggested by bas-reliefs at Prambanan. In Vietnam, as pointed out above, a Chinese preference for ground-level houses nearly led to the disappearance of building wooden structures on piles. Reid suggests (1988: 62) that in northern Vietnam and Java large timbers had become scarce by the sixteenth century in the most densely populated areas. Thus houses were built at ground level. The point is that in some aspects of culture, the Hispanicized Filipino is more traditionally Southeast Asian than some of his neighbors.

One criterion therefore for defining a Southeast Asian architectural communality would be the use of the house-on-stilts. But this criterion could be broadened to include as well all responses to the physical environment and to the preexisting traditions in the region. Thus defined, Vietnamese temples and palaces can be regarded as fitting the tropical landscape. Though influenced by Chinese ideals of architecture, they differ in not having ceilings and interior wall dividers (Bezacier 1955: 34). Rafters and interior columns are well-articulated, perhaps as a response to the need for maximum ventilation in the tropics. Even Filipino churches dating from the sixteenth to the nineteenth centuries, often termed "Spanish," may be "Southeast Asian" after all. Because of the frequency of earthquakes, they tend to be relatively low in height. Their ceilings are of wood rather than of stone. At times the woodwork of the roof is exposed in Mudejar fashion. Moreover, Chinese motifs appear in the treatment of clouds and garment folds in statuary and in the belfries. In Spain and Spanish America, towers are integrated into the facade and are four-sided. In contrast Philippine towers are often polygonal from base to dome, may rise in tiers, and are sometimes separated from the church as freestanding structures. They thus evoke the pagoda, as the Spanish historian, Pedro Armengol Ortiz, has casually suggested in conversation.

Religious rituals

Processions are essentially demonstrations where the faithful pray while accompanying religious images along a determined route. The most popular procession in many Filipino towns and cities is that of the Santo Entierro (sacred burial) or "Christ in the Coffin." This takes place every year on Good Friday evening to mark the anniversary of Christ's death on the cross. Lifesize ensembles of wooden and/or ivory statues, clothed with gold- and silver-trimmed brocade and velvet, dramatize scenes from the passion and death of Christ. The ensembles are carried on silver floats decorated with flowers and lights. Most of the town turns out for this procession. The climax of the procession is the statue of Christ in a gold-trimmed glass bier, followed by the statue of the Mater Dolorosa (grieving mother) robed in black velvet trimmed with silver. At first glance, the procession could not possibly have any connection with Southeast Asia. But it has, for the procession has continuities with the cult of the ancestors.

In pre-Hispanic times, upon the death of the chief, he was mummified and his body was kept in a coffin in the innermost part of the house together with family heirlooms (Chirino 1969 [1604]: 88). The belief seems to have been that his spirit would protect the house from intruders. The Ifugao of the Cordillera Mountains would keep the ancestral corpse in a sealed coffin underneath their houses (Barton 1946). In pagan times, the Batak of Sumatra kept the dried corpse of their ancestor in a boat-shaped coffin hanging from the eaves outside their house for from one to ten years (Sibeth 1991: 70–71). The custom of keeping the dried remains of the ancestor inside or close to the house may have been widespread in Indonesia at one time but is no longer so, because of Indian-introduced cremation. This has caught on even among non-Indianized groups in the outer islands, for instance among the Dyak of Borneo who burn the remains of their ancestor in a large ceremony called *tiwah* (Bambang and Prijanti 1990: 61).

To go back to the Philippines, this time to the Hispanicized lowlands: some rural Bicolanos keep the bones of their ancestors. After these have dried up and have been exhumed from the first burial, they are wrapped with cloth into a bundle and hung from the rafters for their power to protect (Cannell 1991).

Ancestors were revered and prayed to in pagan times all over Southeast Asia; they are prayed to even today by Hispanicized Filipinos. Among the Ilocanos in Northern Luzon, people lay aside a portion of any newly pre-pared roast meat or sweetmeat for the deceased ancestors of the house. While such offerings do not take place in Metro Manila, friends confide that they do pray once in a while to a deceased grandparent or parent for help.

Christian missionaries came in the late sixteenth century from a West where attention was focused on the passion and death of Christ rather than on his resurrection. They promoted religious statuary because these drama-tized religious events and important persons. What differentiates the Philip-pines from Spanish America and Spain is that processional statuary is owned and kept at home by Filipino families. In Spain and Spanish America, they are owned and kept either by the Church or by confraternities. In Filipino towns, families vie with each other to own an ensemble or single statue that is taken out in procession during Holy Week or the town fiesta. They keep the images in the innermost part of their house: the bedroom where they also keep their other prized possessions. And the icons that signify that the owners are at the social pinnacle are: the Mater Dolorosa and the body of Christ in the coffin (Santo Entierro). It used to be that those who owned either of these two were the oldest and wealthiest families in town, accord-ing to the expert on processions, Basilides Bautista. Finding that the cult of the deceased chief was so entrenched, the missionaries of previous centuries may have decided to allow the faithful to keep large processional icons in their homes, as substitutes for the mummy. Significantly enough, the icons are referred to using parental terms. Mary becomes *Ina* (Mother); while Christ, who was the Son of God, is called *Ama* (Father).

Conclusion

Because the Association of Southeast Asian Nations (ASEAN) exists and closer exchanges among Southeast Asian countries are growing, the question of "What is Southeast Asia?" has become an important one. People look for symbols that can make them feel that they share something which differentiates them from the rest of the world. As a starting point, we should avoid projecting our present desires to the past. A "Southeast Asia," conceived as a felt unity, like "Western Europe" or "Islam" has never existed. Historically the latter two have been ecumenes with vivid, deeply felt, shared symbols. Countries within the presently defined boundaries of Southeast Asia have not formed a single ecumene. At present these countries participate in four different Great Traditions: the Indic, the Sinic, the Islamic, and the Western. It would be a mistake to develop a Southeast Asian identity only around communalities derived from a common Indic heritage; or conversely, only around aboriginal elements which lie outside these Great Traditions. Either option effectively excludes Sinicized central and northern Vietnam and Hispanicized Luzon and the Visayas. Such an attempt may also tend to alienate devout Moslem Malaysians, Filipinos, and Indonesians. It is better to stress a variety of communalities:

1. Responses to a similar environment, e.g. fish sauce or the house-on-stilts.

2. Motifs brought about by common myths and behavior generated by speaking closely related languages, Austroasiatic, Austronesian, and Tai, such as the cult of the ancestors or the relatively higher status of women.

3. Influences of the four Great Traditions which create a sense of community. Necessarily this will emphasize specific cultural areas within the overall cluster that is Southeast Asia. Aside from Malaysia, Indonesia, and the southern Philippines, there are pockets of Moslems in southern Vietnam, Cambodia, southern Thailand, and Burma. They will naturally feel an affinity for each other. On the other hand the widespread use of English as a literary medium creates bridges between Filipinos, Malaysians, and Singaporeans.

4. Influences from the outside which create a common ground but which thus far have not fostered an all-embracing ecumene. For instance, the pervasive influence of Chinese migrants has created a common culinary symbol throughout the region: the noodle and a common motif of turn-of-the century houses, traceried woodwork. But both have not been accompanied by the transmission of Chinese script, classics, and temple architecture to the ordinary Southeast Asian.

Analyzed on these four levels, "Southeast Asia" has space for the Hispanicized Filipinos. Many of their characteristic artifacts and rituals do indeed link them to the Hispanic world, but also to Southeast Asia. Their cooking style, their national costume, their traditional urban houses, and even their Good Friday rituals bridge two worlds: Southeast Asia and the Hispanic world. Such a Southeast Asia would have space for the Sinicized Vietnamese as well. In some American graduate schools, one favorite question is: "Does Vietnam belong to Southeast Asia or to the Far East?" This parallels the question raised for the Philippines: "Does it belong to Southeast Asia or to the Hispanic world?" My answer would be a counterquestion: "Why not to two or more worlds?" Malaysia and Indonesia belong to both Southeast Asia and the Islamic world and this is not questioned. A more dynamic definition of Southeast Asia also creates space for Chinese enclaves like Singapore, whose traditional shop houses, with their Chinese roofs, Corinthian pilasters and Portuguese tiles, obviously combine several traditions.

To imagine "Southeast Asia," a more inductive approach is needed, as has been adopted for instance by Anthony Reid in his synthesis (1988). Instead of assuming that the defining characteristic of Southeast Asia is Indianization, he sorts out different aspects of Southeast Asian life: the material culture, social organization, festivals and amusements, and he articulates the patterns cutting across them. His approach is rich in data and detail. Moreover, it embraces both the Philippines and Vietnam. Hopefully, someone in the future will show how these communalities have been changed by, and at the same time have changed, the four Great Traditions. At present the world is conceived of as a giant jigsaw wherein each part has a defining essence. "Asia" is supposed to have an essence, so likewise its subregion, "Southeast Asia" is also assumed to have one. It is more realistic to imagine the latter as a configuration of cultural traditions of different shapes and textures overlapping with and interconnected with each other.

Notes

1 The exact term for this type of culture in both Arnold Toynbee's work and the Anglo-American tradition of archaeology is "civilization," that is, culture where the state and the city (the word *civitas* in Latin can be translated in both ways) are both present as institutions and which can embrace a wide variety of cultures to create an ecumene (see Toynbee 1972: 43 ff.) However, this precise use of "civilization" as a type of culture is not observed by many writers. Instead they use "civilization" and "culture" interchangeably. To avoid confusion, I prefer not to use the term in this essay.

2 "Culture area" is a concept which is much used in American anthropology. I have not used it because it tends to connote a bounded geographical area where different cultures share similar traits. So defined, it is similar to common responses to an ecosystem and is only one way to classify cultures together.

3 Recently, a copper plate with an Old Malay text in the Early Kawi script used at one time in Bali (Indonesia), Thailand, and Champa (central Vietnam) was unearthed in Laguna. It is a semiofficial certificate of acquittal of a debt incurred by a person in high office, together with his entire family. It can be dated to around A.D. 900. Place names referred to in the text still exist to this day in the region in and around Manila (Postma 1992). This raises anew the question: to what extent did Indianizing influences penetrate northward? And still another: why did this influence, if present, not lead to the formation of a monarchy? Also, why did the script fall into disuse?

4 Still, one has to qualify what this Indian Great Tradition would mean today. Over the course of centuries, participating cultures have become isolated from each other: first because of the advent of Islam and the conversion of Java and Sumatra; second, because Western colonialism created new political boundaries. As a result, Bali has gone on its own separate course. Perhaps the Indian Great Tradition no longer exists as an all-embracing tradition but as several autonomous traditions. In contrast, Islam may be diverse, but there are focal points in the tradition, like the pilgrimage to Mecca, which create a vivid sense of universal community.

5 Singapore is both Sinic and Western. Its unequalled efficiency suggests that it has internalized Western notions of public and business administration far more than its neighbors, including the Philippines.

References

Alcina, Francisco Ignacio (n.d.) The Munoz Text of Alcina's History of the Bisayan Islands (1668). Transliteration from a microfilm of the Spanish text in the Biblioteca del Palacio, Madrid, by Victor Baltazar. Chicago: Philippine Studies Program, Department of Anthropology.

Barton, Roy. 1946. *The Religion of the Ifugaos*. American Anthropological Association Memoir 65. Washington DC: American Anthropological Association.

Bambang Harsrinuksmo and Prijanti Pakan. 1990. "Adat dan tata cara penguburan," pp. 69–75 in *Ensiklopedi Nasional Indonesia*, vol.1. Jakarta: Cipta Adi Pustaka.

Bellwood, Peter. 1985. *Prehistory of the Indo-Malaysian Archipelago*. Sydney: Academic Press.

Bezacier, Louis. 1955. *L'Art Vietnamien*. Paris: Editions de l'Union Française.

Bhusan, Jamila Brig. 1958. *The Costumes and Textiles of India*. Bombay: Taraporevala's Treasure House of Books.

Cannell, Fenella. 1991. "Catholicism, Spirit Mediums and the Ideal of Beauty in a Bicolano Community, Philippines." Ph.D. dissertation, University of London.

Chirino, Pedro. 1969 [1604]. *Relacion de las Islas Filipinas/ The Philippines in 1600*. Manila: Historical Conservation Society.

Coedès, George. 1964. *Les Etats Hindouisés d'Indochine et d'Indonésie*. Paris: E. de Boccard.

Coedès, George. 1968. *The Indianized States of Southeast Asia*. Honolulu: East-West Center Press.

Delacour, Catherine. 1994. "Des guerriers japonais," in *Un Trésor sous la Mer*, eds. Dominique Carré, Jean-Louis Desroches and Frank Goddio. [Paris?]: Association Française d'Action Artistique, Ministère des Affaires Etrangères.

de la Torre, Visitacion. 1986. *The Barong Tagalog: The Philippine National Wear*. Manila: A. Bautista Press.

Fayol, Fray Joseph. 1903–09. "Affairs in Filipinas, 1644–47," pp. 212–75 in *The Philippine Islands, 1493–1898*, 35, eds. Emma Blair and James Robertson. Cleveland: Arthur H. Clark Company.

Fifield, Russell Hunt. 1958. *The Diplomacy of Southeast Asia: 1945–1958*. New York: Harper & Brothers.

Fox, James F. 1987. "Southeast Asian religion: insular cultures," pp. 520–26 in *The Encyclopedia of Religion*, 13, ed. Mircea Eliade. New York: Macmillan Publishing Company.

Francisco, Juan R. 1985. *Indian Culture in the Philippines: Views and Reviews*. Kuala Lumpur: University of Malaya.

Fraser-Lu, Sylvia. 1988. *Handwoven Textiles of Southeast Asia*. Oxford: Oxford University Press.

Gilmore. David D. 1982. "Anthropology of the Mediterranean area," *Annual Review of Anthropology* 11: 175–205.

Harrison, Brian. 1968. *South-East Asia*. London: Macmillan.

Ho Tai, Hue-tam. 1985. "Religion in Vietnam: a world of gods and spirits," pp. 22–40 in *Vietnam: Essays On History, Culture and Society*, eds. David W.P. Elliott et al. New York: The Asia Society.

Hutterer, Karl L. 1976. "An evolutionary approach to the Southeast Asian cultural sequence," *Current Anthropology* 17: 221–42.

Jones, E.L. 1991. "A framework for the history of economic growth in Southeast Asia," *Australian Economic History Review* 31: 5–19.

Keyes, Charles. 1987. "Southeast Asian religion: mainland cultures," pp. 513–20 in *The Encyclopedia of Religion*, 13, ed. Mircea Eliade. New York: Macmillan Publishing Company.

Kennett, Frances. 1994. *World Dress*. London: Mitchell Beazley.

La Gironiere, Paul de. 1962 [1853]. *Twenty Years in the Philippines*. Manila: Filipiniana Book Guild.

Lincoln, Bruce. 1987. "Indo-European religions," pp. 198–204 in *The Encyclopedia of Religion*, 7, ed. Mircea Eliade. New York: Macmillan Publishing Company.

McCloud, Donald G. 1986. *System and Process in Southeast Asia: The Evolution of a Region*. Boulder, Colorado: Westview Press.

Magos, Alice 1986. "The Ideological Basis and Social Context of Ma-aram Practice in a Kiniray-a Society." Ph.D. dissertation, University of the Philippines.

Maxwell, Robyn. 1990. *Textiles of Southeast Asia: Tradition, Trend and Transformation*. Oxford: Oxford University Press.

O'Connor, Stanley J. 1988. "Southeast Asian sculpture," pp. 401–03 in *Encyclopedia of Asian History*, 3, ed. Ainslie T. Embree. New York: Charles Scribner's Sons.

Osborne, Milton. 1983. *Southeast Asia: An Introductory History*. London: George Allen & Unwin.

Pitkin, D. 1963. "Mediterranean Europe," *Anthropology Quarterly* 36: 120–29.

Postma, Antoon. 1992. "The Laguna copper-plate inscription: text and commentary," *Philippine Studies*, 40, pp. 183–203.

Redfield, Robert. 1956. *Peasant Society and Culture: An Anthropological Approach to Civilization*. Chicago: University of Chicago Press.

Reid, Anthony 1988. *Southeast Asia in the Age of Commerce, 1450–1680, vol 1, The Lands Below the Wind.* New Haven: Yale University Press.

Rios de Coronel, Hernando. 1903–09. "Memorial y relacion para su Magestad, 1621," pp. 183–297 in *The Philippine Islands, 1493–1898,* 19, eds. Emma Blair and James Robertson. Cleveland: Arthur H. Clark Company.

Sibeth, Adim.1991. *The Batak: Peoples of the Island of Sumatra.* London: Thames & Hudson.

Taylor, Keith Weller. 1983. *The Birth of Vietnam.* Berkeley: University of California Press.

Tilman, Robert O. 1987. *Southeast Asia and the Enemy Beyond: ASEAN Perception of External Threats.* Boulder, Colorado and London: Westview Press.

Toynbee, Arnold. 1982. *A Study of History.* New York: Weathervane Books.

Unabia, Carmen Ching. 1986. The Bukidnon Batbatnon and Pamuhat: A Socio-Literary Study, 2–I: 1–4, narrated by Anastacio Saway, narrator; translated by C.C. Unabia and Danilo de la Mance. Unpublished ms.

Wicks, Robert S. 1988. "Southeast Asian architecture," pp. 86-87 in *Encyclopedia of Asian History,* 1, ed. Ainslie T. Embree. New York: Charles Scribner & Sons.

Winzeler, Robert L. 1976. "Ecology, culture, social organization, and state formation in Southeast Asia," *Current Anthropology* 17: 623–39.

Wolters, O.W. 1982. *History, Culture, and Region in Southeast Asian Perspectives.* Singapore: Institute of Southeast Asian Studies.

Woodside, Alexander B. 1971. *Vietnam and the Chinese Model.* Cambridge, Mass.: Harvard University Press

Zialcita, Fernando N. and Martin I. Tinio. 1980. *Philippine Ancestral Houses: 1810-1930.* Quezon City: GFC Press.

Chapter 3

Cultural Knowledge, Nation-States, and the Limits of Globalization in Southeast Asia

TONG Chee Kiong and LIAN Kwen Fee

The Mediation of Cultural Universes

Culture enables people to make sense of their lives by making available ideas and meanings, with which they are able to articulate their experience of the world. It enables individuals and groups to traverse the U-turns and dead ends which inevitably come with the business of living, and helps to resolve the contradictions and uncertainties of such experiences. However in a world made smaller by the expansion of capitalism, technological revolutions, economic interdependence, and the rise of nation-states, the cultural resources for making sense of an increasingly complex world have multiplied several times. These sources of cultural knowledge may be global or universal, regional, national, and communal – all of which are arbitrated by the individual or the group.

The cultural significance of globalization

The "global" refers to post-capitalist society in which the everyday lives of people are dominated by consumption and the economy, and the type of culture in such a society may be described as consumer-utilitarian. Such an economy has more than just utilitarian significance. As Schudson (1994: 32) describes, "In modern society, many goods are mass produced and widely distributed, and these goods may become not only devices of practical import but symbolic structures that command attention and evoke devotion or allegiance for their own sake and from the fact that they have been shared." Common consumption patterns and lifestyles, and their dissemination through a widespread communications network have been primarily responsible for creating a new consciousness in which the world is regarded as a single place or locale.

Regional associations

While the influence of consumer culture has been pervasive in most societies, regional associations are a more recent development and their origins may be traced to the Cold War years. Regional groupings such as the European Union, ASEAN, and NAFTA have subsequently emerged as loose economic and political unions – mainly to facilitate freer movements of trade and industry. Such groupings may also include "pan"-nationalisms, which Smith (1990: 186) defines as attempts to unify several states into a single political community on the basis of common cultural characteristics such as a lingua franca. He cites as examples of these pan-Arabism, pan-Africanism, and even pan-Latin Americanism. While he refers to these as incipient regional cultures, their influence has been more patchy than real.

Imperatives of nation-building

The emergence of the nation-state is a modern phenomenon in so far as it has evolved over the past two centuries, a period which saw the development of industrial society and the expansion of capitalism. In contrast to the diffuse influence of regional and global cultures the nation-state has exercised a dominant and comprehensive influence in the lives of its citizens as a source of cultural knowledge. As an institution actively engaged in constructing society and community, the nation-state makes available public symbols and ideas which can be invoked as blueprints for these ideals. It sets the parameters within which the "good society" should operate and individuals' personal and collective identities should be subsumed. Nation-building is ideological work because it is highly articulated, self-conscious, and attempts to provide comprehensive solutions to both contemporary problems and those anticipated to appear in the future.

Nation-building consists of three processes. First, it requires state elites to formulate a common or national ideology. In Southeast Asian states this often involves explicitly setting out certain ideas and values which are deemed desirable for their citizens. Hence *pancasila*, multiracialism, and *rukunegara* have been espoused as national ideologies in Indonesia, Singapore, and Malaysia respectively. Second, a public culture compatible with the tenets of the national ideology is promoted. Although this may be confined to public occasions and celebrations, such visible displays of culture have symbolic significance and serve as reminders to the population that they belong to a single community. Third, the careful construction and articulation of a common ideology and public culture is necessary for the purpose of nurturing a collective or national identity. Individual citizens expect some consistency between their private identities and the symbolic contents upheld by public authorities, the latter being expressed in public institutions and celebrated in public events (Breton 1984: 124–5).

Moreover, the imperatives of nation-building require the state to essentialize and totalize (Chun 1996: 70). To essentialize something means to reduce it to its supposed pure form and to treat that form as if it exists in reality. For example, states in Southeast Asia often essentialize ethnicity by assuming that ethnic groups possess inherently different cultural or behavioral characteristics; these are then used to distinguish them for the purpose of government. By way of illustration, the state essentializes "Chinese-ness" in Singapore as much as "Malay-ness" in Malaysia and "Javanese-ness" in Indonesia. To totalize is to apply the relevant classification to as many of the inhabitants as possible in order to facilitate government. In this way, the nation-state homogenizes, categorizes, and absorbs in order to eliminate ambiguity (Bauman 1990: 165–66). If physical borders separate states spatially and are zealously maintained in order to assert the identity of the state, then cultural boundaries are equally important in distinguishing different groups in the minds of the population for the same end. A nation-state is a conceptual community because it attempts to impose a cultural homogeneity on its population (Giddens, cited by Schlesinger 1991: 167).

Community and tradition

The final source of cultural knowledge is found in the communal or ethnic community. It is one of the most enduring of human organizations, it antedates the rise of the nation-state and has premodern origins (Smith 1988). Cultural resources deriving from the ethnic community are also described as "traditions" (Swidler 1986: 279). These are articulated cultural beliefs and practices, but unlike ideology they are usually taken for granted, are partial rather than all-inclusive, and are diverse and not always enthusiastically supported, particularly when they are no longer appropriate to modern conditions. They may be used against the state or for the state. They frequently offer resistance to the ineluctable expansion of capitalism and to the development of a global consciousness. Because the nation-state and globalization share to an extent a common goal in homogenizing the diversity of "natural" communities, the latter often find themselves in a position of having to offer "cultural resistance" to preserve their identities. As Chun asserts, one can view such discourses of identity "as interpretive mechanisms through which specific people, institutions or cultures localize (or indigenize) diverse global flows in order to negotiate a meaningful life space or position themselves within a situation of power" (Chun 1996: 69).

All four sources of cultural knowledge – global, regional, national, and communal – more or less impinge on the personal consciousness and identity of individuals, and all of them derive from wider collectivities. Giddens (cited in Schlesinger 1991: 166) describes these collectivities as "locales of operation." Locales are physical settings in which typical interactions occur. They are constituted by interactions in time and space, and are necessary for sustaining meaningful communication between actors. Locales may be as diverse as shops and empires. When the four locales referred to in this discussion are taken together, they form a complex culture with which individuals and groups continually have to cope. Individuals, groups, and organizations are involved in an endless process of mediation between the locales or levels of cultural sensibility. They seek to resolve inevitable tensions, conflict, and contradictions which arise when the locales intersect. This paper addresses how, in particular, nation-states in Southeast Asia attempt to mediate between the global and communal constituencies as sources of cultural knowledge for individuals and groups.

The limit of globalization: the nation-state

We begin by reiterating Giddens' point that "the emergence of the nation-state was integrally bound up with the expansion of capitalism" (cited in Schlesinger 1991: 166). It is therefore a modern development (see Gellner 1983; Anderson 1983). As we alluded to earlier, globalization has its origins in the expansion of capitalism. Contemporary globalization is a postcapitalist development and its effect on nation-states is to make the boundaries between them more porous. The nation-state is the site in which the universalizing tendencies of globalization are articulated. However the nation-state, despite the remote possibility that it may dissipate in the face of universalization, sets its limits according to the logic of its existence. The explanation for this may be sought in the nature of global and national cultures (Smith 1990: 177–9). Smith argues that a global culture is essentially calculated, artificial, and technically oriented. It is a mélange of disparate influences drawn from everywhere and nowhere. For this reason it is timeless, ahumanistic, and decontextualized. In contrast national cultures are particular, time bound and expressive, and their eclecticism operates within cultural constraints. They are historically conscious and are therefore contextualized. It is the decontextualizing proclivities of globalization, for example the preoccupation with material consumption, which dehumanizes individuals and communities – whose identities are only meaningfully enunciated in context. As a consequence the nation-state, while it is committed to development, must moderate the "homelessness" inherent in globalization. For this purpose it appeals to communal or ethnic traditions as the basis of national identity; in doing so it has to contend with the danger that such appeals may easily slide into ethnic chauvinism that may prove the undoing of plural societies. Hence such traditions are reinterpreted and neutralized to head off the possibility of polarization, and to make them more acceptable to a heterogeneous population.

Because of the need to contextualize national identity, state elites often go back into history to resuscitate premodern traditions, which may then be used as the basis of national ideology and public culture. The use of "invented tradition" as discussed by Hobsbawm and Ranger (1989: 1–14), involves identifying particular practices and beliefs which help to inculcate certain values and norms of behavior. Such traditions are also attempts to establish continuity with an appropriate past. If they are repeated often enough, the practices may then be routinized in the public institutions of the state and adopted as public culture.

In spatial-symbolic terms, the connection between national and communal cultures may also be framed as center-periphery relations. Shils (1975) argues that a society has a cultural center from which its influence radiates. The center refers to a central order of symbols, values and beliefs that govern society. The periphery is that social space which, because of its remoteness, is relatively free of control from the center. National culture is viewed as emanating from the center and is homogenizing whereas communal culture is peripheral and resistant to such homogenization. Despite the apparent tension between the two, both national and communal cultures are context-bound and may be seen as competing against each other. A global culture is contextless and, although pervasive and unavoidable, it is refracted through nation-building to make it palatable to traditional communities. Identities, whether of nation-states or communities, are only sustained by anchoring them in historical experiences and memories, and in cultural specificities. Because the emergence of the nation-state, as we referred to earlier, is interwoven with capitalist development and globalization, it has necessarily involved itself with the homogenizing tendencies of the latter. In doing so, the nation-state is in danger of losing the distinctiveness on which its identity and existence are dependent. From time to time, it must "pull back" and reaffirm its historical lineage and cultural roots to revitalize its identity. Hence although the "traditional community" may be an obstacle to nation-building, the nation-state is unable to do away with it.

Transnationalization: a challenge to the nation-state

In the discussion of Indonesia and Malaysia, this essay will illustrate the contradictory roles of the nation-state in the face of globalization. It examines the interplay between global, national, and communal cultures as they work out some kind of accommodation with each other in these Southeast Asian societies. So far we have dealt with these cultural universes as if their influences are discrete. One of the other consequences of globalization and the development of postindustrial society is a more recent phenomenon, namely the process of transnationalization, which not only involves the migration of labor but also the movement of capital across national boundaries.

Transnationalization has produced what Basch *et al.* (1994: 7–8) call "transmigrants." The essential element of transnationalism is the multiplicity of involvements that transmigrants sustain in both home and host societies, and their identities manifest themselves in transnational terms. In contrast to Indonesia and Malaysia, cultural development in Singapore has taken a different turn. This is because Singapore's strategic location and economic origins forced it to come to terms with cross-national influences much earlier than either Indonesia or Malaysia. The discussion of Singapore will address this issue.

Indonesia

The ideology of pancasila

When Indonesian nationalists declared independence from colonial rule after the Japanese surrendered to the Allied Forces in 1945, they also took the opportunity to formulate an ideology for the independent nation called *pancasila* which they incorporated into the new constitution. At first reading, the five principles laid down in *pancasila* – namely, belief in God, humanitarianism, nationalism or national unity, democracy, and social justice – would appear to reflect the liberal influence of Western political theory and a commitment to economic development. However, an understanding of the nationalist interpretation of these ideas quickly dispels the view that *pancasila* was an unquestioned affirmation of Western notions of political and economic progress. For example, when both Sukarno and Suharto referred to the democratic principle, they had in mind an idealized concept of traditional village government in which consultation and consensus were essential to any decision-making (Ramage 1995: 13). The principle, as far as they were concerned, did not refer to Western forms of parliamentary democracy. Of the other tenets, humanitarianism emphasized the practice of tolerance and respect between all Indonesians, and nationalism required the submergence of regional and ethnic loyalties to an allegiance to the Indonesian state. All these were attempts to formulate a national philosophy which respected and accommodated the plural character of Indonesian society. The fifth principle, social justice, is a commitment to egalitarianism which can only be realized through sustained economic development and rising standards of living. This was a central preoccupation of the New Order government of President Suharto, which saw the active encouragement of direct foreign investment after 1965 when Indonesia abandoned the socialist path along which the growing local communist movement had been taking it. In sum, the implementation of *pancasila*, conceived of as the basis of Indonesia's national ideology, and its subsequent interpretations have consisted of attempts by the nation-state to mediate between the demands of global economic development and the loyalties of local communities and traditions.

National culture vs. cultural traditions

Given the geographical extent of Indonesia and the cultural diversity of its population, the state is particularly sensitive to the omnipresent danger of the politicization of regional, ethnic, linguistic, and religious differences. These have from time to time erupted into separatist movements since the founding of the republic. The fall of Suharto in 1998 precipitated calls for varying degrees of independence ranging from outright secession in East Timor and Aceh to a limited autonomy in Riau. These have underlined the tenuous hold the Indonesian state has over its far-flung provinces. For this reason, the state has taken great pains to forge a "philosophy," in Geertz's words, "soft enough to soothe 'cultural' sentiments, and hard enough to contain them with the carefully fenced preserve of the officially unpolitical" (Geertz 1990: 79). Acciaioli (1985: 151–53) illustrates how the rich cultural traditions of Indonesia's local communities have been emasculated by the practice of such a state ideology. *Adat* or "customary usage which has been handed down from the ancestors" has been the basis of regulating the social behavior of the more than three hundred ethnic groups in the archipelago. Over the years, first with the colonial administration and later with the extension of the nation-state over much of Indonesia, the practice of *adat* in many communities has increasingly been restricted and does not enjoy the authority it once had. Instead it has been relegated to the performance of ceremony or ritual, and its value is primarily aesthetic. The expansion and promotion of tourism under the New Order also gave to the state an opportunity to neutralize the political potential of cultural differences by restricting cultural expressions to performance and display (Acciaioli 1985: 158).

While *pancasila* philosophy, in recognition of humanitarian and democratic principles, allows for the practice of different cultures out of respect for the heterogeneous composition of the population, these are subsumed within the overriding requirement of national unity. National culture in Indonesia is defined as a hybrid mix of the best of existing cultures in the nation, but the political dominance of the Javanese has meant that greater prominence has been given to their influence (Hooker and Dick 1993: 4). Hence official culture has drawn on Javanese traditions which have been reinterpreted within the requirements of *pancasila* and a pan-Indonesian identity (ibid: 7). The articulation of *pancasila* ideology, particularly under the New Order government, has been developmentalist; and the presentation of national culture has necessarily been plural, eclectic, impartial, and cosmopolitan (Geertz 1990: 89). Carried to its extreme, the state may find itself in the unwitting position of decontextualizing its national identity. If this happens its legitimacy may be called into question, as will be elaborated in a moment. It is therefore unable to abandon its Javanese roots not only for this reason, but also because its political support is dependent on Javanese society. Furthermore, in Shils' terms, Java is the "cultural-spatial center" from which it must operate in order to maintain its influence over the periphery, the outer islands of Indonesia. However, recent events in Indonesia have shown that Javanese political dominance in the past, translated into Suharto's authoritarian rule, was no longer acceptable to the people of these islands.

Reinterpreting development

Since the early 1970s, urban Indonesian society in particular has been flooded by the consumer culture associated with international capitalism, and has undergone rapid economic and social change. Since the late 1980s, growing concern has been voiced by many Indonesians that such changes, achieved under the New Order government, should be balanced by a reevaluation of the spiritual and mental well-being of the population (Hooker and Dick 1993: 1–2). As a consequence, the state finds itself in an ambiguous position. As Foulcher (1990: 302) comments, "On the one hand middle class consumerism is an essential component of 'development' as it is conceived in Indonesia, while on the other the lifestyle which it spawns is viewed with

apprehension, as the location of the negative 'side-effects' of development."
In response, the state and its representatives have attempted to reconstruct
"Indonesian" values and traditions to ameliorate the perception that the effects of "development," which is so central to the policy of the New Order
government, may be negative.

One of the ways it has attempted to do this is to use the national language, Bahasa Indonesia, (which is based on Malay), to convey to the population an "Indonesian" understanding of development (Foulcher 1990: 305).
In his Independence Day speech in 1983, President Suharto gave a detailed
list of the qualities which a modern society needs in order to sustain development successfully (Hooker 1993: 279). These included a mental attitude
that is considerate, thrifty and simple, hardworking, conscientious, orderly,
dedicated, honest, and noble. This use of Bahasa Indonesia as an official
standardized language for both native and nonnative speakers throughout
the country helps to shape the behavior and communication patterns of many
communities in line with one dominant orientation (ibid: 273). The
President's speech in 1983 might be interpreted as meaning that if development is disciplined by the values he outlined, then Indonesians need not fear
the excesses of material growth.

Gotong royong

The state is actively involved in reconciling the contradictory forces between capitalist development and the preservation of the identities and practices of local communities. In seeking to do this, the government itself sometimes invents traditions. One of these is the indigenous practice of *gotong
royong* or mutual assistance. *Gotong royong* is practiced in village communities in most parts of Indonesia, and it may take various forms (Bowen
1986: 547–49). As labor exchange, it is commonly employed in major agricultural tasks such as hoeing, plowing, planting, and harvesting. A second
form of mutual assistance is generalized reciprocity, which refers to both a
general obligation and the idea of eventual return. For example, a village
may be obliged to help out in the marriage of a child or the death of a
relative, as a matter of obligation or in return for past favors. A third form
consists of labor that is mobilized as a consequence of political subordination, and is akin to corvée labor commandeered by a local official. These
types of *gotong royong* vary culturally depending on their regional location.
In the New Order, the institution of *gotong royong* was appropriated by the
state to support efforts at top-down implementation of development programs (Bowen 1986: 553). In one such program introduced in the 1980s,
financial grants were given to villages on condition that they provided free

labor and materials not locally obtainable to construct or repair infrastructure such as irrigation, roads, and public buildings.

Gotong royong has been incorporated into national culture and is recognized as such in Indonesia. The significance of this practice is that it facilitates national development, by rendering it in a way recognizable by village traditions. At the same time, by presenting it as an example of the spirit of self-sacrifice and as an expression of the identity of the village community, government officials are able to soften any negative perceptions the villagers may hold toward such development. A cultural practice, which appears to be distinctive to individual communities, has been appropriated and homogenized by the state – and then promoted as official culture and incorporated into the collective identity of Indonesians.

Malaysia

Malaysia introduced its own version of a national ideology, *rukunegara*, soon after Sino-Malay riots broke out in 1969, so that the principles enunciated were a specific response to the dangers of interethnic conflict and a commitment to maintaining national unity. As a formulation of national ideology it has not been subjected to the close scrutiny that *pancasila* has received; neither has it been articulated with the same regularity and intensity. Unlike Indonesia where the government has had to contend with some deeply rooted and long-standing cultural traditions, Malaysia is relatively a new society created by a first wave of intraregional migrants from within the Malay archipelago, followed by a second wave of extraregional migrants from China and India. The interface between these two movements of population was British colonization which spanned most of the nineteenth and the first half of the twentieth centuries. It was during these years that Malaysia was exposed to the capitalist world through the colonial plantation economy. In contrast to Indonesia, where the process took longer because of the size of the country, much of the Malayan peninsula was soon brought within the orbit of the global capitalist economy.

The main beneficiaries of this economic development before 1970 were the non-Malay population, particularly the Chinese who made up a disproportionate segment of the urban bourgeoisie. Based initially on involvement in retailing and mining, their prosperity grew so that now they can be found in all sectors of the industrial and commercial economy. Their economic visibility for most of the years prior to 1970 inevitably led to an acute awareness by the Malays of their own relative deprivation and to increasing resentment of the economic position of the Chinese. This culminated in the fateful general elections of 1969 and the riots which followed, when the Malays were confronted with the possibility that they might for the first time lose their political dominance.

Economic nationalism

The emphasis of Malay nationalism, which had been political in the post-war years, shifted to the economy in the 1970s. The New Economic Policy (NEP) was launched in 1971 for the specific purpose of propelling the Malays to a position of economic parity with the other ethnic communities. Under this proactive policy, by which the state assumed an interventionist role in increasing Malay economic participation and creating a Malay middle class, *bumiputera* or ethnic Malay status was revitalized through privileged access to education, employment, and investment. "The ideology of *bumiputraism*," Lee comments, "was invented to assert Malay indigenousness and justify development policies in favour of concretising Malay modernity" (Lee 1992: 160). As an ascriptive status, the category of *bumiputera* illustrates a significant attempt by the state to mediate the Malay response to capitalist development, albeit in terms which were perceived as interethnic competition. As economic restructuring proceeded throughout the 1970s and 1980s, one consequence was the urbanization of Malay society and the emergence of a nascent class structure, consisting of a Malay proletariat and middle class. The effect of the modernization of Malay society was the appearance of contradictions. According to Lee, these included the contradictory demands made on Malays arising from a new-found individualism and growing state pressures (Lee 1992: 160). The reactions of both the Malay middle class and proletariat to the pressures of development will be discussed below.

Islamic revivalism

In the late 1970s and 1980s, as the full effects of the NEP came to be felt throughout the peninsula and as more Malays were inducted into the capitalist economy, an Islamic revival occurred simultaneously, commonly referred to as the *dakwah* movement. Islamic fundamentalism has developed in two directions. One group is led by the long established rural-based Pan-Islamic Party of Malaysia (PAS), which draws its support from the peasant constituencies of the northern states. The other movement has been described as evangelistic, heterogeneous, and uncoordinated, and it has influence over the more educated, professional, urban middle class, and younger population (Nagata 1984: 81–130). As Couch comments (1996: 171–72), "Unlike their parents, whose practice of Islam was often ritualistic and traditional, the educated offspring came into contact with new religious ideas and interpretations through student organizations, visiting preachers, and Islamic literature." While Islamic revivalism in the conservative rural areas may be interpreted as a reaction against excessive economic development (Lee 1992: 164), it is less clear whether fundamentalism among urban educated Muslims is an anti-modernist response or an adoption of a more intellectual and rational approach to religion. The state's response was to embark on an Islamization program in the 1980s, which included the reaffirmation of what were considered to be good Islamic practices and behavior, and Islamic initiatives in education and banking (Couch 1996: 170–71). Although fears were expressed by the non-Malay population about the government's intention to establish some kind of Islamic state, Couch believes that state-sponsored Islamization is in part an attempt to prevent such a possibility.

The middle class and Malay culture

As a consequence of affirmative action in the NEP, the Malay middle class has expanded. A significant constituency of this middle class is made up of civil servants, educators, and professionals. Many others are employed in the media, state-owned enterprises, and the private sector. This group, though they have benefited from the NEP, are not wholly committed to giving full support to economic modernization and are indeed fearful of rampant commercialism (Kahn cited in Kessler 1992: 146). With the decline of the traditional Malay peasant cultural order in the face of development, "Malay culture" has been revived and romanticized for the consumption of this middle class. Because the cultural images presented in this revival are the antithesis of modern society – rural, personalized and contemplative in contrast to urban, impersonal and rushed – the movement has struck a chord with the urban middle class who are of rural origins but whose links with peasant society today are tenuously maintained (Kahn 1992: 165).

The Malay proletariat

The Malay proletariat has, on the other hand, reacted differently to capitalist development. The industrialization program of the 1970s has created industrial estates in major urban centers on the west coast and multiplied employment opportunities. The exodus of Malay rural migrants to these centers has resulted in housing shortages. In a study of the southern state of

Johore, Guiness (1994: 232–48) describes how Malay workers rejected the unsatisfactory housing provided in the estates and instead chose to live in squatter settlements (representing "traditional" Malay villages) illegally sited on state land on the outskirts of the city. What is uppermost in the minds of such workers are the practical problems of everyday living, in this case finding adequate shelter within an acceptable environment. Guinness argues that despite the illegality, the government has turned a blind eye to Malay squatters particularly because they are a source of cheap labor for industry, and because they provide significant electoral support to the Malay ruling party in opposition to predominantly non-Malay urban constituencies.

The Malaysian examples cited in this discussion show how the Malay middle class and proletariat have reacted to national and global processes in two contrasting ways. On the one hand, "Malay culture" has been repackaged to meet the consumption needs of an expanding middle class. On the other, the urban proletariat has gravitated toward urban *kampongs* as the preferred means of shelter in an industrial environment. As for the state, it has performed sometimes contradictory roles in attempting to balance the needs of both constituencies. When Malays, as an ethnic community, were perceived to be losing out economically to the Chinese, the state dominated by the United Malay National Organization (UMNO) responded by espousing the ideology of *bumiputraism* to justify the privileging of indigenes in economic participation. Similarly, to head off the threat of Islamic fundamentalism, the state has interpreted Islamic practices in modern and pro-development terms.

Singapore

Singapore is a small multicultural nation-state situated at the southern tip of the Malay Peninsula. There are several features of the society that makes it an interesting case study of the impact of globalization and culture. First, Singapore has undergone tremendous social and economic changes in the last forty years. Deciding early on that industrialization was the key to its survival, it opened its economy and society to external influences. Already a cosmopolitan trading society in origin, it was exposed to global forces even further. Secondly, the country is made up of many migrant ethnic groups. The Chinese constitute the largest ethnic group, accounting for 77 percent of the population, while 13 percent are Malays and 7 percent are Indians (300,000 of the population are registered as foreigners). The people of Singapore can thus draw on the cultural resources of the historical civilizations of China, India, and the Malay Archipelago.

Regionalism and transnationalism

Often the debate in globalization theory has been about the polarities of local versus global and the differences between the two (see, for example, Albrow 1990). This paper argues that there are two other dimensions to consider when we examine the processes of globalization in respect to Singapore. One is the increasing emphasis on regionalization, and the other is the process of transnationalization.

The end of the Cold War era has been marked by the proliferation of regional organizations. The most obvious of these has been the drive in Europe towards the creation of a European Union and the adoption of a common currency. In continental America, the setting up of NAFTA, the North American Free Trade Area, which originally consisted of the United States, Canada and Mexico, looks set to incorporate many of the other Latin American countries. Similar processes are happening in Southeast Asia, apparent in the proliferation of acronyms such as APEC, PECC, ASEAN, and ARF – standing respectively for the Asia-Pacific Economic Conference, the Pacific Economic Cooperation Conference, the Association of Southeast Asian Nations, and the ASEAN Regional Forum. The strongly expressed desire of nations who are not yet members to join these regional organizations testifies to their increasing importance in the new global age. Why are regional organizations important?

First, in the new global economic competition, regional organizations provide strength in numbers and influence. This is particularly true in Southeast Asia, where smaller countries with little economic clout, like Singapore and Malaysia, can exert greater influence in international forums through such organizations. In one sense, the new global age has reduced the influence of the superpowers. Whereas in the postwar period the United States was the main engine of world economic growth, the twenty-first century will increasingly be one where there are several regional centers. For example, Asia now controls around 30 percent of the world economy. We will also see more competition between these centers. In recent years, these processes have been seen underlying the negotiations of trade quotas and the allocation of landing rights under the "open skies" policy, both of which are increasingly based on regional considerations rather than bilateral agreements.

In the new global age, national barriers to trade will diminish. We will begin to see the importance of international networks of companies rather than country-specific companies. There has been remarkable growth in capital investments in China, Malaysia, Indonesia, India and Vietnam. We will see greater transnationalization of businesses. Capital has no national boundaries and it will move to where the resources are. In such a situation, there will be decreasing emphasis on national boundaries and a growth in the network of economic linkages and commodity chains. Labor, in the longer term, will follow the way of capital. However, how governments manage migrant labor will be problematic as the concept of citizenship will change more slowly than ways of regulating capital. A significant proportion of the work force in Singapore consists of migrants. The migration of people, or more accurately, the mass movement of labour, will have an effect on the definition of homeland and ethnicity, as will be explained later.

The processes of regionalization and transnationalization are sociologically significant because they provide an alternative way of looking at the relationship between the local and the global. These processes are both local and global at the same time. Regionalization allows countries in the region to maintain, to a large degree, their political autonomy and control of domestic resources, and yet, at the same time, to participate in trade within a large entity. Similarly, transnational companies are situated locally, but are plugged into a regional/global network.

New ethnicities

One interesting consequence of globalization is the creation of new ethnicities. Advocates of primordialism view ethnicity as immutable and static. By adopting a situational view of ethnicity (see Nagata 1984), the debate becomes one about how people assume different identities in different situations and environments. As we move toward a global age, there is a redefinition of what constitutes ethnicity and how it is used. The Chinese diaspora is a good illustration. Over the course of the last century, the Chinese have migrated to various parts of the world. At the present, it is estimated that there are over fifty-five million Overseas Chinese, and there are sizable populations in just about every country in the world, except for some countries in Eastern Europe and parts of Africa.

Tu (1991: 22) suggests that a new kind of Chinese diaspora has appeared in the new global age: "cultural China." This refers to a single universe whose common interest in a modernizing and revitalized China transcends national boundaries and discourses. In a changing global environment that has witnessed once patriotic Overseas Chinese becoming permanently settled in their adopted countries, the dispersal of Chinese intellectuals to the West and Asia, the rise of the four Asian dragons, and the success of the Chinese abroad, Tu raises the possibility of a renewed sense of Chinese-ness, a kind of pan-national imagined community of exiled Chinese intellectuals (cf. Chun 1996).

It is true that, as a result of living with indigenous populations for many years, it is difficult to find any single or set of markers that can be used to define their Chinese-ness. For example, in a recent gathering of Chinese businessmen, one of the authors discovered that the majority did not speak Chinese, practice Chinese religions, or have any real ties with the homeland. Thus, the traditional markers of Chinese ethnic identity – language, education, religion or history – are not central for the Overseas Chinese. Yet, there is a primordial sense of being Chinese. Part of the reason for this is the expansion of opportunities for investment in China, followed by conferences organized by the Chinese diaspora and gatherings of Chinese businessmen. For example, the First World Chinese Entrepreneurs' Conference held in 1989 attracted delegations from all over the world. There have been similar gatherings of Hokkiens and Teochews. Because of the Chinese proclivity to emphasize *guanxi* and the preference to work with *ziji ren*, these meetings of the Chinese facilitate the networking of Chinese businessmen.

This new "Chinese-ness" is essentially an "economic identity." It is no longer based on common cultural and sentimental attachments. People identify themselves as Chinese without reference to the conventional markers of identity. It is a pragmatic and instrumental identity based on shared economic interests. The influences of global culture, trade flows, and transnationalism have created a transnational identity that transcends political and geographical boundaries, and is characterized by interlocking nodes and networks.

While clearly a transnational identity is emerging in some groups and in some societies, we should be cognizant of the influence of local space, history, and sensitivities. Critics view the homogenization of this new Chineseness as evidence of the rise of Chinese chauvinism. This has caused concern to some governments in countries that have a sizable Chinese minority. The resultant product of this tension between indigenization and globalization, and of the local place versus transnational space, will be, in our view, an ethnicity that operates at multiple levels. As Chan and Tong (1995: 9) argue:

Contact between cultures and groups has potential integrative and divisive consequences; it creates conditions for cooperation and fusion, as well as conflict and differentiation, partly because sameness and differentness are simultaneously accentuated by the groups' co-presence. Also, global culture homogenises group differences but is rarely not met with the respective groups' own idiosyncratic attempts at indigenization and incorporation ... Local cultures decide when and in what form they are being homogenised by the global culture.

Friedman (1994) suggests that one of the features of globalization is the crisis of identity, precipitated by the weakening of national identities and the appearance of new identities. This will call into question the concept of citizenship – the abstract meaning of membership grounded in a territorially defined and state-governed society – and its replacement by an identity based on primordial loyalties, such as ethnicity, race, local community, language and other culturally concrete forms. The idea of an ethnocentric nation-state is increasingly problematic in the new world order, and there have been reconfigurations in national identity. However, to suggest that they are being replaced by ethnic identity is to overstate the case, and to underestimate the power and resilience of the nation-state. As we have argued earlier, the globalization process is mediated by local interpretations.

In Singapore, there is a tension between the ideas of citizenship and the rights of citizens on the one hand, and the demands created by the internationalization of Singapore society and its economy on the other. This is operationalized in the concept of "Singapore Unlimited," a term coined by the Prime Minister, Goh Chok Tong. In order to maintain its economic viability, Singapore needs to be a part of the international grid. Yet the obligations and responsibilities of citizenship at home (for example, three years' compulsory national service in the army for all able-bodied male Singaporeans) require the maintenance of national identity. In Singapore, this is operationalized by using the Swiss model, where one third of all Swiss citizens live and work outside the country. To maintain ties with home, Singaporean clubs and international schools have been established in countries with a significant Singaporean population. Using a computer analogy, Singapore provides the central node and Singaporeans overseas become nodal points. The justification for such a network is overtly economic, especially with the drive to regionalize the economy. However this may also be viewed as a necessary consequence of modernity. The idea of a bounded nation is important, but it may not be a sufficient condition for fostering nationalism. A sense of being Singaporean, irrespective of place, is. Thus, being Singaporean in the twenty-first century may be nonspatial and unbounded, but it will not necessarily be replaced by alternative cultural practices.

Conclusion

Globalization, as we understand it, is the logical development of capitalist expansion. It is a postcapitalist phenomenon in which people's lives have become consumption-conscious and utilitarian-oriented. The consequence of this is that the boundaries which have separated communities and states are now increasingly permeable, and the identities individuals and groups hold are less certain. The emergence of nation-states in the eighteenth century, in part a response to capitalist development, has contributed to the maintenance of these boundaries and identities but it has also been responsible for diluting them. In particular, the nation-state has been instrumental in mediating between the local community, which is a reference point for most individuals, and the universalizing influence of postcapitalism. The limit of globalization is its inherent capacity to decontextualize social existence, and the nation-state plays an important role in countering the rootlessness of such existence. However, labor migrations and capital flows have been responsible for a recent phenomenon that is described as transnationalization. This raises the question of whether groups and individuals, caught in the full tide of these transnational flows, will develop multiple identities and loyalties, and whether this will pose an alternative to the nation-state.

This essay has attempted to look at how three Southeast Asian societies, with different geopolitical histories and cultural traditions, have responded to the making of their own nation-states in the face of globalization and deculturalization. No attempt has been made to document these responses in any comprehensive manner. Instead, we have sketched in broad terms how the processes of localization, regionalization, and globalization have operated in these societies.

Indonesia's preoccupation with the construction of a national culture is comprehensible in a situation in which ethnic traditions have been so deeply embedded in such diverse localities. Malaysia, more exposed to capitalist development and globalization, has been concerned with how the Malay community can adapt successfully to economic change in comparison with the Chinese. The economic origins of the island state of Singapore, on the other hand, forced it early on to come to terms with the free flow of capital and labor which inevitably accompany the expansion of capitalism. In doing so, the Singapore government has been quick to respond innovatively to the issues which confront most modern states today – namely migration, citizenship, democracy, and the construction of national identity. In sum, the responses of these three Southeast Asian societies represent points on a continuum. Singapore, because of its geopolitical history and a predominantly migrant population, has been able to absorb with relative ease the full effects of globalization. Malaysia is not far behind, but the ethnic constitution of the society reveals examples of localization, in which both modern and traditional elements are juxtaposed. Indonesia appears to be the most resistant to globalization, given the remoteness of many of its ethnic constituents and the depth of some of its cultural traditions. However Indonesian cultural syncretism may produce a few surprises in the next decade, as the country struggles to come to terms with economic change introduced from the outside.

References

Acciaioli, G. 1985. "Culture as art: from practice to spectacle in Indonesia," *Canberra Anthropology* 8 (1 & 2): 148–72.

Albrow, M. 1990. *Globalization, Knowledge & Society*. London: Sage.

Anderson, B. 1983. *Imagined Communities*. London: Verso.

Basch, L., Schiller, N. and Blanc, C. 1994. *Nations Unbound*. USA: Gordon and Breach.

Bauman, Z. 1990. "Modernity and ambivalence," *Theory, Culture & Society* 7: 143–69.

Bowen, J.R. 1986. "On the political construction of tradition: *gotong royong* in Indonesia," *Journal of Asian Studies* 45 (3): 545–61.

Breton, R. 1984. "The production and allocation of symbolic resources: an analysis of the linguistic and ethnocultural fields in Canada," *Canadian Review of Sociology and Anthropology* 21 (2): 123–44.

Chan, K.B and Tong, C.K. 1995. "Modelling culture contact and Chinese ethnicity in Thailand," *Southeast Asian Journal of Social Science*, 23 (1): 1–12.

Chun, A. 1996. "Discourse of identity in the changing spaces of public culture in Taiwan, Hong Kong and Singapore," *Theory, Culture & Society*, 13 (1): 51–75.

Couch, H. 1996. *Government and Society in Malaysia*. Ithaca: Cornell University Press.

Foulcher, K. 1990. "The construction of an Indonesian national culture: patterns of hegemony and resistance," pp. 301–320 in *State and Civil Society in Indonesia*. Ed. A. Budiman. Monash University (Monash Papers on Southeast Asia, No. 22).

Friedman, J. 1994. *Cultural Identity and Global Process*. London: Sage.

Geertz, C. 1990. "'Popular art' and the Javanese tradition," *Indonesia*, 50: 77–94.

Gellner, E. 1983. *Nations and Nationalism*. Oxford: Basil Blackwell.

Giddens, A. 1981. *A Contemporary Critique of Historical Materialism*. London and Basingstoke: Macmillan.

Guinness, P. 1994. "The politics of identity: Malay squatters in industrializing Malaysia," pp. 232–48 in *Modernity and Identity: Asian Illustrations*, ed. A. Gomes. Bundoora: La Trobe University Press.

Hobsbawm, E. and Ranger, T. eds. 1989. *The Invention of Tradition*. Cambridge: Cambridge University Press.

Hooker, V. and Dick, H. 1993. "Introduction," pp. 1–23 in *Culture and Society in New Order Indonesia*, ed. V. Hooker. Kuala Lumpur: Oxford University Press.

Hooker, V. 1993. "New Order Language in Context," pp. 272–93 in *Culture and Society in New Order Indonesia*, ed. V. Hooker. Kuala Lumpur: Oxford University Press.

Kahn, J. 1992. "Class, ethnicity and diversity: some remarks on Malay culture in Malaysia," pp. 158–78 in *Fragmented Vision*, eds. J. Kahn and F. Loh. Sydney: Asian Studies Association of Australia with Allen & Unwin.

Kessler, C. 1992. "Archaism and modernity: contemporary Malay political culture," pp. 133–155 in *Fragmented Vision*, eds. J. Kahn and F. Loh. Sydney: Asian Studies Association of Australia with Allen & Unwin.

Lee, R. 1992. "Modernity, anti-modernity and postmodernity in Malaysia," *International Sociology* 7 (2): 153–71.

Nagata, J. 1984. *The Reflowering of Malaysian Islam*. Vancouver: University of British Columbia Press.

Ramage, D. 1995. *Politics in Indonesia*. London: Routledge.

Schlesinger, P. 1991. *Media, State and Nation*. London: Sage.

Schudson, M. 1994. "Culture and the integration of national societies," pp. 21–43 in *The Sociology of Culture: Emerging Theoretical Perspectives*, ed. D. Crane. Oxford: Blackwell.

Shils, E. 1975. *Center and Periphery: Essays in Macrosociology*. Chicago: University of Chicago Press.

Smith, A. 1988. "The myth of the 'modern nation' and the myths of nations," *Ethnic and Racial Studies* 11 (1): 1–25.

Smith, A. 1990. "Towards a global culture?" *Theory, Culture & Society* 7: 171–91.

Swidler, A. 1986. "Culture in action: symbols and strategies," *American Sociological Review* 51 (2): 273–86.

Tong, C.K. 1989. *Religious Conversion and Revivalism : A Study of Christianity in Singapore*. Singapore: MCD.

Tu, W.M. 1991. "Cultural China: the periphery as center," *Daedalus* 120 (2): 1–32.

Yasuaki, O. 1996) "In Quest of Intercivilizational Human Rights." Center for Asian Pacific Affairs Occasional Paper No. 2.

Part II

The Local, the National, and the Transnational

in Southeast Asia

Chapter 4

How to Live a Local Life: Balinese Responses to National

Integration in Contemporary Indonesia

Haruya KAGAMI

Introduction

A simple, coherent, broadly defined ethnic structure, such as is found
in most industrial societies, is not a residue of traditionalism but an
earmark of modernity. But how this reconstruction of the system of
primordial affiliation takes place, the stages through which it passes,
the forces that advance or retard it, the transformations in personality
structure it involves, all are largely unknown. The comparative sociology
(or social psychology) of ethnic change remains to be written. (Geertz
1973: 308–309)

Thus wrote Geertz more than thirty years ago in his paper discussing the
problem of national integration in new, multiethnic states. While his concept
of "primordial affiliation" which he put forward powerfully in his paper –
or, more precisely, the tendency to look upon such affiliation as "primordial"
– has been seriously criticized in the current debates on ethnicity, the
interrelated processes of national integration and local ethnic response still
remain among the key issues in an analysis of the contemporary situation of
these countries, and the task of understanding them has yet to be fully
accomplished.

The Republic of Indonesia, which was presented as a "new state" in
Geertz's paper, has experienced vast social change during the thirty years
since. In spite of Geertz's rather gloomy predictions of the future path of the
new states, for many years it experienced steady economic growth and the

development of a high level of political integration, especially under Suharto's New Order regime until its demise. These development processes were guided by the policies of a highly centralized government and were sustained by the authority of the armed forces.

What then were the local responses to the central governmental policy of national integration during this period of development? Did people in different parts of the country simply submit to the governmental plans, or did they demand and attempt to secure a special place in the state? This process of interaction between the state and the local peoples within it is the question which Geertz urged us to investigate, and it is the task to be pursued in this paper with particular reference to the case of the Balinese.

The Balinese originate from the island of Bali which, together with some small islands nearby, has constituted one of Indonesia's provinces since 1958. The population of this wet-rice cultivating island stood at around three million in the late 1990s, and the majority (more than 90 percent) of the Balinese are Hindus. While the size of the population might be modest compared to other ethnic groups in Indonesia, they are a true minority in terms of religion in a state where 90 percent of the population are Muslims. As will be discussed below, this situation has contributed to the distinctiveness of their response to policies of national integration.

As Geertz's remarks in the paper cited above suggest, the integrative process in new states is not simply an economic and political matter, but also one of identity. His problematic assumption of "primordial sentiments" aside, national integration requires the subjective involvement of the local peoples, and as a result it also has to deal with local identities. The situation confronted by the local peoples, however, may not always involve clear alternatives as much as groping towards a satisfactory relationship between local culture and the national scheme of things.

In this cultural domain, too, the Indonesian New Order government made conspicuous efforts to domesticate local cultures and to integrate them into the national culture. One obvious example of such a plan can be seen in the "Beautiful Indonesia in Miniature" Park, sponsored by Mrs. Suharto and inaugurated in 1975 in the suburbs of Jakarta (see, for example, Pemberton 1994: Chapter 4). The core area of the park is arranged to exhibit twenty-seven building complexes, each built in one of the traditional styles of the provinces making up the nation. The buildings represent the national motto "Unity in Diversity." This strategy of the parallel positioning of representative local cultures can also be found, for example, in various government-sponsored traditional arts and dance festivals.

The emphasis on material culture such as architecture, arts and crafts suggests the government's intention to depoliticize the local cultures. On the other hand, the central government has carefully managed their religious and customary domains, for the existence of varied religious traditions and local customs has potentially been one of the most dangerous factors threatening the unity of the Indonesian state since its independence. Religious matters at the national level have been managed almost exclusively through the Ministry of Religion, while local customs have been subordinated to the national laws enforced in each area. In this regard, the key strategy of the central government in domesticating the local cultures seems to have been to separate them from the management of local affairs.

Local responses to such a central governmental policy, then, seem to lie in efforts to revive local cultures in a form in which they can be reintegrated with the national scheme. Although not all local cultures can succeed, success is still possible, and the Balinese case discussed below is perhaps the best illustration of this. The next section describes general government policy in the New Order era and the part which was played by the Balinese government, or which was imposed upon it during this period. The following two sections analyze the provincial government's policy of promoting Balinese local customs as a basis for the reconstruction of the local cultural identity. The disparity between the provincial government officials' intellectual approach and the responses of ordinary village people will be also discussed.

Bali and the New Order Developmental Policy

The most prominent achievement of Suharto's New Order government lay in the state's economic growth. After taking over the political leadership from President Sukarno in the mid-1960s, Suharto's government put the utmost emphasis on the development of the domestic economy. First it aimed to improve agricultural productivity, especially that of rice, by introducing high-yielding varieties. The plan was implemented intensively throughout Indonesia in the 1970s, and the government was able to declare the country self-sufficient in rice in 1984. The national economy was also supported by the high price of oil and natural gas on the international market throughout the 1970s. After the fall in oil prices in the early 1980s, the government shifted its emphasis to the promotion of the manufacturing sector. From 1986 it started to introduce a series of measures aimed at economic liberalization, which provided domestic industry with conditions suitable for export-oriented development, thus supporting further economic growth (see, for example, Hill 1994).[1]

Within this economic developmental policy, the province of Bali has contributed to national economic growth through both the agricultural sector and the service sector, especially tourism. The major part of the wet-rice region of Bali accepted high-yielding varieties in the mid-1970s, and achieved high growth rates in productivity. More impressive still was the development of tourism, both international and domestic, since Ngurah Rai International Airport began to operate in 1969. The tourist industry in Bali included not only service facilities such as restaurants, accommodation, and transportation, but also artistic performances and the manufacture of souvenirs which helped raise the local standard of living in the villages.

A less visible but equally important achievement of the New Order government was the enactment of domestic legal and administrative reforms. The most important of them in relation to national integration were two ordinances concerning local governance: the Ordinance on Regional Government (Undang-undang RI No. 5 Tahun 1974), and the Ordinance on Village Government (Undang-undang RI No. 5 Tahun 1979).[2] Through these ordinances the government succeeded in establishing a uniform system of local government throughout the country.

This new form of local administrative organization, especially at the village level, did not necessarily coincide with the local customary social units, and problems brought about by the enforcement of the ordinance have been reported, for example, from the province of Riau (Kato 1989). The Balinese, too, were quick to respond to the enactment of the village government ordinance in various ways which will be described in the next section.

Long before the establishment of village organization by the government, the Balinese had their own autonomous local units, the system of customary villages (*desa adat*). As the size of the customary villages was usually smaller than that of the government's administrative units, many of these units in Bali included several customary villages, thus providing the setting for the co-existence of the two systems. Though not totally destroyed, the autonomy and effectiveness of the customary villages could have been seriously challenged by the existence of the administrative units which now had sole juridical legitimacy. However harmoniously the two systems coexist, the Balinese still have to deal with government policy if they want to preserve the effectiveness of the customary village system as the basis of their local communities. The crucial point about Balinese responses to government policy in relation to village administration, as well as local customs in general, is that these customs, including the customary village system, are basically related to religion. Thus, the Balinese customary village system revolves around religious activities and sanctions. Villagers are obliged to participate in the management of their village temples and temple festivals, for they reside on communal plots owned by the temples. The Balinese farmers' organization, namely the irrigation society (*subak*), also has its own temples and religious sanctions. Even many of the artistic performances which have contributed to Bali's reputation as a tourist destination are based on ritual performances. Considering the religious nature of Balinese custom, it can be understood how Balinese responses to the New Order government's developmental policy were not only economic and political but also cultural in nature, and that the Balinese themselves saw these issues as religious. They tried to reconstruct their local cultural identity by placing the Hindu religion at its center, as will be discussed below.

The Hindu religion, however, is not always taken into account in the Indonesian context. In the highly politicized situation in relation to religion in the early period after Indonesian independence, the only officially recognized religions which could obtain full legitimacy and support from the state were Islam and Christianity (both Catholicism and Protestantism), while Balinese Hinduism was classified as one of the "indigenous beliefs." After the ardent Balinese promotion of Hinduism as a candidate for official recognition, an unusual political movement in modern Balinese history in that it involved the whole island (Robinson 1995: 183), Hinduism obtained the legal and administrative status of a religion in 1965. This success was achieved through the efforts of Balinese intellectuals to reform their customary religious activities, such as the designation of holy texts, the institutionalization of the priesthood, and doctrinal rationalization. These efforts at reform have been continued through the activities of the Hindu Council (Parisada Hindu Dharma Indonesia), which was established as the body representing Balinese Hindus in 1959, and which is now the sole official organization for the nation's Hindus as a whole (see, for example, Forge 1980). Hinduism, which the Balinese see as the basis of their local culture, is itself a result of historical (re)construction in contemporary Indonesia.

Provincial Government and Local Customs

Under the developmental policy of the New Order government, Bali experienced vast and rapid social, political, and economic changes. Economically, the development of tourism led to the spread of a unique lifestyle in which the peasant look was preserved, even though it was largely dependent on income from the service sector, even in the rural areas. Politically, the region became more and more integrated into the national system. In this kind of situation, the response of the Balinese, led mainly by the provincial government, consisted of efforts to reform and strengthen their local customs.

Chronologically, the provincial government's policy of promoting Balinese local customs followed the enactment of the local governmental ordinances mentioned above by the central government. Considering the delicate position of local customs in national policy, this can be said to have been a fairly bold local response to central governmental policy, and one which was quite unique at that time.

The policy was introduced by the provincial government in 1979, just after the inauguration of the new governor, Ida Bagus Mantra. He was a Balinese of high caste origin and was also an academic. He studied in India in the 1950s, obtained a master's degree in cultural history, and held the post of Dean and then President of Udayana University in Bali in the 1960s. From 1968 to 1978 he served in Suharto's cabinets as Director-General of Culture in the Department of Education and Culture. There have been few governors in Indonesia with this kind of background.

As the governor of Bali, Ida Bagus Mantra promoted not only Balinese customs but also Balinese arts as well. The Bali Arts Festival, the most popular and spectacular event for the promotion of Balinese arts by the provincial government, began to be held annually in 1979. This was apparently a response to the beginning of mass tourism in Bali in the 1970s. The aim of the festival itself, however, was not primarily that of a tourist attraction. Rather, it was aimed at urging the Balinese people themselves to recognize the value of their own artistic tradition, and to encourage them to become involved in artistic activities. This might result in the promotion of tourism in Bali, but only as a by-product. The primary aim was clearly stated by the governor himself in his speech at the opening ceremony of the first Bali Arts Festival in 1979 (Bali Provincial Government 1991: 8).

This event is not simply an arts festival, but ranges widely over Balinese culture. It is financed by the provincial government and lasts for a month, and the most important and popular events on the program are the interegional contests in gamelan music, the revival of old dances and dramas, and the presentation of newly created performances. But it also includes contests and exhibitions in various other fields such as traditional costumes, making ritual offerings, cookery, reciting classical literature, and so on. A large number of Balinese, not only artists but also ordinary villagers, are involved in these activities as participants and also as spectators.

The promotion of local customs by the government was also aimed at the revitalization of Balinese traditional culture, in this case customary organizations such as the customary village, irrigation societies and so on. Throughout the 1970s, Bali experienced steady and rapid social change, brought about by the New Order government's development policies including promoting tourism, agricultural reform, and family planning. In this situation,

Balinese customary organizations proved themselves to be effective in carrying out these government plans. Many of the irrigation societies, when properly consulted, showed themselves able to contribute to the growth of rice production. The family planning program in Bali gained greater acceptance than in other regions with the help of promotional propaganda from the customary villages. Local communities suffered little serious disruption in the face of mass tourism thanks to the strength of their local customs. These experiences might have persuaded the provincial government to adopt a policy which was unique in Indonesia, that of promoting local customs and reactivating customary organizations.

It should be noted here that local customs in general had often been viewed negatively as feudal institutions during the preceding Sukarno era. Although the Balinese customary village and irrigation systems had maintained their organizations and activities, some of their practices, especially those concerning status differences, had often been criticized by the Balinese themselves in the political atmosphere of the Sukarno period, with its emphasis on class struggle. It is rather ironic that the efficacy of the old customs began to be reevaluated during the following period which stressed development and modernization.

In 1979 the provincial government founded a semiofficial organization called Majelis Pembina Lembaga Adat (Committee for Guiding Customary Organizations). The membership of the committee consisted of provincial government officials, academic specialists in law and representatives of the Hindu Council. Its primary task was to consult and give advice to the local customary organizations, especially concerning legal matters. Through this committee, the Bali provincial government began to adapt Balinese customary organizations to developmental policies and the process of modernization which resulted from them.

At the beginning of the 1980s the provincial government started a unique program to implement this policy, consisting of a set of interregional contests. These included a customary village contest (*lomba desa adat,* dating from 1983), an irrigation society contest (*lomba subak,* dating from 1981), a dry-field society contest (*lomba subak abian,* dating from 1983), and a village youth association contest (*lomba sekaa teruna,* dating from 1985). Both the customary village and the irrigation society are long-standing indigenous organizations, while the dry-field society and youth association are newly invented ones which have been promoted by the provincial government, especially since the 1980s. These contests are interregional, involving competitors selected from each subdistrict at the district level, and then the winners from each district at the provincial level. They are held annually with financial support from the provincial and district governments and under the supervision of a committee.

The items to be judged and the rules of the competition are decided in detail by the committee and are approved by the provincial government. The composition of the items is based on the Hindu concept, *tri hita karana*, which refers to the three domains of the cosmos, consisting of the divine, human, and material worlds. The divine sphere concerns the management of, and activities in, Hindu temples owned by the various customary organizations; the human sphere involves issues of organizational management; and the material sphere covers the material conditions under which the activities of the organization are carried out.

Each of the three spheres is further divided into more detailed areas. Thus, for example, the divine sphere is composed of ten areas which are judged competitively in the customary village contests. Judges look at the condition of the village temples, the shrines within them, the house-yard temples, temple festivals, sacred dances, ritual, daily prayer by the village members, and so on. The human sphere is made up of thirteen areas concerning the composition, management and activities of the organization. And the material sphere consists of seven areas related to the material composition and arrangement of the village and its environment. In the contest, these areas are evaluated one by one by a team of judges, based on prescribed criteria. The closer the approximation to Hindu religious ideals, the higher the scores.

Before the judging, each competing group receives help from a team of instructors sent by the district and provincial governments. The composition of the team is roughly the same as that of the team of judges: both are composed of government officials, committee members, and members of the Hindu Council. This provides the team with a chance to show the villagers how the customary organizations should be organized and how they should function. This guidance is not only a preparation for the contest but also an opportunity for the provincial government to guide the customary organizations in the right direction.

Another important element of the customary organization contests is the effort to codify the customary law prescribed and observed by each organization. These customary laws have evolved in the meetings of the organizations, and have usually been passed down orally from generation to generation. One of the crucial elements in the provincial government's policy is the effort to codify this oral tradition of customary law in order to provide a legal basis for the customary organizations.

In these contests between customary organizations, the codification of the customary law by each competing organization is also one of the elements which is judged. Participating organizations are urged to codify their customary law before the contest if they have not yet done so. A local government official who is a specialist in law is sent to meet with the members of the organization for consultations about this codification. What is discussed in this meeting is not only the content of the customary law, but also its correct legal transcription.

The government official never intervenes in deciding the content, which must be decided by the members of the organization themselves. The official gives advice on revising the law only if its contents are inconsistent with the national ordinances. Through this process, every customary organization which has participated in the contests now has a body of codified customary law.

In support of this codification program, the Balinese provincial government enacted an ordinance concerning official recognition of the customary village in 1986 (Peraturan Daerah Propinsi Daerah Tingkat I Bali No. 6 1986). Balinese customary villages have consequently obtained full legal rights and support, together with the codification of their customary law. The crucial point is that the law is linked to the management of village temples and their activities, and it recognizes the temples' ownership of communal land, both residential and agricultural.

The customary organization contests have been held annually since the early 1980s. The nomination of the participants is usually arranged in rotation so that all existing organizations may eventually participate at least once. To take an example, Gianyar district has 268 customary villages dispersed in seven subdistricts. Each subdistrict nominates one candidate for the district level contest each year. A simple calculation shows that ninety-eight villages participated in the contest during the fourteen years from 1983 to 1996, or approximately one third of all the customary villages in the district. According to a local official, about sixty villages in the district have already had their customary law codified and officially recognized.

These, then, have been the provincial government's activities in promoting Balinese local customs and guiding customary organizations since the end of the 1970s. During the course of the contests, the present conditions of the participating organizations are evaluated and the winners are offered a prize by the government. The essence of the contests, however, seems to lie in the process of guidance and instruction before the evaluation, through which the provincial government encourages the Balinese people to take an active part in regional as well as national development.

Restructuring Local Customs, and People's Responses

As I pointed out earlier, the management of local customs has been a sensitive matter in the Republic of Indonesia since independence. While their existence has generally been recognized judicially and their practices taken into consideration in many governmental policies, they have hardly been given full legitimacy. The most crucial and controversial problem is the one concerning communal land rights. In this situation, the Balinese case described above seems to present a challenge to the central government.

The officially announced aim of the policy of promoting customary organizations by the Bali provincial government is to recognize the positive contribution of grass-roots organizations in the period of economic development and to mobilize them to achieve the goals of development policy. This has often been stated in government documents, as well as in speeches by government officials. This official explanation, of course, fits well with the central government's developmental policy. As a regional government within the nation state, the provincial government is not allowed to oppose the central government's policy.

The provincial government of Bali started to revitalize customary organizations, including customary villages, just after the central government enacted the Ordinance on Village Government which was intended to apply a uniform village governmental structure throughout the nation. Given this timing, the Bali government's innovative and subtle policy of promoting customary organizations may appear surprising. The preamble to the central government's ordinance states that village government should be uniform as far as possible; however, careful consideration should also be given to existing forms of village organization and local custom which still sustain the governance of the local village, in order to mobilize the people for development and effective village administration (Undang-undang RI No. 5 Tahun 1979: Preamble B). Although this might have been intended as mere lip service to the diversity of local customs on the part of the central government, the Balinese provincial government seems to have taken this statement as legitimation for commencing a policy of promoting customary organizations. The central government finally authorized this kind of policy at the provincial level in 1984 with the introduction of a regulation by the Minister of Domestic Affairs agreeing to the promotion of local customs in so far as they do not conflict with national developmental policy (Peraturan Menteri Dalam Negeri No. 11 Tahun 1984).

The provincial government of Bali has been headed by Balinese governors since the time of Ida Bagus Mantra, and the majority of the officials have also been Balinese. These officials are also members of customary villages in their respective residential areas. During the course of customary organization contests, officials who are members of instruction and evaluation teams may also join the other villagers in receiving instruction. This may explain the provincial government's commitment to promoting their local customs and customary organizations, as they are clearly siding with the Balinese people on this issue. The crucial point in this response to central government is that the Balinese customs and customary organizations which are officially prescribed by the provincial government are based on the Hindu religion, which occupies a fairly minor position in Indonesia as a whole. As has already been noted, the Balinese have gone to great efforts to get the state to recognize Hinduism as an official religion. The result is that Hinduism in Indonesia is almost synonymous with Balinese culture, although there are other non-Balinese Hindus, and not all Balinese are Hindus. It is therefore quite understandable that Hinduism occupies a central position in Balinese cultural identity.

Official pronouncements relating to Balinese culture by the provincial government can be found in governmental documents and publications. To cite some examples, the provincial government defines Balinese customary law as that which "is based on the Hindu doctrine and socially recognized tradition" (Peraturan Daerah Propinsi Daerah Tingkat I Bali No. 6 Tahun 1986: Chapter I Article 1–i), and it describes local culture in Bali as "a local culture based on the customary villages which have been founded on the Hindu doctrine" (Peraturan Daerah Propinsi Daerah Tingkat I Bali No. 5 Tahun 1993: Naskah Chapter III A-8). These show clearly that the Hindu religion is seen as the fundamental basis of Balinese cultural identity.

The concern with Hindu doctrine can also be found in the actual programs for promoting customary organizations. As was already described, the system for judging customary organization contests relies largely on Hindu concepts and ideals. They not only cover religion and the ritual activities of these organizations, but also penetrate the whole range of members' activities.

Not all customary practices, however, have actually originated from religious prescriptions. In fact, the provincial government's stress on Hinduism as the basis of Balinese culture is itself an effort to adjust local culture to the national scheme. Given strict national policies on religion, Hinduism itself has experienced a process of reform led mainly by the Hindu Council. Relying on an officially recognized religion seems to be a key strategy in the promotion of the local culture by the provincial government.

Here a disparity arises between the position of the provincial government and that of the ordinary villagers concerning local customary practices, which can be seen in the customary village contest itself. One of the criteria for judging the contest is the practice of personal prayer three times a day, a religious obligation recently introduced by the Hindu Council to meet the standards of an official religion, but one which was never practiced by the villagers before. During the course of the contest, the villagers are required to answer questions concerning basic Hindu concepts of the type also to be found in school textbooks. In this case the position of the provincial government is quite instructive.

Behind this disparity lies a discrepancy between the religious and customary domains. The provincial government's policy is not always consistent, and in some cases it encourages secular customary practices which have little relevance to religious prescriptions. In the course of customary organization contests, the participants are advised to wear traditional dress. The members of the instruction team and the evaluation team also dress in this way. In the preparatory meetings and on the occasion of the judging, both the villagers and the judges speak in polite Balinese. The use of traditional dress and the local language on these occasions has scarcely any religious rationale. Local costumes as well as local languages are rather issues concerning local culture, not only in Bali but in Indonesia as a whole. Thus, exhibitions of traditional costumes and Balinese pop song contests are among the most popular events in the Bali Arts Festival. Contests between customary organizations can also be viewed as colorful cultural events performed by the Balinese villagers and government officials.

This emphasis on the particular elements of local culture which concern the cultural identity of the local people may disguise the instructional role of the provincial government, and may also give rise to a sense of commitment among the participants, both villagers and officials. It is true that not all members of an organization participate spontaneously in the government contests, and that participation in the event is usually considered by the common villagers to be a duty forced on them by the government. It should be recalled, however, that the officials acting as instructors or evaluators on the government side may also play a role as members of a customary organization on another occasion. Here they may be influential in helping the other members meet the requirements of the contest. Through this process, and through the promotional policy in general, the provincial government has encouraged the commitment of the Balinese people to the promotion of their local culture.

Some problems still remain. While the programs for promoting local culture have largely been led by the provincial government, ordinary people may respond in their own way. An example can be seen in the recent popularization of particular styles of ritual costumes (Kagami 1995). While the only official prescription on ritual costume by the Hindu Council is that those who pray to God must put on at least a white or yellow sash over a clean garment (Parisada Hindu Dharma 1978: 69), people have come to use a more formal style of dress which is recognized as being appropriate on ritual occasions. Recently, more systematic use of different costume styles according to the kinds of occasions involved has also appeared. For example, a white shirt, a white headcloth and a yellow sash are now seen as normal for ritual occasions dedicated to God; batik cloth is seen as appropriate for secular formal occasions such as a village meeting; gold or silver brocade cloth is suitable for weddings, and so on. This trend is looked on favorably by the provincial government as reflecting people's heightened consciousness of their own local customs (Dinas Kebudayaan 1994: 25–26). A more controversial trend is the wearing of black at funerals. This fashion has appeared and spread since the mid-1980s, perhaps inspired by Christianity. Hindu intellectuals have criticized it because black symbolizes the god Wisnu, the preserver of life in Hindu mythology, and also because Hindu doctrine has no concept of mourning for the dead because death is the emancipation of the soul from this world. Though criticized on these grounds in newspapers and official speeches, the fashion seems to be still in vogue.

These examples illustrate how the ordinary Balinese people have responded in their own ways to the rapid social changes of the period of development and to the provincial government's policy of promoting local culture. This kind of local-level response can also be seen in other domains, such as the proliferation of Balinese-style carvings in house decoration. Some of these trends have been welcomed as realizing the policy of promoting local culture, while others have been criticized as deviations from Hindu religious doctrine. Although the provincial government has defined Balinese customs as those based on Hindu ideals, there still seems to lie a vast gulf between the officially recognized Hindu religion and the socially maintained local customs.

It is obvious, however, that as Hindu religious doctrine has undergone rationalization and reform in response to the Indonesian government's policy on religion, so Balinese local customs have evolved in response to the developmental process and the policy of promoting local culture by the provincial government. And it cannot be denied that the provincial government's policy has certainly led to an increase in people's consciousness of their local customs, resulting in some of the modern trends mentioned above.

Concluding Remarks

During a period of increasing national integration under Suharto's New Order regime, the Balinese made outstanding efforts to protect their local cultural forms and their identity within the Indonesian state. The provincial government of Bali, as the representative of the Balinese, pursued a strategy of supporting and mobilizing customary organizations on the basis of Hinduism as an officially recognized religion. Because of this strategy, as well as a series of new legal arrangements, the central government had little reason to curtail the Balinese people's desire to strengthen local cultural forms and local identity.

The same strategy, however, has brought about a disparity between the officially prescribed forms of Balinese culture and the customarily maintained social practices. The officially recognized Hindu religion is one which has been constructed recently through a process of reform and rationalization, in line with government policy on religion. If official doctrine is applied too dogmatically, it will probably fail to cover the whole range of Balinese culture. The ordinary villagers' local cultural identity still seems to lie not in Hindu doctrine but in the socially recognized local customs.

Apart from this disparity between the intellectuals and the ordinary people, the provincial government's cultural policy can be judged as having been fairly successful in that it heightened people's consciousness of their own local culture. It at least showed a way in which local cultures can be maintained in the face of the forces of national integration and uniformity.

The Balinese success in their cultural demands can be explained from several points of view. Their unique culture has been a major tourist resource and has provided the province with considerable income. The Hindu religion, the key issue in the provincial government's policy, holds merely a minor position in Indonesia as a whole, with very little influence in national politics. The fact that the Balinese ethnic boundaries and regional boundaries coincide has also contributed to the effectiveness of the provincial government's policy. And, finally, the nomination of a scholar-politician, Ida Bagus Mantra, as governor fitted the situation at the time. He is still remembered among Balinese intellectuals as the most eminent protector of Balinese culture.

Although the Balinese case is perhaps the best example of a local culture prevailing in the face of the Indonesian national order thanks to the factors mentioned above, it is not an isolated one. Following the Balinese provincial government's policy, similar cultural policies and activities in several provinces have flourished since the second half of the 1980s. Thus, for example, we find the Yogyakarta Arts Festival (beginning in 1989, at Yogyakarta, Central Java), the Mulayu Cultural Festival (beginning in 1987, at Medan, North Sumatra), and the Toraja Cultural Festival (held for the first time in 1997, in Tana Toraja, South Sulawesi). We can also note the activities of regionally established committees concerning local customs such as the Lembaga Adat Riau (Riau Institute for Local Customs), the Lembaga Adatdan Kebudayaan Aceh (Aceh Institute for Local Customs and Culture), and so on. These may not be entirely similar to the Balinese case, and each situation has its own characteristics. It is obvious, however, that appeals to local culture have recently flourished in Indonesia and that the Balinese case is one of the earliest and most obviously successful cases. However exceptional it may be, it shows a negotiating process in which a local "primordial" society is linked to a national "civil" society, and hence to the rest of the world, through the codification of customary law and the rationalization of religion.

As Geertz predicted, peoples' appeals to local culture have been the key issue in national integration. Given the highly centralized developmental policies in Indonesia under the New Order, local peoples' aspirations to establish a secure cultural identity seemed more and more acute and urgent. Examining these processes is an indispensable task in understanding the contemporary situation of the Indonesian state and the local peoples within it.

Notes

1 As has been widely observed, the Indonesian economy has experienced an abrupt decline and a period of stagnation since the currency crisis in 1997. This, however, was largely brought about by the illegal economic maneuvers of Suharto's family and cronies rather than by problems of the economic structure of the state itself.

2 After Suharto's resignation from the presidency in May 1998, these two ordinances were openly criticized as leading to too much centralization, and their amendment was agreed by the Peoples' Supreme Council. Though not completely decentralized yet, the local governmental system may become one which allows a much wider range of local government discretion with the enactment of further amendments.

References

Forge, Anthony. 1980. "Balinese religion and Indonesian identity," pp. 221–33 in *Indonesia: The Making of a Culture*, ed. James Fox. Canberra: Australian National University.

Geertz, Clifford. 1973. "The integrative revolution: primordial sentiments and civil politics in the new states," pp. 255–310 in *The Interpretation of Cultures*. New York: Basic Books.

Hill, Hall. 1994. "The economy," pp. 54–122 in *Indonesia's New Order: The Dynamics of Socio-economic Transformation*, ed. Hall Hill. St Leonards: Allen & Unwin.

Kagami, Haruya. 1995. "Girei no seisô rongi ni miru Bari no shûkyô jijô" [The state of religion in Bali: the implications of the debate over ritual dress], *Minzokugaku Kenkyû* 60 (1): 32–52.

Kato, Tsuyoshi. 1989. "Different fields, similar locusts: adat communities and the Village Law of 1979 in Indonesia," *Indonesia* 47: 89–114.

Parisada Hindu Dharma. 1978. *Upadesa tentang Ajaran-ajaran Agama*

Hindu. Denpasar: Parisada Hindu Dharma.

Pemberton, John. 1994. *On the Subject of "Jawa."* Ithaca: Cornell University Press.

Robinson, Geoffrey. 1995. *The Dark Side of Paradise: Political Violence in Bali*. Ithaca: Cornell University Press.

Government documents

Bali provincial government. 1991. *Pesta Kesenian Bali*. Denpasar: Cita Budaya.

Dinas Kebudayaan Propinsi Daerah Tingkat I Bali. 1994. *Tata Busana Adat Bali*. Denpasar: Dinas Kebudayaan Propinsi Daerah Tingkat I Bali.

Peraturan Daerah Propinsi Daerah Tingkat I Bali No. 6 Tahun 1986 tentang Kedudukan, Fungsi dan Peranan Desa Adat Sebagai Kesatuan Masyarakat Hukum Adat Dalam Propinsi Daerah Tingkat I Bali.

Peraturan Daerah Propinsi Daerah Tingkat I Bali No. 5 Tahun 1993 tentang Pola Dasar Pembangunan Daerah Propinsi Daerah Tingkat I Bali Tahun 1994/1995–1998/1999.

Peraturan Menteri Dalam Negeri No. 11 Tahun 1984 tentang Pembinaan dan Pengembangan Adat Istiadat di Tingkat Desa/Kelurahan.

Undang-undang RI No. 5 Tahun 1974 tentang Pokok-pokok Pemerintahan di Daerah.

Undang-undang RI No. 5 Tahun 1979 tentang Pemerintahan Desa.

Chapter 5

The Impact of Tourism in Three Tourist Villages in Bali

Wayan I GERIYA

Introduction

Tourism is a modern phenomenon that has had an intense impact on Balinese social life and culture. It has dominated and encouraged changes in the economic organization of Balinese society, shifting it from an agrarian to an industrial and service structure. Tourism has also widened the social networks of the Balinese community, crossing ethnic and national borders on an international and global scale. It has also introduced mass culture and new values into Balinese culture and the lives of the Balinese people. Through tourism, Balinese society and culture are being transformed in a "melting pot" in which the Great and Little Traditions, the traditional and the modern, and local, national and global cultures all come together (McKean 1973; Geriya 1983).

Balinese culture has a clear identity based on Hinduism. This culture has very deep historical roots, as well as religious, communal, educational, and recreational functions. Despite the small size of Bali and its isolation from the rest of the Hindu world, its culture draws on the universal aesthetic principles of Hinduism manifested in the philosophy of *tri hita karana*, together with the arts, including dance, music, and the fine arts.

Balinese culture is supported by the established traditional institutions of the customary village (*desa adat*) and village section (*banjar*). These traditional institutions are based on various sets of relationships and boundaries, such as place, kinship, and common interests. In essence they are also based upon religious, emotional, and communal sentiments, combined with a creativity that strengthens the sustainability of the culture. The dominant values of Balinese culture therefore combine religious and aesthetic values with those of solidarity and harmony. These are expressed through a system of symbols, both religious and secular, which emphasize the paradigm of harmonious relations with nature. Even though the Balinese are strongly bound to a variety of social groupings, including those of village, kinship, administrative unit, and caste, historically they have been open to outside influences, selectively adapting foreign elements from Indian, Chinese, Dutch, and Japanese cultures. This has also been the case in relation to neighboring cultures such as those of Java and Sasak.

Historically speaking, the Balinese encounter with tourism really began in the 1920s when the Dutch company, KPM (Koninklijke Paketaart Maattchapij) promoted the island and attracted European visitors to it. Mass tourism, however, has become part of the Balinese social and cultural system over the last thirty years, from the early 1970s onwards. This has been due to developments in the tourism sector such as the extension of Ngurah Rai International Airport, and the expansion of hotels, restaurants, tourist attractions, tourist promotion, and so forth. The total number of foreign visitors coming directly to Bali through Ngurah Rai International Airport more than doubled during the five years from 1988 to 1993. In 1988 Bali had 360,413 foreign visitors, and the number increased to 885,516 in 1993. The total foreign exchange earned by tourism in 1993 was approximately U.S.$88.2 million.

From a regional perspective, since 1994 the tourist resorts that used to be concentrated only around Sanur, Kuta, and Nusa Dua in Badung regency have spread to other areas. There are now over twenty resorts scattered over eight regencies and one municipality. The number of Balinese people who are involved in the tourism sector has increased significantly. An increase can also be seen in the number of villages affected by tourist development, as places which tourists visit or in which they stay.

Interaction between the Balinese and the tourists is encouraged by different but complementary motives. Visitors look for aesthetic experiences while the Balinese seek economic benefits. These two underlying motives mean that both groups have something to gain from the other (McKean 1973). Communication between hosts and guests has been intensified thanks to the fast-growing world tourism industry that has resulted from the revolutions in transportation, telecommunication, and trade.

In the view of Robert Wood, the interaction between Balinese society and culture and tourism has very wide implications, because it has a knock-on effect in other areas of social life such as the economy, environment, health, education, religion, and culture (Wood 1993). For this reason, the study of the impact of tourism and the identification of the factors that support Balinese cultural resiliency have become increasingly relevant and urgent.

Tourism in Bali over the last seventy years, as in other societies, has developed through a number of distinct phases, from discovery by the outside world, through the development of responses by the local people, to the institutionalization of the tourist industry. While various forms of local response have developed, tourist activities have also been institutionalized within a framework of government regulations, such as those concerning cultural tourism.

Two types of local response are visible. The first is that local people are taking advantage of the positive impact of tourism through participation in the economic opportunities that it presents. The second is their increasing resistance to negative cultural influences from outside in order to protect and sustain Balinese culture itself on which, ultimately, cultural tourism is based. This paper will focus on the discussion of three main problems relating to these issues:

1. To what extent has tourism had an impact on Balinese culture? Here I focus on Balinese symbolic structures, social and cultural institutions, values, and religious institutions.

2. How far has Balinese cultural resistance been successful in dealing with the impact of tourism, and what factors have played an important role in shaping this resiliency? Here I consider the role of human resources, traditional institutions, Balinese self-identity, and the dynamic aspects of cultural processes.

3. What are the main patterns of participation by village communities in the economic opportunities opened up by the growth of tourism? Here I analyze the situation in three customary villages which were selected as research sites: Tenganan in Karangasem regency, Sangeh in Badung regency, and Ubud in Gianyar regency.

Cultural Tourism and Balinese Villages

The existence of modern tourism is supported by two historical traditions in Balinese life: the Great Tradition of Hinduism, and the Little Tradition of Bali itself, or *Bali aga*. However, tourism as a service industry is also dominated by modern technology, the money economy and labor relations.

The conceptual basis of tourism development in Bali is that of "cultural tourism." This principle was laid down in Perda (Regional Government Regulation) No. 3, 1974 which was later revised as Perda No. 3, 1991. Cultural Tourism is defined as tourism which takes into account Balinese culture, which is in turn part of the national culture, and makes use of it as a basic resource in development. On the one hand culture is expected to provide a focus for tourism, while, on the other, it is hoped that tourism will develop in harmony with culture.

The result has been intense interaction between the cultural sector and tourism, that is to say between the traditional and modern sectors. Balinese cultural resiliency with respect to the impact of tourism is based strongly upon the main pillars of Balinese tradition: the symbolic system, traditional institutions, the value system, and the Hindu religion. The ability of Balinese culture and the Balinese people to create, select, and adapt is being tested as they interact with tourism. The mode of participation in this process may develop either through individuals or groups in the form of institutions like the customary village.

In Bali villages are defined in two ways. First, there is the *desa adat* or customary village. Secondly, there is the administrative village, the local unit of district administration within the formal government structure. There are 601 administrative villages in Bali and 1,610 customary villages. Conceptually, the customary village is a both a unit for the purposes of *adat* or customary law, and a community whose unity is based on Hindu customs and traditions. It is linked to a village temple, controls its own region and property, and has the right to administer its own internal affairs autonomously. It is formed on the basis of the threefold *tri hita karana* principle, which includes (1) *parhyangan* (space for worship), (2) *pawongan* (the village community), and (3) *palemahan* (the village area). The customary village is subdivided into smaller units called *banjar*, of which there are 3,449 in Bali.

There are five basic principles underlying the existence of the customary village in Bali: (1) material and spiritual harmony; (2) mutual cooperation, unity, and the ideology of the family; (3) diversity according to variations in space, time and customs; (4) the use of deliberation to obtain consensus; and (5) a degree of autonomy.

Participation in tourism involves four main components (Margono 1995): (1) information about opportunities; (2) the motivation to participate; (3) the ability to render participation effective, including mental and physical capabilities, education, and skills; and (4) the opportunity to participate. Village participation in tourist development in Bali is relatively a new phenomenon. It started with the growth of the customary village as a tourist attraction. It later continued with the development of the customary village as a coordinating institution managing tourist activities within the village. Recently greater efforts to develop village tourism based upon the customary village have been noted (Oka 1993). Village tourism as a type of cultural tourism aims to develop the *desa adat* as a tourist attraction and is concerned with local arts, handicrafts, natural beauty, institutions, and the system of local government. Its aim is to promote the more even provision of social welfare. The village thus has a dual role as both the object and the subject of tourist development. The pattern of participation in tourism of the three villages studied is based on three main variables: (1) initiative to participate, (2) scale of participation, and (3) pattern of participation. The three villages vary in terms of the information available, and in their will, ability and opportunities to participate.

In terms of development, Tenganan is an agricultural village, with a compact settlement pattern and a relatively closed social structure. Sangeh is also agricultural, though more scattered. The *banjar* which make it up are more clearly separated from each other and the social structure is more open. Ubud is a village which produces arts, handicrafts and services, though originally it was also agricultural. It has a scattered layout and an open social structure like Sangeh. In relation to tourism, Tenganan receives relatively short visits from tourists interested in cultural tourism, with comparatively little interaction between the residents and the tourists. Sangeh is visited by tourists interested in both natural and cultural tourism. They come to the village mainly in the morning, and there is fairly intensive interaction with the local people. Ubud in contrast is a place where tourists both visit and stay, so that very intensive interaction occurs between the visitors and the local residents. Thus while Tenganan has experienced tourist development on a small scale, the developments in Sangeh are on a more significant scale, while the developments in Ubud are both far-reaching and complex.[1]

Despite their links with the modern sector of the economy through tourism, the unity of all three villages investigated is still based on tradition in relation to values, institutions, ways of thinking, patterns of interaction with the environment, and village dynamics. These involve both religious and aesthetic values, as well as a stress on solidarity and harmony. Village institutions are characterized by the *tri hita karana* principles of collective orientation, mutual cooperation, and harmony. They also share a degree of autonomy, regulation, a leadership system and clear geographical and social borders. In terms of ways of thinking, even though religion and social solidarity are both strong, so is the spirit of entrepreneurship which has grown up in response to the opportunities opened up by tourism. The village community also places great importance on a harmonious relationship with the environment. Finally, from the point of view of the dynamics of village life, despite their openness to new ideas and innovations, the villagers are still solidly determined to preserve the existing principles on which their lives are based in the face of the changes which are taking place. The local response of Balinese society to tourism involves active participation in different tourist activities, including providing attractions, accommodation, transportation, and services. The more recent institutionalization of the industry has largely been based on the concept of cultural tourism and government regulations aimed at promoting tourism around the customary village.

The initiative to participate in village tourism began with individual local villagers and was later developed institutionally by the customary village, which now coordinates and manages all tourism activity in the village. Income from tourism comes from four main sources: a fee for entering the location, souvenir kiosks, and photographic and parking services. There have been efforts to diversify tourist attractions and develop local accommodation facilities, in order to expand tourism further. Generally, however, the pattern of participation by the local people is collective, through the institution of the village.

The resulting tourism has affected different villages in Bali in different ways. Villages can be classified under three headings: villages where tourists live, villages which are visited by tourists, and supporting villages. The three case studies below illustrate the degree of variation.

Tenganan

Tenganan is an isolated mountain village in Karangasem regency. The compounds in the village share a similar layout, technology is traditional and simple, and the population is socially homogeneous. The majority are farmers, with some traders, artisans, and employees. Many of the traders sell souvenirs to the tourists, and some houses in the village also function as souvenir shops. Social organization is based on place of origin and kinship. Social institutions of mutual cooperation within the customary village are still strong, though the administrative village also plays an important role. The whole village is Hindu, religious institutions are strong, and the complex ritual system continues to function and develop. This, together with types of sacred art such as *rejang* and *selonding*, have become cultural assets which attract visitors. Various local handicrafts such as textiles and woodcarving have also been important in tourist development. The village is one of the oldest in Bali, and the social life of the village community combines traditional *Bali aga* culture with its own distinctive traditions. These relate to village membership, young people, the life cycle, informal education, burials, art and ritual, village gatherings and *adat* meetings, mutual cooperation, and environmental maintenance and preservation.

The structural and architectural homogeneity of the village is unique. The settlement pattern is based on the family, with six rows of buildings separated by three village roads. Each family compound has a similar layout consisting of four types of buildings. The village provides some facilities for tourists such as a parking area, souvenir kiosks and shops, and small market stalls. Restaurants and accommodation are easily found in the Candi Dasa tourist resort located about two kilometers to the south.

Sangeh

The village of Sangeh in Badung regency is a village in the plains and is less isolated geographically. It has a scattered settlement pattern and is made up of separate *banjar*. The population, like that of Tenganan, is homogeneous from the point of view of religion and ethnicity, but it is becoming more heterogeneous in terms of occupation. A number of buildings designed for tourism facilities such as kiosks are concentrated around the village.

The inhabitants of Sangeh village work as farmers, traders, providers of services, employees, and laborers. The concentration in trade and services has developed around tourism, and there is more use of modern technology than in Tenangan. Social differentiation and stratification are more complex, in line with the complexity of occupational and social structures. The community of Sangeh village is also Hindu. The arts of music and dancing are well developed in the village, in contrast to painting and carving which are not as developed. The supplies of goods for the tourist souvenir shops come from outside the village, generally from Gianyar regency.

The main object of tourism in Sangeh village is actually the natural environment, a natural tourist park. This includes an area of homogeneous forest consisting of approximately fourteen hectares of nutmeg trees and a population of thousands of monkeys. The trees in the forest are arranged in terms of structure, leaf density, and type of trunks and branches so that the corridor underneath them appears to be an artistically created space. The Sangeh park is a mix between a botanical garden and a zoological garden. The characteristics of its forest and fauna make the area a natural tourist resort. Within this forest there are four separate temple compounds (*pura*): Pura Pule, Pura Tirta, Pura Melanting and Pura Bukit Sari. The park's attraction lies in the harmony between the forest, the monkeys (both wild and tame), and the religious images. It is visited by both international and domestic tourists, especially during holidays, from morning till noon. Around it there are facilities available such as a parking area, food stalls, souvenir kiosks, and photographic services.

Ubud

The village of Ubud in Gianyar Regency has also developed as a tourist resort. Like Sangeh, Ubud also has a scattered settlement pattern and consists of separate *banjar*. The population seems to be more heterogeneous in terms of ethnicity, religion, and occupation. They are also highly mobile. Tourist facilities such as kiosks, "homestays" (local houses which are available as accommodation), restaurants, and art shops are found scattered all over the village. The majority of the Ubud population make their living as traders, providers of services, and artisans. Only a small number of people work as farmers. The growth of Ubud village as a tourist resort has resulted in the rapid development of the modern sector in the village, including the adoption of modern technology in the fields of communication and transportation. In terms of the structure of the community, traditional institutions in Ubud have developed alongside formal institutions such as the village administration, and private institutions such as associations for the local hotels, travel companies, homestay providers, and artists.

The majority of Ubud people are Hindus. There are also a number of newcomers looking for jobs in tourism who come from different religious backgrounds, either Muslim or Christian. The periodic rituals which take place according to the Hindu Balinese calendar system are a major attraction for tourists. Ubud has a rich artistic life, including the fine arts, carving, and dancing. A number of art museums and galleries have developed in the village, including Puri Lukisan Museum, Ratna Warta, Neka Museum, and the Agung Rai Museum of Art. Ubud Palace as a cultural center also organizes daily performances of the *legong* and *kecak* dances for tourists.

Ubud village was well known as a tourist destination long before Indonesian independence in 1945. It started as a center for cultural tourism, specializing in the fine arts and dancing. It was already famous in the mid-1920s, thanks to the work of a local pioneer, Tjokorde Gede Agung Sukawati. In order to provide unity and encourage creativity, especially in the fine arts, an association of artists called Pitha Maha was formed in 1931, including both local artists such as Tjokorde Gede Agung Sukawati and Gusti Nyoman Lempad, and foreigners such as Walter Spies and Rudolf Bonnet. Its aim was to improve the quality of the work being produced and to help in marketing it.

More recently the village has seen a growth of various kinds of tourist facilities, such as hotels, restaurants, art shops and museums, and homestays. This has resulted in an increase in participation by members of the community, either as individuals or as groups. The varied and relatively large scale of activity required a higher level of professional management, and the Yayasan Bina Wisata was formed for this purpose. This institution is organized by the Ubud LKMD (Lembaga Ketahanan Masyarakat Desa), a village preservation association.

The institutionalization of tourism can be at the level of the family, *sekaa* (associations), and the village, as well as in the development of institutions such as Yayasan Wisata Desa Ubud. Since 1994, the village of Ubud has been officially designated by the provincial governor as one of twenty recognized tourist resorts in Bali Province. In addition to the increasing enthusiasm for the arts, religious ritual has also seen a revival, from the level of the family to that of the *banjar* and customary village as a whole. There seems to be a positive correlation between the economy, culture and religion. This enthusiasm reflects the vitality of the local culture and its function in the life of the community.

The Impact of Tourism on Culture

The impact on culture has taken place in two ways: first, through the interaction between the visitors and local community; and second, through increasingly open communication and dialogue between local cultures in both the national and global contexts. The process of interaction between visitors and the local community, as stated previously, takes place in a context of interdependence and complementary expectations. The visitors expect an aesthetic cultural experience, and this provides economic opportunities for the local community. The economic impact on the community has, on the one hand, encouraged the development of certain attitudes and types of behavior such as commercialization, individualism, and materialism. On the other hand, the growth of the economy has also been significant and meaningful for the local community in terms of the revitalization of its physical structure as well as its society and culture. The cultural communication and dialogue taking place in relation to tourism have encouraged the growth of a tourist culture with new values in terms of the economy, science and technology, individualism, and new forms of secular social institutions. In addition, the spread of new forms of expression and values, together with the dialogue between diverse cultures, has opened up opportunities and challenges, accelerating innovation, creativity and cultural enrichment.

In Tenganan, the development of the village as a tourist site has encouraged the development of handicrafts, including *tenun gringsing* (woven cloth), and lontar leaf crafts, and has opened up job opportunities in service industries. On the other hand, the rapid growth of souvenir kiosks in the settlement area has also disturbed the traditional pattern of settlement and the harmony of the village environment.

In Sangeh, the development of a village tourist industry has accelerated the increase in income of the village community and of the customary village as a tourism-managing institution. Furthermore, the impact of this economic growth has included the restoration and renovation of the tourist sites, the increased distribution of the income to the *banjar* as subunits of the village, and increased support for the village's ritual and cultural life. The data from 1993 to 1995 suggest that around four hundred village members had gained job opportunities in the tourism sector and that the income of the customary village from this sector was substantial. From 1993 to 1995 it amounted to over fifty million rupiah (about U.S.$22,000) annually.

In Ubud, the development of the village as a tourist object and resort has encouraged the growth of the fine arts, performing arts, and handicrafts. The strength of the village's enthusiasm for art and culture based on economic motives is reflected in the efforts to create, preserve, and collect art in museums. There is also considerable enthusiasm for religious rites at the family, *banjar* and customary village levels. This enthusiasm reflects the vitality of local culture and its function in the life of the community.

On the other hand, commercial and tourist art have also developed, but these consist of rather routine, monotonous, secular mass production. The transformation of land ownership and acquisition has also occurred as local people have disposed of land to people from outside the village. In addition, there has been a transformation of the physical and social structure of the village, as it has become more dynamic, crowded and heterogeneous. Social relations are no longer confined to the boundaries of the village or kinship group, but have crossed ethnic, religious, and racial boundaries to become a network of national and global relations. The coordination and management of the various village tourism activities are no longer carried out by the customary village, but rather by a specialized organization, the Yayasan Bina Wisata.

The above discussion shows briefly that the impact of tourism on culture in the three research locations has both positive and negative characteristics. There have been superficial changes in relation to physical symbols, cultural products, activities, and material culture. However, the attitudes of the village community, the functions of social institutions, the relationship between the village community and traditional institutions, the ways and patterns of community life, and its physical, sociocultural and spiritual environments all remain strong, protecting the basic spirit of the culture. The basic values of solidarity and harmony are still strong enough to provide the village with its identity and to influence the physical structure and the life of the community. There is still continuity despite the changes taking place through the processes of Balinization and globalization. A very strong consciousness of culture has developed which has accelerated both creativity and participation in the wider society (cf. McKean 1973; Picard 1993 : 73).

However, the impact of tourism on culture can be seen as both positive and negative. The intensive cultural communication in tourist activities crossing local, national and global boundaries has resulted in challenges to the existence and function of local culture. Cultural resistance has grown stronger in response to tourism and the new environment with its rapid and dynamic development.

These challenges have different dimensions, both internal and external. The internal challenges are related to development of a sustainable culture, able to keep its identity as a major attraction in Balinese tourism, in accordance with the concept of cultural tourism. The external challenge includes different kinds of negative impacts from the rest of the world on the local community and culture. These can be classified as: (1) the growing density of tourist resorts with their various problems such as prostitution, narcotics, crime and other forms of harassment; (2) commercialization accompanied by materialism, secularization and individualism; (3) conflicts of values, especially between traditional values (religious, social, aesthetic); and modern values (economic, technological, and individualistic); and (4) the transformation of the ownership of land and other natural resources.

The thirty years of tourism that these three villages and Bali in general have experienced as a tourist destination in Indonesia indicate that despite the increasingly rapid changes taking place, Balinese culture is still strong enough to resist them, because of four factors. The first factor is that of the Balinese people who are responsive, active and creative in reacting to the development of tourism. This has allowed them to take advantage of the various opportunities, and the economic, social and cultural benefits arising from tourism. The second factor is that of the strength of the traditional social and cultural institutions in Bali. These have been able to adapt to the changes taking place, while still retaining a hold over the community. This phenomenon is clearly apparent in the function of the customary village in the three research locations of Tenganan, Sangeh, and Ubud. The third factor is the cultural tourism development policy of the regional government of Bali with its various strategies and supporting regional regulations, such as the prohibition on the use of temples as objects of tourism, the required use of Balinese traditional architecture, and the ban on hotels higher than the height of a coconut tree. The fourth factor is the Hindu religion which has become the essence of Balinese culture and the basis of the identity of cultural tourism. The historical experience of communication between Balinese and outside cultures has also supported the ability of Balinese culture to resist change.

Conclusions and Implications

From the anthropological analysis of the three villages as objects of tourism in Bali some conclusions can be drawn. The impact of tourism on local culture is still very superficial, and the basic Balinese culture is still strongly protected by local attitudes, social institutions, ways of life, and sense of community. The interaction between tourism and culture has led to cultural revitalization and change on the surface, but underlying these changes are many continuities as the processes of Balinization and globalization have continued. The economic, social, cultural, and ecological opportunities and challenges cross local, national and global borders. These opportunities are positive and varied, while the challenges are also large and significant. The opportunities include employment, an increase in income, the extension of social relations, the development of creativity, and cultural revitalization. The challenges can be identified as the varied problems arising from increasing density of development, a strong current of commercialization, the rise of value conflict, and the transformation in the ownership of land and other natural resources.

On the one hand, Balinese culture is strong enough to cope with these various challenges due to the fact that the society and culture are responsive, active, and creative. On the other hand, the resiliency of the culture is also strongly supported by responsive human actors, established traditional institutions, strong tourism development policy, and the solid identity and spirit of Balinese culture. The implications in relation to the development of tourism in Bali during the twenty-first century include the following.

First, the strategy of sustainable tourism development must be able to improve tourism and culture in accordance with the basic concept of cultural tourism.

Second, the development of tourism should aim to provide a high level of economic benefits, while still maintaining the quality of Balinese culture, preventing its secularization, improving the quality of service, and always preserving the environment.

Third, tourism development should encourage an increase in community participation, in which the role of the traditional sector is complementary to that of the modern sector.

Fourth, the improvement and extension of tourism should be able to maintain the existence and integrity of Bali island in accordance with the motto: "Tourism for Bali, not Bali for Tourism."

Note

1 The information used in this study was collected through fieldwork research on social life, culture and tourism in the research locations, as well as from documentary sources and the results of previous studies. Structured in-depth interviews were carried out with key informants, including village heads, *adat* chiefs, *banjar* heads, tourism entrepreneurs, and selected groups of villagers who could provide detailed information on the problems of tourism. Participant observation was also used to collect information on the activities of the local community in response to tourism, the management of tourist sites, village businesses, and attractions and entertainment for tourists. Close consideration was given to the patterns of life and culture of the local community in relation to tourism, and the villagers' own views of the relationship between the customary village and tourism development. Interviews were carried out both with individuals and groups. Many of them were recorded, and information was cross-checked where possible.

References

Geriya, Wayan I. 1995. *Pariwisata dan Dinamika Kebudayaan Lokal, Nasional, Global: Bunga Rampai Antropologi Pariwisata.* Denpasar: Upada Sastra.

Haryati, Soebadio. 1991. "Kesinambungan Nilai-nilai Budaya Indonesia dalam Era Kebangkitan Nasional II." Unpublished seminar paper, Faculty of Letters, University of Udayana, Denpasar.

Hitchock, Michael, Victor T. King, and Michael J.G. Parnwell eds. 1993. *Tourism in Southeast Asia.* London and New York: Routledge.

McKean, P.F. 1973. "Cultural Involution: Tourism, Balinese and the Process of Modernization in an Anthropological Perspective." Ph.D. dissertation, Brown University.

Picard, Michel. 1993. "'Cultural tourism' in Bali: national integration and regional diffrentiation," in *Tourism in Southeast* Asia, eds. Michael Hitchock, Victor T. King and Michael J.G. Parnwell. London and New York: Routledge.

Soedarsono, R.M. 1993. "Industri Pariwisata: Sebuah Tantangan dan Harapan bagi Negara Berkembang," in *Kebudayaan dan Kepribadian Bangsa*, eds. Tjokorde Rai Sidharta et.al. Denpasar: Upada Sastra.

Sutjipta, Nyoman et.al. 1990. *Partisipasi Masyarakat dalam Pembangunan di Daerah Bali.* Denpasar: Bappeda in association with Unud.

Wood, Robert. 1993. "Tourism, culture and the sociology of development" pp. 48-70 in *Tourism in Southeast* Asia, eds. Michael Hitchock, Victor T. King and Michael J.G. Parnwell. London and New York: Routledge.

Chapter 6

Gamelan Degung: Traditional Music in Contemporary

West Java

Shota FUKUOKA

Gamelan degung is a type of traditional ensemble music among the Sundanese people of West Java. The *degung* ensemble is rather smaller than that used in Javanese court gamelan music. Contemporary *degung* has two different types of repertoire. One consists of classical instrumental pieces which are now called *degung klasik*, and the other consists of pieces composed more recently called *degung kawih*. In this paper I focus on the process of development of these *degung* repertoires since the 1920s when the *degung* tradition known today is said to have been established. I also discuss these two types of repertoire as representing two contrasting approaches to traditional music which have been the main driving forces in the development of *degung* in contemporary Sundanese society.

Sundanese musicians following the first approach have tried to pass on the heritage of traditional *degung* pieces. Of course this process is not a mere imitation of the musicians of former generations, but the reevaluation, recontextualization, or, in some cases, the recreation of tradition in the ever changing society of West Java. In other words, they see as their task the establishment and maintenance of the Sundanese musical tradition. Other Sundanese musicians, on the other hand, have also created a newer repertoire to make *degung* music attractive to a wider audience. They have introduced female singers, borrowed pieces from other genres of Sundanese music, and devised new arrangements. In doing so, they have tried to popularize *degung*, and in the process they do not seem to worry so much about "tradition."

Shota FUKUOKA

Degung in Sundanese Music

Jaap Kunst has written that *degung* has been, from ancient times, the gamelan of the highest status groups in West Java (Kunst 1973: 387). The high status of *degung* is derived from its association with the Sundanese aristocracy. *Degung* was once the prerogative of the *bupati* or regent under Dutch control, and was played for state receptions, dinners, and public appearances of the regent himself, as a symbol of his presence and power (Heins 1977: 61–62). *Degung* was also played on *pesta raja*, the birthday of the Queen of the Netherlands (*Soeara NIROM* 21 August, 1938: 32).[2] It was thus the ceremonial music of the rulers at the center of Sundanese aristocratic culture, in the same way as the Javanese courts served as the centers of Javanese aristocratic culture. *Degung* therefore once had symbolic significance for the Sundanese aristocracy. Max Harrell has written that *degung* was the sacred possession of the hereditary rulers, more important than a crown (Harrell 1974: 8).

The Sundanese aristocracy has another musical genre with which they are associated, namely that of *tembang sunda cianjuran*.[3] This is vocal music accompanied by one or more zithers, and a bamboo flute or a bowed lute. The most significant difference between *cianjuran* and *degung* is that *cianjuran* was sung by the *menak* (aristocrats) themselves, while *degung* was played by musicians who served them. This also affected the directions of development of these two genres after Indonesia's independence. Today, *cianjuran* is still patronized by the descendants of the aristocracy as a way of expressing their feelings of nostalgia for their glorious past. In contrast, we can no longer find any meaningful association between the artistocracy and *degung*.

Besides *degung*, Sundanese have other gamelan ensembles, *goong renteng* and *gamelan salendro* or *gamaelan pelog*. *Goong renteng* (or *gamelan renteng*) is found in remote mountain villages and played exclusively for ritual. The instruments used in the ensemble in Lebakwangi village, for instance, include a *bonang* (gongchime), a *saron* (a multi-octave metallophone), two *goongs* (suspended knobbed gongs), a *kenong* (a knobbed gong placed with its boss upward), a *kecrek* (a set of four small cymbals), and a *beri* (a pair of hammer-beaten cymbals) (see Heins 1977). As it is played for ritual, its social function is comparable to that of *degung*, and the appearance of the instruments is also similar. *Goong renteng* can be said to be an equivalent of *degung* in village areas, and Heins suggests that *degung* has probably evolved from *goong renteng* (Heins 1977: 94). Today *goong renteng* is still found in a few villages in West Java.

The other type of gamelan music widely found in West Java is one that is usually referred to simply as *gamelan*, often with the names of types of

96

scales added, such as *salendr o* or *pelog*. The composition of the ensemble of instruments in this type of gamelan is similar to that of Javanese court gamelan, but with a smaller number of instruments. It is associated with the rod puppet theater, *wayang golek*, and with various dances and dramas. Its basic musical structure is widely shared with other forms of Sundanese traditional music, with the exception of the original *degung* and *cianjuran* pieces, and this enables an exchange of repertoire between genres of Sundanese music.

Sundanese people often refer to *degung* and *cianjuran* as *lemes* or refined musical genres in contrast to *kasar*, coarse or simple ones. This axis of evaluation basically contrasts aristocratic music with that of the common people and places musical genres in a hierarchical order. We can also find hierarchy within the repertoire of a single musical genre. Zanten suggests that the repertoire of *panambih*, the supplementary metrical songs associated with *cianjuran*, is considered less refined than the *mamaos* repertoire, the main *cianjuran* repertoire sung in a rubato style (Zanten 1989: 23). *Panambih* songs in *cianjuran* are classified as *kawih*, which may be defined as metrical songs, in contrast with *mamaos*.[4] Zanten, however, defines *kawih* as the simpler (*kasar*), less refined form of vocal music (Zanten 1989: 16). Since 1950, the *kawih* repertoire in *cianjuran* has increased (Zanten 1989: 23), and become an important part of the genre.

In gamelan performances, *kawih* music used to be associated with girl singers and dancers (*ronggeng*), who were also thought of as prostitutes, and therefore it often had negative connotations (Zanten 1989: 45; Kunst 1973: 394). However, Nano and Warnika have written that today the term *kawih* tends to designate pieces that are composed rather recently and it has come to be distinguished from *sindenan*, meaning traditional songs sung by a *sinden* or female singer in gamelan performance (Nano and Warnika 1983: 23). According to them, this type of *kawih* has come to be used in education, and people like Machjar Angga Kusumadinata, Mang Koko, O.K. Jaman and Ujo Ngalagena have edited songbooks for this purpose (Nano and Warnika 1983: 23). The use of *kawih* in education began in the 1930s. Kunst noted that in 1933, Kusumadinata was requested by the Director of Education and Religion to attempt to reverse the decline of Sundanese vocal music. In the space of twelve months, Kusumadinata managed to teach the music to a number of schoolteachers, and Sundanese popular vocal music was saved from being lost (Kunst 1973: 394–95). Songbooks edited by Kusumadinata in the 1930s indicate that he taught many *kawih* songs.

These *kawih* songs were also popularized through radio and 78 rpm records. One example is the song composed by a female singer named Moersih[5] which became popular around 1937, "Es Lilin." The name of this song began to appear in the radio program guide, *Soeara NIROM* around October 1937, and in February 1938 it was also broadcast in Surabaya and described as a piece that was popular in West Java (*Soeara NIROM*, 20 February, 1938: 19). Other popular *kawih* songs like "Sorban Palid" were also often broadcast in radio programs. R.A. Darja pointed out that radio influenced the emergence of a new trend in *sindenan*, a playing technique called *dirangkap* which means "playing in double beats" (Darja 1949: 8).

The Establishment of the *Degung* Tradition

Degung is played by a standard ensemble of instruments today consisting of a *bonang* (a set of about fourteen small gongs placed on a wooden frame), a *jengglong* (formerly called *degung*, a set of about six medium sized gongs suspended in a wooden frame), a *goong* and a *kempul* (a large gong and a smaller one suspended in a wooden frame), a *panerus* and a *pekin* (metallophones with about fourteen bars), a *suling* (a bamboo end-blown flute), and a set of *kendang* (three double-headed barrel-shaped drums, one large and two small). Sometimes it also has additional instruments like a *kacapi siter* (a box-shaped zither), two *saron* (one-octave metallophones), a *gambang* (a xylophone) and a *rebab* (a bowed lute). Kunst however has argued that the *degung* ensemble was not standard, and that the only essential item was the *degung* (*jengglong*) itself, the instrument after which the ensemble was named (Kunst 1973: 387). Clearly, over the last fifty years there has been a progressive standardization of the ensemble. The Bandung musical style prevails throughout the whole of West Java, and the repertoire and musical style of *degung* is also dominated by it. This style is taught at the National Institute of Performing Arts and the National High School of Music.

According to the oral traditions of *degung* musicians, the *degung* tradition in Bandung was established around the year 1920 by a legendary musician called Idi, though it is not known exactly how this happened. Harrell has suggested that the tradition was based on the *degung* of Cianjur and Sumedang (Harrel 1974: 15), while Nanda has written that Wiranatakoesoema V, the former *bupati* of Cianjur, brought his musicians from Cianjur when he was appointed as the Bupati of Bandung, and they established the tradition at Bandung (Nanda nd: 28), although today there is no evidence to confirm it.

Nor do we know about the *degung* of Bandung before 1920. Kunst and Wiranatakoesoema (1921) wrote that the ensemble of *degung* instruments had been passed down from generation to generation in the

Wiranatakoesoema family. We also have an account that states that when the capital of the West Java regency was moved from Dayeuh Kolot to Bandung, *degung* and *gamelan salendro* accompanied the procession (Prahiangan 1930: 798). But, again, we do not know whether the repertoire and musical style of *degung* before 1920 and after 1920 were identical or not. There are few pieces in common even between the repertoire which was described by Kunst and Wiranatakoesoema in 1921 and that of today.

In spite of all this, it seems without doubt that Wiranatakoesoema V and Idi laid the foundations of a new era of *degung* in Bandung around 1920. This coincided with the foundation of the Java Institute which began to show an academic interest to Sundanese music. In 1921, the second conference of the Institute was held in Bandung and one of the focuses was Sundanese traditional music. According to the details of the conference schedule described in the journal, *Djawa*, *degung* was introduced and played in addition to other forms of Sundanese traditional music such as *tarawansa*, *renteng, celempung*, and *angklung. Degung* was also played at the beginning and the end of the program. An academic interest in Sundanese music, including *degung*, was becoming apparent, especially in the paper by Kunst and Wiranatakoesoema (1921), recognized as the first ethnomusicological research on the subject. The activities of the Institute contributed to the establishment of a sense of tradition in Sundanese music, which began to be regarded as *Pusaka Sunda* (the title of one of its journals), part of the Sundanese heritage which should be preserved.

This does not mean that they tried to freeze the *degung* tradition in an unchanging form. It was also an important task to construct and develop the tradition, and from the beginning there were various creative attempts to do this. The repertoire played during the conference of the Institute included some pieces which from the 1930s were no longer regarded as *degung*. In addition, Idi and his colleagues are said to have composed many *degung* works during this period (Natapradja and Harrell 1974: 231–32). Thus in the 1920s there may have been a process through which the repertoire was established and organized. During the conference of the Institute, *degung* was also used as one of the accompaniments for *Lutung Kasarung,* a musical drama of a type known as *gending karesmen*, accompanied by Sundanese traditional music. This usage in drama already went beyond the traditional uses of *degung* in the regency. In 1927 and 1928, *degung* was used as an accompaniment for a silent movie version of *Lutung Kasarung*. It also replaced *tanji-dor* and became popular as a form of entertainment at wedding and circumcision feasts, or *hajat* (Natapradja and Harrell 1974: 225).

In this way, *degung* became recognized as a form of traditional music by a wide range of Sundanese people. Radio also contributed to the process.

McDaniel writes that in the Dutch East Indies in the 1930s, radio provided local groups with an early opportunity to share their performing arts and culture (McDaniel 1994: 39). It also contributed to the construction of a shared performing arts tradition among the Sundanese. In the first half of the 1930s in Bandung, the Bandung Radio Society transmitted *Bumiputera* (indigenous Indonesian) and *Tiong Hoa* (Chinese) programs in addition to their European program in Dutch (McDaniel 1994: 39). NIROM (Nederlands Indische Radio Omroep Maatschappij), a private corporation licensed by the Dutch government, commenced operation on 1 April 1934 (McDaniel 1994: 39). Besides its Dutch programs, NIROM also broadcast Asian programs. In 1936 these were operated by indigenous listeners' organizations subsidized by NIROM in Betawi (now Jakarta), Yogyakarta, Surakarta and Semarang, and by NIROM itself in cooperation with advisory committees in Bandung and Surabaya (*Soeara NIROM* 16-30 October, 1936: 3–4). Their role was taken over by NIROM on 1 January 1937 and the subsidy for listeners' organizations was decreased (*Soeara NIROM* 1–15 January, 1937: 4–5). On 1 November 1940, the operation, apart from the technical section, was taken over by PPRK (Perhimpoenan Perkoempoelan Radio Ketimoeran, or the Alliance of Eastern Radio Groups), founded in March 1937 for the purpose of realizing truly indigenous broadcasting (McDaniel 1994: 40; *Soeara NIROM* 27 October, 1940: 1–2).

Sundanese music occupied an important position in the Eastern programs of NIROM and PPRK, along with *kroncong*, Hawaiian, Javanese, Balinese and Chinese music, radio drama, and news (see *Soeara NIROM*). The Sundanese music which was broadcast included *degung, cianjuran, gamelan salendro*, and *orkes kacapi*. In the Dutch East Indies, there were more than thirty thousand licensed radio receivers by 1937 (McDaniel 1994: 40). Although this meant that only a limited number of people could listen to the radio broadcasts of this period, radio still had a considerable influence on Sundanese music (Suadi 1997). In 1935, the year that radio broadcasting by the VORL (Vereeniging voor Oostersche Radio Luisteraars, or Eastern Radio Listeners Organization) began, a distinction was being made between *klasik* and modern in the Sundanese performing arts, especially in drama or *wayang*.

Degung developed rapidly after 1920 and became popular as a genre of Sundanese music. In this process only the Bandung tradition survived and prevailed throughout West Java. Other traditions practically disappeared. On the other hand, *degung* developed beyond its limited use by the regency. It came to be used as a form of entertainment for feasts, and to be broadcast on the radio.

The Development of *Degung* after Indonesian Independence

Under Japanese rule, many gamelan instruments, including those used in *degung*, were confiscated by the Japanese army to provide materials for the production of weapons (Heins 1977: 65). Tjarmedi writes that it seemed as if *degung* had been buried with Idi who died in 1945 (Tjarmedi et al. 1997: 13). After its declaration of independence Indonesia suffered from the war against the Dutch army which came back to colonize Indonesia again. These years produced profound changes in Indonesian society. In West Java, the aristocrats lost the institutional base supporting their social status, and could no longer maintain *degung* music.

Radio also contributed to the process of development of *degung* after Indonesia's independence. The establishment of Radio Republik Indonesia (RRI) was announced on 11 September 1945, although it suffered hardships in its early days. The Dutch came back to Indonesia and tried to reestablish control. They soon took over the radio stations and began broadcasting again. However, the Indonesians removed the broadcasting equipment and began broadcasting programs from the places where they had taken refuge, such as the temporary station at Tasikmalaya established by RRI Bandung (*Pedoman Radio* 1950b: 5).

In 1948, the Renvile Agreement was reached and the army of the republic was withdrawn from West Java. The Pasundan state was founded, which was to form the Republic of the United States of Indonesia, and the former *bupati* (regent) of Bandung, Wiranatakoesoema, was elected head of state. At the same time, the Radio Foundation of the Transition Period (ROIO) began to broadcast. It had programs both in Dutch and in Indonesian, and music occupied a large part of both of them.[6] In the Indonesian program, *degung* music performed by the group Purba Sasaka was broadcast thanks to Wiranatakoesoema. It was probably the last major link between *degung* and the aristocracy.

After the transfer of sovereignty based on the agreement of the round table conference at the Hague, the radio stations in Java were taken over by the Ministry of Information, and Radio Rebublik Indonesia started to broadcast. Performances of *degung* by Purba Sasaka, the group led by Oyo, continued to be broadcast. On Sunday morning, *degung* was on the air alternating with *kendang penca*, music to accompany *penca silat*, a form of martial arts practiced for exercise.

RRI had already become the institution supporting *degung* in place of the regency before independence. Many popular and traditional musicians were employed as full-time and part-time staff. They began to perform *degung* under the leadership of Tjarmedi around the mid-1950s.[7] *Degung* music was used at the opening of the local news program in Sundanese, and as a result, it left a deep impression on the Sundanese people.[8] From that time to the 1980s the RRI was regarded as a stronghold of *degung*.[9]

Tjarmedi (1924–1995) became known as *tokoh*, a *degung* master. He learned it from his uncle, Oyo, and was active as a *degung* specialist at the RRI, as well as a player of *ketuk tilu* and gamelan. He often supervised the music of *gendeing karesmen* dramas. According to his wife, the gamelan singer Imik Suwarsih, his desire to innovate in *degung* seemed to increase after he was appointed as musical director for a drama by the former regent of Ciamis, R.T.A. Sunarja, and he brought about many changes. He speeded up the standard tempo of performance and added a female vocal part.[10] He also taught at the schools of traditional performing arts both at the university and the high school level. He was so influential in matters of traditional *degung* that his style is now dominant in West Java.

At the same time as Tjarmedi was trying to develop the *degung* tradition, the interest of ordinary people in Sundanese music increased and many amateur groups began learning to play *degung*, including children's groups, women's groups and student associations.[11] It is important that the revival of *degung* was carried out by these people and not restricted to the aristocracy. Before, *degung* used to be played only by experts, but now it was opened up to a wide range of Sundanese players.

People no longer associated *degung* with high status, but saw it as an indigenous art form and a symbol of the region (*Pedoman Radio* 1950a: 4). It was freed from the value system of the aristocracy which made a strict distinction between *lemes* and *kasar* music, and was enriched by a number of creative experiments.

The appearance of groups of female *degung* performers around the end of the 1950s clearly marked the change in its character. Before, all the players were male. Female musicians were almost all *sinden* who sang and sometimes danced for male audiences, and this had negative connotations.[12] As a form of *lemes* music, *degung* had excluded female players. In the other genre of *lemes* music, *cianjuran*, all the singers were male until the early twentieth century. The first women who participated in *cianjuran* gatherings were only allowed to sing *panambih* songs which were considered less "refined."[13]

However, as the former aristocratic standards became more relaxed or were no longer relevant, women came to participate in *degung* performance as in other social activities. Female *degung* groups must have greatly impressed the Sundanese. These flamboyant groups soon became popular and were often requested to play at *hajat*, or circumcision, feasts. The hosts invite many guests to these feasts, receive congratulations and gifts from them, and treat them to a buffet. If the hosts are relatively wealthy they may hire a group or groups of performing artists to entertain the guests. *Degung* is one of the most popular entertainments at feasts, together with *jaipongan* dancing. But the classical *degung* repertoire, *degung klasik*, is rarely performed, and most of the pieces played belong to the *degung kawih* repertoire.

Commercial cassette tapes also influenced the process of development of *degung kawih*. In Indonesia they replaced records in the early 1970s and spread rapidly throughout the country. For example the state-owned record company, Lokananta, ended production of records in 1973, and started to produce music cassette tapes exclusively (Yampolsky 1987: 2). Music cassette tapes could be produced with less capital and simpler equipment than records, and recording companies producing tapes were founded, not only in Jakarta, but also in cities in regions like Bandung.[14] These companies mainly recorded regional music and sold cassette tapes locally. They were able to cover a wide range of regional music, and they also helped in establishing new regional trends.

For example the Sundanese dance called *jaipongan*, which was created by a choreographer, Gugum Gumbira, at the end of the 1970s, based on a variety of Sundanese folk dances and music, developed together with the commercial cassette tape industry. Many commercial cassette tapes of *jaipongan* music were produced and distributed.[15] Private *jaipongan* dance schools were opened all over West Java, and even in Jakarta and cities in Central and East Java. In these the dance was taught using commercial cassettes. In a relatively short time *jaipongan* became one of the most characteristic types of performance in West Java.

The cassette tape also serves as a medium for the dissemination of new pieces of music. *Degung* players memorize pieces which have become popular and play them at feasts. In the 1960s, before the arrival of the cassette tape, Lokananta had released records of *degung* which contained classical pieces performed by Lingkung Seni Parahyangan, the group led by Tjarmedi. In the first half of the 1970s, private recording companies also recorded many classical pieces from traditional music genres, including *degung*, but since then, most of the music recorded on tape has shifted from classical to newly composed pieces.[16]

If we compare the situation with that of Central Java, the differences are striking. According to Sutton, commercial music tapes in Central Java provide authoritative examples of traditional gamelan pieces performed by gamelan musicians. Students of traditional music imitate the performance. As a result, the music tapes contribute to the process of the homogenization of performance practice (Sutton 1985: 25–27). By contrast, in Sundanese society which had already escaped from the traditional value system of the Sundanese aristocrats symbolized by the *lemes-kasar* distinction, music tapes provide the opportunity for musicians to show their creativity. Thus the music tapes have contributed to a diversification of the tradition.

However, *degung* has another problem. While the *degung kawih* repertoire is popular as an entertainment at feasts and is also growing rapidly through the mass media, *degung klasik* is increasingly rarely performed, and some people are anxious about this decline. The Indonesian government is therefore trying to preserve the *degung* tradition. For example, in 1995, the section for education and culture of the provincial government of West Java published a textbook on *degung* and distributed it to the elementary schools in the region with sets of *degung* instruments. The West Javanese newspaper *Pikiran Rakyat* (16 November 1995) reported this as follows:

> It is because *degung* is being gradually pushed aside by the products of the modern arts that [the government of West Java] has distributed sets of *degung* instruments and the book. If some groups perform *degung* at a circumcision feast or wedding the pieces played are newly composed ones. In contrast, we rarely hear classical pieces.

Here, "modern arts" may refer to the popular music being disseminated by the mass media. The government is therefore trying to prevent classical *degung* pieces from disappearing in the face of popular music and newly composed *degung*.

Many other efforts have also been made to pass on the tradition. For example the provincial government of West Java, as well as the national government, often holds *degung* contests in West Java. In these contests the set pieces are usually from the *degung klasik* repertoire, as are the optional pieces selected by the participants. *Degung* is taught in some elementary and junior high schools. The *degung klasik* repertoire is also taught as part of the curriculum at the High School of Traditional Arts and the Indonesian Performing Arts Institute in Bandung. Conscious efforts are therefore being made to preserve it.

The Degung Repertoire

Degung klasik

The original degung repertoire is now called *degung klasik*, mainly in contrast to the rather newer repertoire of *degung kawih*. As we have seen before *kawih* is considered a *kasar*, or less refined, musical genre, and the *degung kawih* repertoire is therefore also considered *kasar* compared with original *degung* pieces.

In the 1920s and 1930s, *degung* was the ceremonial music of the Sundanese aristocracy, and the repertoire was mainly maintained by the regency musicians. The legendary musician, Idi, and his colleagues composed many pieces for *degung*, and they now comprise the main repertoire of *degung klasik* (Natapradja and Harrell 1974: 231–232). One of his colleagues, Oyo, also helped maintain the tradition of *degung*. He was active from the 1920s until the 1960s, and he led the group, Purba Sasaka, which often played *degung klasik* outside the regency and on the radio.

Although Tjarmedi was regarded as an innovative musician during his career,[17] he was also considered as a successor to the *degung klasik* tradition because he learned it from Oyo, and he came to be associated with the orthodox tradition of regency *degung*. Today, since the RRI has declined as a center of traditional Sundanese music, the SSTI (Indonesian Institute of Arts) has replaced it. Some lecturers have been researching *degung* music and its history, and some experienced musicians are being appointed as part-time lecturers.

Most of the *degung klasik* repertoire overlaps with what is called *lagu gumekan*. This name is derived from a *bonang* playing technique, in which both the right and left hands combine to play one melody line. In other words, in the *degung klasik* repertoire the *bonang* plays the main melody and leads the performance. Other instruments are played according to the contour and pivotal tones of the phrases played by the *bonang*, so that all the musicians have to know the *bonang* melody.

The structure of the *degung klasik* repertoire also depends on the melody played by the *bonang*. As in other gamelan music, the large gong acts as a marker for the constituent units of a piece, which are called *gongan*. In *degung klasik*, the length of the *gongan* is determined by the *bonang* melody and not every *gongan* has the same length, although it usually consists of four, eight, twelve, or sixteen *matra* or measures.

Tjarmedi added a female vocal part to the *degung klasik* repertoire, which is sung by several singers in unison. The song may be called *kawih* because it is metrical, but it is usually distinguished from other *kawih*, because it involves *rampak*, or singing together. The melody of the vocal part is based on that of the *bonang*, so the musical structure remains the same as in the *degung klasik* repertoire.

Degung kawih

The music of *degung kawih* basically consists of a vocal part and a comparatively simple pattern of accompaniment. This type of piece is also called *lagu kemprangan* and is derived from the *bonang* playing technique. *Kemprangan* refers to a technique where the right and left hands play the same tones in octaves simultaneously.[18] The musical form and playing patterns of the instruments in *degung kawih* are identical with those of the repertoire called *rerenggongan* in *gamelan salendro* or *pelog*. *Panambih* songs in *cianjuran* also have the same musical form. So these musical genres can share a *kawih* repertoire.

The patterns of accompaniment in *degung kawih* do not depend on the contours of the entire song melody but only on the final tones of each phrase. Thus different songs may have the same accompaniment if the final tones are the same. The various combinations of these skeletal tones are called *patokan*. Indeed, many songs are composed based on a few *patokan*, and thus musicians can accompany many songs for several hours at a feast using only a few playing patterns. This means that young inexperienced female players can also perform on stage. It is one of the reasons that Sundanese musicians consider *degung kawih* easy to play.

A striking change in the music of *degung kawih* has occurred with the development of commercial music cassette tapes. In contrast to the traditional patterns of accompaniment, playing patterns of the pieces that are recorded on cassette tapes are arranged beforehand and performers have to play the melody that a composer or arranger specifies for each song. Although the actual playing patterns of some sections might be left to the players to play in the traditional way, they are also integrated into the total plan of the composition. Thus each song has its own pattern of accompaniment and it cannot be used for other songs. For example, the introductory section of a song (*intro*) is especially elaborately arranged, and becomes a kind of trademark of the song.

The ways of performance have also changed. Recording in studios using the new technologies, including multitrack recording, have become common. In multitrack recording only one part is recorded on each track. If the studio has several separate rooms, musicians can play their parts in them at the same time. If the studio does not have separate rooms, they record one part at a time. Traditional gamelan performance is based on close communication between musicians without a conductor. In contrast, musicians in recording studios are often separated both in space and time. They can no longer enjoy the kind of improvisation which depends on close communication.

Conclusion

Now I will summarize the differences between *degung klasik* and *degung kawih*. *Degung* once was a ceremonial form of gamelan for the rulers. Most forms of ceremonial gamelan like *goong renteng* in West Java, *gamelan sekaten* in Cirebon, or *kodok ngolek* and *monggang* in Central Java do not have a vocal part. The addition of a vocal part to *degung* marked a change in its character. While in most cases *degung klasik* is played by male musicians, the *kawih* element in *degung kawih* is sung by female singers. This has historical connotations. Female singers, who were often also dancers, used to serve men, with the result that the Sundanese aristocracy classed *kawih* as low status music, in contrast to *mamaos* which was sung by male aristocrats.

However, the audiences, on the other hand, want songs sung by women. A female musician has a strong appeal especially for a male audience. Today, even in *cianjuran*, many cassette tapes show an attractive (even sexy) picture of the female vocalist on the box (Zanten 1989: 49). In Sundanese folk music, males used to perform on instruments while females sang and danced. Today, this custom has been imported into the musical genres of the Sundanese aristocracy. In *cianjuran*, which used to be a genre for males, female singers outnumber males, while professional instrumentalists are still almost all male. Female song has been imported into *degung*, which formerly did not have a vocal part. In *degung kawih* female musicians even play the instruments, though instruments considered difficult to play are still usually played by male musicians. In recording studios male musicians still play the instruments.

Musical styles or forms are also different between the two repertoires. *Degung klasik* has a characteristic form which consists of *gongan* which vary in length according to the melody played by the *bonang*. In contrast, *degung kawih* has a form consisting of the repetition of *gongan* of the same length, identical with the form of the *rerenggongan* repertoire of *gamelan salendro* and *pelog*, as well as with *panambih* in *cianjuran*. As for the playing patterns of the instruments, *degung klasik* has its own distinctive patterns, while *degung kawih* shares patterns with *gamelan salendro* and *pelog*. As a result, the *degung kawih* repertoire can be shared by other genres of Sundanese music.

The recognition that *degung klasik* is the original repertoire peculiar to *degung* has led to an awareness of the need to preserve the tradition. Before, the regency used to maintain the tradition, and provided opportunities for performance. As a result, when this aristocratic base broke down, *degung* seemed destined to disappear. However, as it became recognized as part of their ancestral heritage, the Sundanese began to feel that it was necessary to preserve it as a repertoire of established works. In contrast, the repertoire of *degung kawih* is still growing, based on its contemporary appeal.

Notes

1 In the remainder of the paper, I will simply call this ensemble simply *degung*.

2 On 31 August 1938, *degung* was performed to celebrate the birthday of Queen Wilhelmina. It was also performed also for the birthdays of the prince and princess.

3 In the remainder of the paper, I will simply call this genre *cianjuran*.

4 Zanten points out some exceptions. According to him, *pantun* recitations, lullabies, children's songs, or working songs are not necessarily metricized, though all are classified as *kawih* (Zanten1989: 15).

5 In *Soeara NIROM*, the title was spelled "Ys Lilin" or "Ijs Lilin."

6 For the contents of the program, see *Pedoman Radio* (Radio Guide), published twice a month by ROIO. It was taken over by the RRI, Ministry of Information.

7 Until the mid-1950s, RRI continued to broadcast *degung* performance by Purba Sasaka whose members seem to have been RRI staff members.

8 Personal communication with Sundanese composer Nano S., and *suling* (end-blown flute) player Ahmad Suwandi in 1997.

9 Until the late 1980s, musicians who were considered masters like Sulaeman Sutisna, Samin Batu, and Tosin Muchtar were active at the RRI. However the older generation retired from the RRI at the end of the 1980s or the beginning of the 1990s, and many musicians outside the RRI told me that it no longer served as the center of Sundanese traditional music as before.

10 Personal communication with Imik Suwarsih in 1997.

11 Personal communication with Enoch Atmadibrata in 1997.

12 Nano S. told me that when he was in KOKAR (the conservatory for traditional music, which later become SMKI) at the beginning of 1960s, there were some people who threw stones at it, shouting "*Sinden* school!"

13 Personal communication with Apung Wiraatmadja in 1997.

14 Recording companies which released cassette tapes of Sundanese music were founded from the end of the 1960s, for example; Asmara (Bandung, founded around 1968), Hidayat (Bandung, producing music tapes from 1969), and Suara Parahyangan (Bandung, producing music tapes from 1971).

15 In August 1988, I counted 144 albums available in cassette shops in Bandung.

16 Personal communication with Teddy Jauhari in 1988. He runs a wholesale store for music cassette tapes called Tropic, and also produces many

Sundanese music tapes. He is known as the "king of cassette tapes" in Bandung.

17 Harrell wrote that Tjarmedi [Carmedi] was concerned with the creation of new music and new instrumentation (Harrell 1974: 3).

18 In *lagu kemprangan*, the *bonang* may also be played using the *cacagan* or *carukan* technique. *Cacagan* is a rhythmic variant of *kemprangan*. *Carukan* is the technique by which two instruments, in this case *bonang* and *panerus*, are combined to form a melodic pattern.

References

Darja, R. A. 1949. "Lagu Sunda didepan Tjorong Radio," *Pedoman Radio* *34* (20 February 1949): 8.

Harrell, Max L. 1974. "The Music of the Gamelan Degung of West Java," Ph.D. dissertation, University of California, Los Angeles.

Heins, Ernst. 1977. "*Goong renteng*: Aspects of Orchestral Music in a Sundanese Village." Ph.D. dissertation, University of Amsterdam.

Kunst, Jaap. 1973. *Music in Java: its History, its Theory and its Technique.* 2 vols. The Hague: Martinus Nijhoff.

Kunst, Jaap and R.T.A. Wiranatakoesoema. 1921. "Een en ander over Soendaneesche Muziek," *Djawa* 1: 235–52.

McDaniel, Drew D. 1994. *Broadcasting in the Malay World: Radio, Television, and Video in Brunei, Indonesia, Malaysia, and Singapore.* Norwood, New Jersey: Ablex Publishing.

Nanda. n.d. "Riwayat Perkembangan Seni Degung," *Belletin Kebudayaan Jawa Barat: Kawit*, 11: 28–30.

Nano S. and Engkos Warnika. 1983. *Pengetahuan Karawitan Daerah Sunda.* Departemen Pendidikan dan Kebudayaan, Direktorat Jenderal Pendidikan Dasar dan Menengah.

Natapradja, Iwan trans. and M.L. Harrell ed. 1974. "Report of a meeting of experts concerning gamelan degung," pp. 218–34 in "The Music of the Gamelan Degung of West Java," M. Harrell. Ph.D. dissertation, University of California, Los Angeles, pp. 218–234.

Pedoman Radio. 1950a. "Minggu Ini," *Pedoman Radio* (20 August 1950): 4.

Pedoman Radio. 1950b. "Siapa Dia Diseberang Gelombang," *Pedoman Radio* (25 June 1950): 5–6.

Prahiangan. 1930. "Bedja ti Bandoeng," *Parahiangan* 2 (50) (11 December 1930): 798.

Suadi, Haryadi. 1997. "Riwayat Radio di Indonesia (8): dari Lagu Sunda Sanggian Baru sampai Kecapi Berkawat 7 Tuan Koko," *Pikiran Rakyat*

(2 October 1997).

Sutton, R. Anderson. 1984. "Who is the Pesindhen? Notes on the female singing tradition in Java," *Indonesia* 37: 119–33.

Tjarmedi, E. et al. 1974. *Penuntun Pengajaran Degung.* Bandung: Pelita Masa.

Tjarmedi, E. et al. 1997. *Pedoman Lagu-lagu Klasik dan Kreasi Gamelan Degung Jawa Barat.* Bandung: Dinas P dan K, Propinsi Daerah Tk.I Jawa Barat.

Williams, Sean. 1989. "Current developments in Sundanese popular music," *Asian Music*, 21(1): 105–36.

Yampolsky, Philip. 1987. *Lokananta: A Discography of the National Recording Company of Indonesia 1957–1985.* Madison, WI: Center for Southeast Asian Studies, University of Wisconsin.

Chapter 7

Batik as a Commodity and a Cultural Object

Teruo SEKIMOTO

This paper is about Indonesian batik, colorful cotton cloth intricately dyed using the wax-resist technique. This art form has won international fame for its fine handiwork and the artistry of its unique designs. However, this paper does not deal with the "arts and crafts" aspects of batik. Instead, it first examines the way batik-making in Java has adjusted itself to the ever changing circumstances of modern society and developed as a form of economic enterprise since the last century. A brief sketch of the development of the batik industry in Java will demonstrate how a textile tradition with a rich heritage from premodern times has emerged as a contemporary tradition under the conditions, both favorable and difficult, imposed by modernity. In order to think about tradition in a meaningful manner, I assume that it is not a product of the past but a particular conceptual framework through which we see the things around us. In other words, it does not belong to the past but to our own contemporary experience.

Secondly, this paper deals briefly with the problem of what I call the "traditionalist" discourse surrounding batik which emphasizes the protection and preservation of past tradition. There is sufficient reason to invoke the past, for the batik industry in the modern history of Indonesia has often been a weak player in the competitive economy, subjected to one difficulty after another. It has had to compete with cheap mass-produced textiles from large factories equipped with large capital and advanced technology, especially since the 1970s. The changing lifestyles during the same time period also have threatened the survival of the industry. Those people who are devoted to batik-making, as well as those who love batik, therefore often appeal to the preservation of past glory. There is, however, a pitfall in this argument if the traditionalist view of batik is formalized into an official discourse, resulting in the separation of past tradition from the contemporary realities of batik-making. This official discourse, while praising batik as something belonging to times past, sees the people who are actually making batik and earning their living in the face of many difficulties as if they also belong to the past. By turning them from active agents on the cultural periphery into passive ones needing protection, the traditionalist discourse rather adds strength to the modernism on which the cultural hegemony of the power center rests. What is really meaningful to us is not to look for a preserved cultural asset in a fossilized form but to see the people who engage in batik-making as existing on the periphery of cultural hegemony. The dichotomy between the old and the new, tradition and modernity, is a misleading one. The traditionalist discourse which attributes tradition only to the past is just another version of modernism. Tradition is a living part of contemporary reality, albeit in a marginalized form. The real dichotomy is not that between tradition and modernity but that between the power center which subjugates and dictates the nature of traditions, and marginalized realities, including living traditions which escape the official discourse about "tradition."

Batik as Cultural Object

There is in Japan a small but consistent demand for Indonesian batik which is met by importers and retailers, not only in large cities but also in small, local urban centers. Even as early as the 1920s, there was a Japanese firm, Fuji Yoko, in Yogyakarta, Central Java, making batik products, including broad waistbands (*obi*) for traditional Japanese clothes, and exporting them to Japan (Kat Angelino 1930–31: 175, 189). The Japanese import of batik has been small in quantity compared to other major commodities imported from Indonesia such as crude oil, gas, plywood, fish, textiles, or garments. However, batik has its own characteristics which are different from those of other major imports. Whereas for most commodities the country of origin is irrelevant to consumers, batik is recognized as a uniquely Indonesian product. Unlike garments or plywood, countries other than Indonesia and Malaysia do not enter into batik production, even if there is a sizable market for this particular commodity. Commodities in general know no national boundaries, but this economic dictum does not fit batik.

Batik is produced mostly in Indonesia, and especially in Java. The term "batik" originated in Javanese and Malay, although the term is now employed in English to denote any dyed cloth made using wax-resist methods. In the eyes of those who are fond of batik, the Javanese nature of batik is a plain fact which calls for no specific explanation, as batik is deeply rooted in the history of Java and Indonesia. Already in the sixteenth century European travelers reported the production of colorfully painted cloth in Java (Elliott 1984: 36). There also are theories that batik production in Java began much earlier than that but they are hard to prove. One might maintain that batik's value lies exactly in the good old tradition of Java, and therefore it cannot be transplanted to other countries. One could argue further that batik in essence is not a commodity but a cultural object.

Such a view of batik, which is based on a dichotomy between economy and culture, is not totally wrong. In present-day Japan, for example, batik is seen mainly as a cultural object. Articles dealing with batik tend to appear in the culture sections of Japanese newspapers. When the Japanese emperor made a state visit to Indonesia in 1991, Ardiyanto's Gallery, an exclusive batik shop in Yogyakarta, was included in his itinerary because – as Japanese senior officials must have seen it – it represented Indonesian cultural tradition, not modern industrial development.

Changing Techniques of Production

We, however, should note that this view of batik as exclusively a cultural object ignores the modern history of the batik industry since the nineteenth century in which the dichotomy between economy and culture has not been self-evident. For example, imitation batik was produced in Japan and exported to Indonesia from the 1930s on (Japan Textile Design Center 1960: 19). Produced at large textile factories in Japan without the wax-resist method, these imitation prints were aimed at meeting the demand for inexpensive batik among Indonesian consumers. In the early decades of this century the use of Western-style trousers or skirts was still very limited in Indonesia. Though the different types of jackets, shirts, and blouses of European origin became common among an increasing number of the population, both men and women wore local styles of wraparound waistcloths. Batik waistcloths, which for centuries were exclusively worn by the Javanese elite, were adopted more widely by commoners as well, as the cash economy and wage labor made inroads into Javanese cities and the countryside in the latter part of the nineteenth century (Shiraishi 1990). Since there was a huge demand for batik in Java and nearby areas, first British, then Dutch textile manufacturers had already begun manufacturing imitation batik using newly invented printing methods and then exporting it to Indonesia in the early nineteenth century. The Japanese manufacturers were latecomers in the competition for this market. These efforts to export batik to Java continued into the twentieth century. They were, however, never very successful as foreign manufacturers could not compete with Javanese batik makers. Whether it came

113

from Europe or Japan, the imitation batik failed primarily because the colors were not fast (Brenner 1991: 37). People wear the inexpensive types of batik for everyday use. Since they wash their clothes by beating them and drying them under the tropical sun almost daily, the colors fade quickly unless superior dyeing methods have been used. With the printing methods then available in Europe and Japan, the imitation batik was ultimately no match for Javanese products in which time-consuming wax-resist methods were applied on both sides of a piece of cloth.

At the time when Japanese manufacturers tried to export batik to Indonesia, batik makers there made the inexpensive type of batik by the cap or stamp method. In the wax-resist method of Indonesian batik,[1] melted wax is applied to those parts of a piece of cloth which are not to be dyed with an intended color. The waxed cloth is then soaked in the dye solution until the desired color is obtained. The same process is repeated for each color until all the intended colors are obtained. In an older method of hand drawing, *tulis*, a copper tool with a reservoir, roughly similar to a fountain pen, is filled with melted wax. A female worker holds the tool, applying wax to the cloth just as if drawing a picture. It is a highly time-consuming method. The cap method then appeared, supposedly in the northern coast area of Java in the 1840s (Rouffaer and Juynboll 1914), and eventually came to revolutionize batik-making. The "cap" is a copper stamp by which a wax pattern is pressed on cloth at a far greater speed than the hand drawing method can accomplish. As many minor improvements were added to the stamp over years, it gradually developed into a more sophisticated, larger tool, increasing the productivity of batik-making tens or even hundreds of times. Now batik-making could be done in two ways. The hand drawing method was used to make quality batik in smaller quantities while the stamp method turned out inexpensive batik in much larger quantities.

Along with the new method of cap printing, new batik firms grew up throughout Java and parts of Sumatra, each employing tens or even hundreds of workers. The technical innovation made possible the mass production of batik at a much cheaper cost, which then created new demand, further increasing the scale of production and the number of firms. This was a typical case of economic development triggered by a new technology, even though the cap method still depended totally on manual labor. It thus opened up new opportunities for modern business enterprises to the non-European population in Indonesia, especially to the Javanese. Since the major industrial sectors in the Dutch East Indies were then dominated by Europeans, batik-making, along with the manufacture of silverware and clove cigarettes, provided one of precious few niches in which Javanese entrepreneurs could prosper.

Batik and History

There are only a few historical sources about batik production before the nineteenth century when it began developing as a modern business activity. Little is known, either, about whether batik was produced for sale in the market. Historical sources indicate that the Javanese courts in the seventeenth and eighteenth centuries had many women at their command who made hand-drawn batik for the princes, courtiers, and their families. The sources also show us that a large amount of fine cloth – both woven and dyed – was imported from India and used by local elites for ceremonial purposes. The Indian textiles, which dominated the world market before the industrial revolution in Western Europe, greatly influenced batik and other textiles in Indonesia. On the other hand, Indian manufacturers often intentionally modeled their products after the local textile designs of Indonesia in order to enhance sales there (Yoshimoto 1996).

When European cotton prints began penetrating the Indonesian market early in the nineteenth century, their chief rival might not have been Javanese batik but Indian textiles. Without the development of the cap method and consequently of the batik industry in Java, European cotton prints might possibly have overwhelmed the domestic production of textiles in Indonesia. Even as late as 1892 several Dutch Residents in Java expressed their apprehension that European imitation batik could eventually destroy the local production of batik (Koperberg 1922: 147). But their foreboding proved wrong as the local batik industry continued to grow.

The productivity of batik further increased early in the twentieth century, as chemical dyes from Britain and Germany gradually replaced the traditional kinds of natural dyes, thus, enabling a much quicker dyeing process. Using the cap method and chemical dyes together the batik industry was prospering all over Java, even though short-term ups and downs were an inevitable part of this indigenous industry. In the 1920s, the owners of thriving batik firms built huge, luxurious houses adorned with imported marble, chandeliers, and automobiles. One can still see the timeworn remnants of these houses in the cities of Solo and Yogyakarta, which show us the past prosperity of the industry. Batik-making was the single most important sector of the economy for Javanese entrepreneurs, and many among the most affluent business people of Javanese descent were batik-makers. Because of their prosperity and luxurious life style people called them "batik kings" (*ratu batik*). One of them was Haji Bilal in Yogyakarta who owned several workshops, and employed 700 workers, selling his products not only in Java but also to Sumatra and Singapore.

Because of its lengthy tradition, one tends to romanticize batik, seeing it as an antithesis to modern capitalism. The fact is, however, that batik has played an important role in modern economic development in Indonesia. The tradition of batik, as we see it today, is as much a result of competition and technological innovation since the latter part of the nineteenth century as it is the continuation of a premodern, more purely indigenous tradition. The aforementioned episode of Japanese-made batik took place within the process of modern economic development in which a technological innovation engendered new demands as well as an increase in production. The technology of printing in the modern textile industry, which in the early twentieth century was not competitive enough to win control of the market from the local batik industry, has greatly advanced today. The latest laser print technology can produce an exact copy of the finest hand-drawn batik. Even the most knowledgeable experts on batik would have difficulty distinguishing between the original and the copy. At the present time, however, such an idea sounds somewhat ridiculous since the commercial value of batik these days is inseparable from the values attached to notions of traditional art, handicrafts, and the Indonesian cultural heritage. Batik in the early twentieth century, on the other hand, was for the most part a common type of textile whose value was judged simply by its price and durability. The production of batik in Japanese factories was not in itself strange so long as it was cheap and competitive. The Japanese-made batik eventually lost out in competition primarily because of its technical shortcomings, namely, the faster deterioration of its colors.

Foreign Influence and the Diversification of Production

It was the cap, or stamp method, that made the modern development of the batik industry possible. Whatever innovations were incorporated into batik-making since the last century, however, the art of hand-drawn batik preceded them and has survived up to the present. Although we lack a detailed description of the "hand-painted cloth made by Javanese women" mentioned by European travelers in the seventeenth and eighteenth centuries, batik at the beginning of the nineteenth century was basically no different in colors and motifs from today's "traditional" batik.[2] In the fields of textile and fashion design, batik has an international reputation. This would not be possible without the aura of age-old tradition surrounding it. Even if the modern batik industry is by and large an economic endeavor, the art of hand-drawn batik may well represent Java's cultural heritage. However, it, too, has undergone changes and developments in the modern social environment. And it is within this social environment, too, that the traditionalist discourse on batik has been developed.

As was mentioned above, batik-making diversified into two sectors after the invention of the stamp method: expensive hand-drawn batik on one hand, and cheaper stamp batik on the other. In most cases, however, a batik firm produced both types of batiks within a single workshop and with a sexual division of labor: men worked on stamp batik while women made hand-drawn batik. Comparatively little is known about the origin of stamp batik, but according to one theory the stamp was invented in the 1840s, not in order to facilitate mass production but to obtain finer, more exact patterns than those which makers of hand-drawn batik at that time could accomplish. The development of stamp technique, then, further stimulated the development of finer, more exact patterns in hand-drawn batik as well.

The different types of hand-drawn batik are ranked by price and quality. Among hand-drawn batiks produced today, those of higher grade are characterized by the machine-like precision in their patterns. This particular attention to small detail may well be regarded as one more example of what Clifford Geertz calls the "involution" of culture in colonial Java (Geertz 1964). The increasing precision of patterns occurred not only in hand-drawn but also in stamp batik. A new technique, which was introduced in 1930, made it possible to remove even the smallest gaps between stamped wax patterns so that uninformed laymen could no longer distinguish hand-drawn from stamped batik (Veldhuisen 1993: 59). The time-consuming effort to obtain extreme precision in patterns is one of the reasons why batik is so greatly prized. It is, however, not a residue of an old tradition preserved statically but the result of a cumulative process through which the modern business of batik-making has developed over the years.

The industrial revolution in Europe also played a role in the modern development of batik. The tradition of batik which we find today is not an isolated local phenomenon but is tightly intertwined with the development of the world economy. Up to the end of the eighteenth century, batik makers utilized either domestic or Indian imported cotton; the former was thick and coarse, while the latter was finer and more highly valued. The first shipments of factory-made cotton from Britain reached the Indonesian market in the early nineteenth century. Then, Dutch cambric started to appear and gradually came to dominate the market. This was a type of cotton cloth woven densely with fine threads producing a textile with a tight, smooth surface. It was cambric which made possible a more intricate patterning of batik than had been possible before (Elliott 1984:38). The Netherlands, with its newly emerging textile industry in Twente, found in Indonesia a very promising export market. As they were not successful in the export of their printed cloth, they eventually concentrated on exporting white cotton as a raw material for Java's batik industry.[3] Thus, the development of the latter was helped partly by an export promotion policy sponsored jointly by the Dutch colonial administration and the textile industry at home. From the 1910s on, however, Japanese cotton exports began making inroads into Java and entered into fierce competition with Dutch cotton, especially in the 1930s (Saraso 1954).

It was not just through the imports of white cotton, chemical dyes, and paraffin that batik was tied to the outer world. Its designs also underwent significant new development in response to foreign textile designs. Since textiles were a major commodity in long distance trade long before the rise of the modern capitalist economy, batik was never isolated from foreign influence. As was mentioned before, Indian influence on batik and other Indonesian textiles was especially strong during the seventeenth and eighteenth centuries. The cap method and the subsequent rise of the modern batik industry, however, brought about a new overall pattern in the production of batik. Besides the older centers of batik-making in inland court cities, new centers were booming in some port cities on the northern coast of Java. While manufacturers in the court cities such as Solo and Yogyakarta largely maintained the older batik designs of court circles, their rivals in the port cities adopted foreign designs much more freely. Brighter colors and motifs of Chinese, Indian, Persian, and Arab origin as well as ornamental designs from modern Europe were taken on board and adjusted to the existing batik tradition. Batik manufacturers in the port cities were ethnically more mixed, and included Chinese, Arabs, and Eurasians working side by side with Javanese. At the time when manufacturers in the court cities, the majority of them being ethnic Javanese, were still largely concentrating on the original kind of batik products – square cloth for Javanese traditional wraparound waistcloths, shawls and headscarves – products in the port cities in the north were more diversified so as to fit the emergent life styles of the urban middle class. Now batik was also being designed which was suitable for Chinese and modern European dress, interior decoration, and so on. It was a type of modern business activity in that it was always seeking to create new demand through the development of a succession of new designs and fashions.

Batik in the Post-War Period

Between 1942 and 1945 when Indonesia was invaded and occupied by Japan, hyperinflation, military seizure of materials and means of production, and the total disruption of overseas trade devastated almost every sector of the economy. Since raw materials were not available, the batik industry almost died. A small amount of batik was produced under Japanese instruction and control with new patterns similar to Japanese traditional textiles.

This batik, known then as "hôkôkai batik," was a rare exception to the general disarray in batik-making during the war period.[4]

Once the war was over, however, the production of batik was gradually resumed, for batik was one of the basic necessities of life for which there was a great demand. In 1948, at the time when the government of the Indonesian Republic was still at war against the Dutch, GKBI, the Indonesian Union of Batik Co-operatives, had already been established by indigenous batik makers with its temporary headquarters in Solo, later moved to Jakarta.[5] In particular, their efforts were aimed at wresting control of the import and distribution of white cotton from the Dutch trading firms and local Chinese merchants. Since the nineteenth century, imported white cotton had been the largest component in the production costs of batik manufacturing. As batik makers suffered chronically from unpredictable fluctuations in the price of cotton, GKBI wanted the batik producers to gain control of its distribution so that they could obtain cotton at a stable price. The political situation just after Indonesia's independence was favorable to the batik makers' cooperative movement. Javanese batik makers could be seen as representing the nationalist ideal of indigenous economic progress. Also, the government's economic policy at that time was much influenced by West European social democracy and cooperative ideas. GKBI's effort gained momentum. After several temporary measures, the government finally granted GKBI the exclusive right to import and distribute cotton in 1955. Now batik makers were organized into local cooperatives, which then distributed white cotton to their members at a fixed price. The amount of cotton individual members received was determined by the number of stamping tables they owned.

Cotton was distributed in this way because stamped batik was still the mainstay of the batik business at that time. Although many batik makers continued producing hand-drawn batik, the sales figures for stamped batik were far larger. The latter also had the advantage of much quicker turnover than hand-drawn batik, which needed a longer span of time both in production and sales. This was very important for batik makers who depended heavily on high-interest loans to run their businesses. During the 1950s and 1960s, the government also regarded batik as one of the basic commodities which people in the middle-to-lower economic strata needed, and not as luxury goods for the well-to-do. Saroso, an economist and high government official who was close to GKBI in the 1950s, even wrote that, whereas the urban middle class no longer needed this traditional type of cloth, a large mass of uneducated people in towns and villages still did (Saroso 1954). The batik industry, in the golden era of GKBI, was not on the periphery but at center stage within the Indonesian national economy. Sukarno often relied heavily on GKBI's financial resources to support his more monumental and grandiose projects. The Jakarta planetarium in the Ismail Marzuki Cultural Center was one such project solely financed by GKBI. At present those who talk about the Indonesian national economy may easily forget about the batik industry, but from the late nineteenth century until the 1960s, it was the batik makers who represented the indigenous sector of the Indonesian economy and business.

With the exclusive distribution rights for cotton, batik makers were thriving. There were more than forty local batik cooperatives spread throughout Java and Sumatra. In the city of Yogyakarta alone there were about nine hundred batik makers organized into five separate cooperatives. Throughout Java local cooperatives built large office buildings, warehouses, meeting halls, schools, clinics, and small factories for low-grade cotton products. The GKBI headquarters also built a large factory in Medali, Yogyakarta, which was equipped with imported machines producing cotton yarn and high-grade cambric. While they monopolized cotton imports and distribution, their eventual aim was to replace imported white cotton with their own products. We can grasp the prosperity of the batik business during this period from the remnants of the cooperative office buildings in every regional center of the batik industry. They are large, impressive structures built in the modernist architectural style which was trendy in the 1950s, though they now often look run-down. Many of them are now leased for other uses. GKBI was the most successful of the many cooperative movements in Indonesia, most of which were doomed to failure. GKBI itself is now mostly out of the batik business, but with its accumulated assets from the past it still continues its operations in the textile and finance sectors.

In the era of GKBI's success in the 1950s and 1960s, the batik industry experienced the second boom period in the twentieth century, following that of the 1920s. GKBI's success and the batik makers' prosperity would not have been possible without its monopoly of cotton imports and distribution. This, however, also had a negative effect on the entrepreneurial spirit of indigenous batik makers. Some of them entered the batik business in the boom period simply to receive a share of cotton at the official price, and then make an easy profit by selling it on the black market. The general economic turmoil surrounding the fall of Sukarno in 1965 and 1966 further accelerated this type of malpractice. The batik industry, however, continued to thrive during the 1970s as there was an ample domestic demand for its products. This sustained demand was partly supported by a new trend in clothing then emerging in Indonesia. Starting in the 1960s several batik designers began utilizing batik for Western-style long sleeve shirts. Though this new fashion looked strange to many people, it became extremely trendy, especially after top ranking politicians and officials adopted it in the early 1970s as a type of formal national dress. The use of batik for all kinds of Western-style clothing spread quickly. In the 1980s, however, the batik industry suffered a serious blow because of the rapid development of print batik.

Print batik is made using techniques of hand screen printing or mechanized roller printing. Since these methods do not involve wax-resist dyeing, it is doubtful whether their products can really be called batik.[6] As we have observed, European and Japanese textiles firms had already exported print batik to Indonesia. According to the late Mr. Soemihardjo, a well-known batik designer and producer in Yogyakarta, an early Indonesian experiment in print batik was carried out in 1950 at the Institute of Textile Technology at Bandung at the suggestion and with the help of the British chemicals firm, ICI (Imperial Chemical Industries) (Soemihardjo, personal communication). Commercial production began in several batik-producing centers in Java in the 1970s. At this initial stage, print batik did not threaten the traditional methods of batik-making because its low quality was obvious to consumers of batik. Printing techniques, however, developed so rapidly during the 1980s that even knowledgeable consumers could hardly tell it from traditional batik. While high-grade batik made with the hand-waxing method could compete with print batik, low-grade batik, whether produced by hand drawing or stamp methods, was hardest hit. This meant that many batik makers lost their most important source of income as the low-grade batik provided them with a large volume of sales and quick turnover.

Besides the threat posed by print batik, the quick development of huge, fully mechanized textile firms in Indonesia since the 1970s has also taken its toll of more traditional batik makers. People now could purchase mass-produced textiles and garments at a price cheaper than that of batik. Many batik makers gave up the business, going bankrupt or turning to other sectors. In the city of Yogyakarta, the number of batik makers, which once numbered over nine hundred, has now decreased to ninety. In Laweyan, a neighborhood of batik makers in Solo which used to typify the prosperity of the batik industry in Java, one can hardly find anybody still continuing to make batik. Ponorogo, a district in East Java which, in the golden age of GKBI, ranked as the fourth largest batik producing center in Indonesia, has suffered the same fate. Print batik now accounts for about 90 percent of the annual production of batik in quantitative terms.

In relation to this technological change from the wax-resist methods to printing, we have to ask whether it is yet another technological innovation within the batik industry, or an external threat to it. This involves the difficult question of the definition of batik. There are people who categorically refuse to accept print batik as batik. Their case is a strong one since the artistic value of batik cannot be separated from the traditional method of wax-resist dyeing. We, however, cannot just ignore the economic reality that print batik is cheap and many consumers cannot distinguish it from

Teruo SEKIMOTO

traditional batik. It only became possible for people in the lower economic strata to wear batik after a wide variety of print batik appeared in huge quantities. Also, some batik makers survived by turning to print batik. It is intriguing to note that the same lamentations and anger that we hear now were also heard when stamp batik developed quickly and flooded the textile markets in Java from the late nineteenth to the early twentieth centuries. Those who highly appreciated the beauty of hand-drawn batik at that time foresaw the death of the batik tradition.[7] That, however, proved wrong and the tradition still continues.

The invention of the method for printing batik is different from the stamp method in its significance. It is seen as lacking some of the fundamental cultural values for which people in Indonesia and abroad love and admire traditional batik. Traditional batik production, however, has not been lost forever. In spite of many adversities, many batik makers and artisans still keep on producing batik with the wax-resist method, and some of them are still at present successful. There is an economic basis for the resilience of the tradition which lies in the diversity of demand for textiles. Unlike some other commodities, the textile market is not totally dominated by the law of the economy of scale. Consumers always seek subtle distinctions and variety from one piece of cloth to another, for cloth is one of the most basic tools used to express personal identities. The market is minutely segmented. That is the reason that some of today's batik designers-cum-producers in Java proudly declare that they never reproduce exactly the same pattern or color of a piece of cloth twice. This kind of subtle distinction can only be attained in handwork.

Today's batik does not survive only as a luxury commodity. Although the most successful makers sell their batik to the quality clothing market, there are also small producers in villages and towns in many different regions in Indonesia still employing the traditional method of dyeing. The quality and prices of their products are also minutely diversified. They can compete with cheap print batik firstly because their products sometimes fit the taste of consumers better in a particular locality or social stratum. Secondly, their way of organizing production is highly flexible, especially in the organization of labor. Many female artisans do their hand-waxing work at home. They receive white cloth and wax from nearby batik makers on credit, then work on it whenever it is convenient for them. When the work is finished, they deliver it to the batik makers, receiving piece-work rates and another supply of cloth and wax. Even those women who work in batik makers' workshops are not subject to strict work discipline, for they are also paid at piecework rates. They are allowed to stay there for days or weeks and go home anytime they like. These traditional types of labor arrangements result in low wages. At the same time, however, it makes it possible for women to stay very close to their homes and divide their time between work and household chores.

This kind of organization of labor illustrates well that the tradition of batik survives today, but it does so on the periphery of society. Some observers of batik only praise the past tradition of batik but deny the value of recent developments. They only see decline in today's batik. But what they see as decline is the contemporary reality of a living tradition. Even print batik finds a market because the production of hand-drawn batik continues to set a central standard for the batik tradition. A nostalgic view of the past only tends to fossilize a living tradition which may be marginalized but which is still alive.

Conclusion

Today's batik represents a tradition of fine handiwork and artistry. This tradition is generally regarded as essentially Javanese and as the antithesis of modernity. According to this view which I have called the traditionalist one, the golden age of batik lies in ancient times and every change the modern era has brought to batik has been negative: modernity always means the decay of tradition. In consequence, batik becomes something which must be protected from the ravages of time.[8] As we have seen, however, today's batik owes a significant part of its fame to innovations and changes since the last century. Ironically, it is this modern development of batik that has given birth to the traditionalist view of it. This view first gained strength among Javanese and Dutch elite circles at the end of the nineteenth century,[9] and since then has been reproduced countless times up to now. The same concerns about the decline and possible extinction of the batik tradition have been repeated for more than a century. This enduring sense of anxiety has some foundation since the batik industry has never been a dominant force in the modern economy. It has had to overcome one difficulty after another, and it still has to overcome them now. It should be noted, however, that batik-making has survived and developed as a form of modern industry representing Indonesian tradition. The very fact that the same concern has been repeated over a century rather paradoxically demonstrates batik's long-term resilience. If the batik tradition had died, the traditionalist concern about batik would have also died long ago.

The traditionalist view of batik opposes tradition and modernity as mutually incompatible, but modernity is a necessary precondition on which any consciousness of tradition in batik is formed. Modernity, however, is not an absolute condition of our contemporary lives, in which many different layers of modernity and tradition exist side by side in continual conflict and contradiction. Jim Supangkat, an Indonesian art critic, writes that "the actual traditional culture has been marginalized, not only by high art, or Western art, modern art and international art. but also by the [locally formed] concept of 'traditional culture' itself" (Supangkat 1997: 84). The reification of culture and tradition by the official discourse only marginalizes actual manifestations of these traditions. "Tradition" or "traditional culture" is meaningful to us not because the past is specially privileged in itself. They are meaningful because both tradition and modernity are living realities of our contemporary lives. Further exploration is needed into the way in which a tradition is established under modern social conditions, thus becoming a part of our lived experience.

Notes

1   For details of the process of batik-making, see Fraser-Lu (1989) and Elliot (1984).
2   We know this from the color lithographs of batik-clad men and women which are included in Raffles' monumental work (Raffles 1978).
3   For the export of European textile to Indonesia in the early nineteenth century, see Van Den Kraan (1996).
4   "Hôkôkai" literally means "association for dedicated service" in Japanese. The Japanese military administration in Java set up this organization to mobilize civilians in occupied territories for Japan's war effort.
5   Chinese batik makers were excluded from cooperative membership because the batik cooperative movement had been, since its start in 1936, motivated by the nationalist cause, which was always tinged with anti-Chinese sentiment.
6   According to the Indonesian Industrial Standards, print batik should not be called "batik" but "cloth with batik-like patterns." Those who are concerned about the tradition of batik often insist that notes be added to print batik on sale so that consumers can tell it from real batik. These regulations and warnings, however, are never included by print batik merchants. What makes the matter more complicated is that final touches of hand-drawn decoration using the wax-resist method are often added to print batik. Such products are called "combination batik," but for the majority of batik traders in retail shops and markets, batik is batik so long as it has batik-like motifs.
7   Kats (1922) was one of those lamenting the death of batik.
8   This traditionalist view of batik is a very common stereotype in Indonesia and abroad. As just one example of this, I refer to a paper by Amri Yahya, an internationally known batik artist in Yogyakarta (Amri 1990). However, since this view is so common, it would be misleading to at-

tribute it to any particular individual.

9 A typical traditionalist view of batik by a Dutch writer was also expressed by Kats (1922).

References

Amri Yahya. 1990. "Batik sebagai media ungkap," paper read at the workshop, "Sarasehan-Diskusi Panel Batik 1990," Yogyakarta.

Brenner, Suzanne April. 1991. "Domesticating the Market: History, Culture, and Economy in a Javanese Merchant Community." Ph.D. dissertation, Cornell University.

Elliott, Inger McCabe. 1984. *Batik: Fabled Cloth of Java.* New York: Clarkson N. Potter.

Frazer-Lu, Sylvia. 1989. *Indonesian Batik: Processes, Patterns and Plates.* Singapore: Oxford University Press.

Geertz, Clifford. 1964. *Agricultural Involution.* Cambridge, Mass: MIT Press.

Japan Textile Design Center. 1960. *Batikku: Jawa sarasa no moyô* [Batik: the patterns of Javanese cotton prints]. Tokyo: Japan Textile Design Center.

Kat Angelino, P. de. 1930–31. *Batikrapport (Deel II, Midden-Java.* Weltevreden: Kantoor van Arbeid.

Kats, J. 1922. "De Achteruitgang van de Batikkunst," *Djawa* 2: 92–95.

Koperberg, S. 1922. "De Javaansche Batikindustrie," *Djawa* 2: 47–56.

Raffles, Stanford. 1978 [1817]. *The History of Java.* Kuala Lumpur: Oxford University Press.

Rouffaer, G. and H. Juynboll. 1914. *De Batikkunst in Nederlandsch Indie.* Utrecht: Oosthoek.

Saroso Wirodihardjo. 1954. *Koperasi dan Masalah Batik.* Jakarta: Gabungan Koperasi Batik Indonesia.

Shiraishi, Takashi. 1990. *An Age in Motion: Popular Radicalism in Java, 1912–1926.* Ithaca: Cornell University Press.

Supangkat, Jim. 1997. *Indonesian Modern Art and Beyond.* Jakarta, The Indonesian Fine Arts Foundation.

Van Den Kraan, Alfons. 1996, "Anglo-Dutch rivalry in the Java cotton trade, 1811–30," *Indonesian Circle* 68: 35–64.

Veldhuisen, Harmen C. 1993. *Batik Belanda 1840–1940: Dutch Influence in Batik from Java, History and Stories.* Jakarta: Gaya Favorit Press.

Yoshimoto, Shinobu ed. 1996. *Shirarezaru Indo Sarasa* [Indian printed cotton]. Kyoto: Kyoto Shoin.

Chapter 8

Globalization and the Dynamics of Culture in Thailand

Anan GANJANAPAN

Introduction

Thailand has, for a long time, subscribed to a policy of an open economy. Such a policy became the main driving force that facilitated the integration of the country into the world market. During the decade from 1986 to 1996, the policy has, on the one hand, encouraged very rapid economic development which can be seen primarily in terms of industrialization. But, on the other hand, the same policy has also committed Thai society to the globalization process.

As a concept, globalization has only developed in academic circles since the second half of the 1980s. It refers both to the compression of the world and the intensification of consciousness of the world as a whole (Robertson 1992: 8). What underlies the process of globalization are basically the dynamics of the capitalist world economy and the revolution in information technology. In this sense, globalization incorporates both material and cultural aspects which are largely under Western capitalist domination. However, it does not entirely imply the hegemony of Western modernity; it is also in some ways a contradictory process which leads to discontinuities and differences (Robertson 1992: 29). In other words, modernist homogeneity and cultural fragmentation, or globalization and localization, are not two opposing views of what is happening in the world today, but two constitutive trends of global reality (Friedman 1990).

Being an integral part of the global economy, Thailand has benefited somewhat from the dynamics of capitalism and experienced rapid industrialization as well as social transformation. Behind this economic miracle lay the role of the emerging Thai middle class as a leading force in society. As representatives of the newly rich, members of this class have had a drastic impact on urban life with their never-ending pursuit of consumerism which has resulted in the commodification of almost everything, including both material and spiritual culture (Thongchai 1995: 116–118; Hong 1996).

The forces of rapid economic change are also fostering the expansion of the major cities at the expense of rural ways of life. As a result, new urban centers are crowded with rural villagers because of internal migration. Lacking roots in the mega-cities, these new urban dwellers cannot avoid being inundated with materialistic capitalist culture within the so-called television society. Many of them have become alienated by the dehumanizing nature of their urban life and work.

With the growing internationalization of the booming Thai economy, inequalities remain prevalent in many areas, especially among rural communities suffering from the impact of marginalization. These communities are increasingly denied the right to control their resources, whether they be land, water or forest. The result is intense competition for resources between the state, the business sector, and the rural population as those resources are mostly managed in favor of the global market. While deeply subjected to commercialism and consumerism through economic participation and the global media in the same way as their urban counterparts, the rural villagers are more isolated from political participation and the control of their own lives.

While most Thai tend to conform with the forces of globalization, this paper will attempt to analyze the complexities and conflicts as various groups in Thai society engage with these forces under different circumstances. Instead of looking at culture as integrating, the focus will be on the contradictions of the dynamics and transformation of culture, in relation to the subjectivity of the Thai people, as seen in the reproduction of popular knowledge and the construction of values, identity, and power. Examples will be drawn from recent studies by both Thai and foreign scholars.

The Urban Revitalization of Religion and Cults of the Supernatural

In the face of strong pressure from the global economic and communications networks, a variety of responses have been generated among the middle class during the past three decades. In the 1970s, various forms of popular knowledge were noticeably revitalized, mainly in urban and suburban areas. For example, within Buddhism there has been renewed enthusiasm for the veneration of meditation monks. This is especially noticeable in relation to a number of famous forest monks who are considered to be saints (*arahant*),

127

and is expressed in an intensified fetishistic obsession with the cult of amulets which has resulted from the development of sectarianism among the followings of these holy monks (Tambiah 1984).

Religious fervor associated with individual charismatic and ascetic monks with meditation abilities has always been a part of Thai history, but this has been the case mainly in the countryside. In the 1980s, the resurgence of Thai Buddhism resulted in a type of reform movement which is more of an urban phenomenon. Such Buddhist reform movements attract quite a large group of participants, especially from the younger and more educated urban middle classes who tend to reject the teachings and the practices of traditional religion. These new religious movements are not entirely limited to Bangkok but also appear in several other urban centers throughout the country (Zehner 1990: 411).

Among the large number of reform groups which are associated with certain charismatic monks, two of the best known and most frequently studied urban Buddhist sects, Thammakai and Santi Asok, have been chosen for discussion here. Considering themselves as reformist, the two groups adopt a more critical stance than that of the established Buddhist organization, the Sangha, by putting more emphasis on an inner-worldly ethic while opposing the "nonnormative" practices of magical ritual. Both movements also encourage their followers to participate in "this-worldly" asceticism to achieve doctrinal goals through certain practices, both through individual concern and collective action (Taylor 1990: 151–52). However, the two groups have opted for completely opposing strategies in their pursuit of religious identity.

Thammakai prescribes meditation as its main religious practice. The term *thammakai* itself means the eternal spiritual essence of the Buddha which is believed to reside in each individual but which can only be discovered with proper meditative insight. In this sense, its meditation methods aim to help its followers to achieve that insight (Zehner 1990: 406–07). The movement focuses on cognitive, moral and doctrinal instruction, a religion of personally immediate experience, and observances consistent with middle-class values of cleanliness, orderliness, and modernity (Zehner 1990: 424). The strong middle-class values can also be seen in its emphasis on symbols of change, progress, purity, and spiritual prowess (Zehner 1990: 403).

However, Thammakai's ideas of modernity reflect mainstream and elitist definitions of reformism, namely through education, technology, management, and the market (Apinya 1993: 198). In order to articulate with the capitalist market, the sect pays more attention to an immanent soteriology and an ethic which fosters material changes in the existing order utilizing an active and flexible modern management strategy with a highly personalized sense of collective power. In fact, the sect set out with the undisguised goal of making money and has invested heavily in many kinds of business ventures. The basic requirement for membership in the sect is the ability to contribute regularly to the monastery and participate in its unorthodox meditation program. Thammakai is said to be the first religious movement in Thailand to have spent such a large sum of money on a sophisticated and costly campaign to propagate its beliefs (Taylor 1990: 139–141). In this sense, it can be pointed out that the Thammakai movement also resembles evangelical Buddhism (Keyes 1989: 135).

In contrast, the Santi Asok is closer to Buddhist fundamentalism (Keyes 1989: 135). This sect strongly opposes the practice of meditation as a useless approach to liberation, and it selectively ignores standard Buddhist texts. Instead, it tends to encourage its followers to apply "moral restraint" consistently in everyday life, which is believed to be helpful in achieving mindfulness and wisdom. Membership of the sect requires working diligently, practicing moderation, and a simple moral lifestyle. It emphasizes an intellectual and reflexive approach to Dharma through discussion groups. In the same way the movement also opposes traditional Pali chanting which is considered useless as few people are able to understand the words, and it debunks the popular belief in the efficacy of various ritual paraphernalia (Taylor 1990: 149–50).

Whereas Thammakai has a market orientation, Santi Asok's response to modernity is an anti-modern and anti-consumerist ethos that focuses on the less worldly in a material sense. This can be illustrated clearly in the sect's adoption of the peasant's cloth as its uniform, implying a premodern Buddhist agrarian community. The Santi Asok movement also consistently calls for self-sufficiency, concern for the environment, and limiting the use of modern technology. This reflects a nostalgia for a reconstructed image of the past and a desire to bring back the good old days when the monk and the temple were the center of community life (Apinya 1993: 199). In its back-to-basics orientation, Santi Asok followers impose strict discipline on themselves. Both monks and laity are vegetarians and continually expound the uselessness of making offerings to images and ritual merit-making for departed kin. Following such an approach, their publicity campaign is directed mainly towards issues of morality and upholding the traditional Buddhist precepts (Taylor 1990: 150).

There are also signs of vitality evident beginning in the 1980s in the area of spirit cults, with an increase in urban spirit mediums who are mainly women. This resurgence is most evident in big provincial centers, particularly Chiang Mai, the second biggest city in Thailand. The belief provides women, and especially poor women, with a symbolic means of regaining their spiritual and social status, which has deteriorated as a result of the decline in the ancestor spirit cults at the village level in which women were once considered to have high ritual authority.

However, in some urban areas of the northern region, the cults of ancestral spirits have recently regained some of their popularity. Ritual offerings to ancestral spirits, known locally as the Phi Mot and Phi Meng cults, are being organized more frequently by descent groups with a greater emphasis on the spirit dance, performed mostly by female mediums. In the past, such rituals were held for the sole purpose of strengthening the well-being and health of the whole group of members of the domestic spirit cult. But the same rituals are, at present, organized in relation to vows made by members of the family for individual purposes, such as success in capitalist enterprises, winning lotteries, and academic success, as well as curing illness and driving away misfortunes (Tanabe 1991: 192–93).

In its modern form, spirit mediumship has to some extent been modified. The most obvious change can be seen in the spirits with which the mediums identify, which are no longer local spirits as in the case of the traditional mediums, but more often Thai national heroes or even the deities of Mahayana Buddhism, especially Kuan Im (or Kuan Yin bodhisattva). But the most significant modification is the increasing association between mediumship and Buddhism. The modern mediums tend to display their Buddhist devoutness through their participation in some popular Buddhist rituals of merit-making. These changes indicate that spirit mediumship can also serve as an avenue for competition and possible material success, as part of the process of the incorporation of traditional medical practices into the market economy, while giving women a means of strengthening their economic position, as well as challenging the power of men (Irvine 1984: 318–22).

In Bangkok, the popular knowledge of spirit cults is taking a new turn, deviating somewhat from the traditional cults of spirit mediumship found in other urban centers. At least two distinctive cults have recently been developing among a wide range of middle-class people, especially those in the business sector ranging from small shop owners to large scale entrepreneurs. The first is the cult of Sadet Pho Ro Ha, while the second one is the cult of Chao Mae Kuan Im.

The cult of Sadet Pho Ro Ha is named after King Rama V of the Bangkok dynasty who initiated the modernization process in Thailand at the start of the twentieth century. It originated simply as hero worship, with ritual offerings being performed by a large gathering of middle-class Bangkok people at the monument of King Rama V every Tuesday which is supposed to be his birthday. The ritual has since transformed the historical figure into the deity of a spirit cult. There is no organized body of members of this cult which is open to all the faithful. In fact, participation in the cult is very simple and taking part in the ritual offerings is not required at all. Anyone can join the cult by having images or photographs of King Rama V in their possession. Normally the faithful will wear these images as ornaments or display photographs in their business premises. This has now become so widespread that it suggests a kind of mass social phenomenon, not only in Bangkok but also spreading out to most other urban centers. As a symbol of modernity, independence and opportunity, the image of King Rama V is believed to bring its holders luck in business as well as protection. In this sense, there are some similarities to the Buddhist cult of amulets (Nithi 1993).

While the cult of Sadet Pho Ro Ha is open to all, another urban cult, that of Chao Mae Kuan Im, is more organized, in the same way as the Buddhist reform movements. Although the two types of cult share the same secular concerns, Chao Mae Kuan Im is more oriented towards the reproduction of morality in a religious sense, given that belief in the goddess Kuan Im is rooted in the bodhisattva concepts of Mahayana Buddhism. In this sense, the cult also incorporates the religious ethos and morality of Mahayana Buddhism, which enhances its position in the eyes of the urban middle class in comparison with the traditional spirit cults. Members of the cult share some basic observances with Mahayana Buddhism, particularly vegetarianism, to remind the faithful of Kuan Im who is believed to be a symbol of kindness.

The cult of Kuan Im is also as widespread as the Sadet Pho Ro Ha cult because of its emphasis on success in business and well-being. In many cases, the photographs of King Rama V and paintings of Kuan Im are even placed together in the same business premises. Huge statues of Kuan Im as well as shrines continue to be set up in many urban centers. This fast-growing social phenomenon is due to the simplicity of the cult and the fact that the cult faithful can have direct communication with the goddess Kuan Im through mediumship, as is the case with traditional spirit cults (Nithi 1994).

Located between the Buddhist reform movements and the cults of the supernatural there is also a resurgence of cults surrounding folk healers, especially in the urban areas of the northern region. These folk healers are generally known as *mo muang* (literally, "town specialists"). They are strong-minded men who gain their moral and charismatic power through their experience in astrology, magic, herbal medicines, and the manipulation of spirits. At present the traditional healers, whether they be herbalists or specialists in treating broken bones, are disappearing. In contrast *mo muang* who specialize in magic and shamanism are very active, and some of them have managed to become charismatic leaders of cult-like groups (*phu wiset*). A number of folk healers are able to gain such a status through the transformation of their position within the structure of the northern Thai moral system, as is partially demonstrated by their devotion to Buddhism. In this manner they are able to attract as clients the emerging rural as well as the urban middle classes who are believers in religious syncretism but who try to dissociate themselves from the belief in spirits in an attempt to find a more rational religious identity for their new social status. Many of the folk healers no longer perform occasional services for local villagers as in the past, but have instead set up formal full-time clinic-like services for a large number of clients who come largely from the town. In this sense, the way in which the *mo muang* organize their activities has been transformed. Even though they are charismatic masters of cult-like groups, they have rationalized the way in which they provide their services in such a way that their operations resemble modern clinics (Anan 1992b).

The Construction of Contradictory Values and the Commodification of Self-Identity

The revitalization of various forms of popular cultural knowledge among the urban middle classes indicates both the dynamism and contradictions of culture as it undergoes changes in the context of ongoing globalization. The common values shared by most of the urban cult movements are more and more individualistic in nature, as is becoming almost universal with globalized culture. But it is paradoxical to find that these universally individualistic values can be realized through local popular culture which used to be more collectively oriented. An explanation for this can be found in the changing discourses among the urban middle classes, since they are not only passively influenced by globalization, but instead are actively involved in the process of constructing their various moralities and self-identities in order to deal with this challenge.

In the process of globalization since the late 1980s, Thai society has undergone drastic social and cultural transformation. With strong control over the communications and education systems, resulting in increasing linguistic uniformity, the Thai state has also managed to strengthen its control over local populations. Due to the open market system and rapid industrialization, the state has had a great impact on marginal rural and ethnic communities. All of these changes contribute considerably to the mobility and migration of rural people into urban areas where they encounter the culture of consumerism as well as industrial and capitalist work discipline, both of which are entirely alien to their rural ways of life.

As these rural people have settled down as new members of urban society, they have experienced a sense of displacement and confusion which can sometimes develop into emotional disorders and psychosomatic disturbances. For instance, Tanabe has shown that the newcomers to a city like Chiang Mai often find that their displacement provokes feelings of anxiety, powerlessness and insecurity in everyday life. He suggests further that such anxiety is the expression of insecurity and uncertainty in areas such as making money, the political future, health, marriage, jobs, relations with bosses, and numerous other aspects of life in urban and industrial settings (Tanabe 1996).

The sense of confusion can also be found among the emerging rural and urban middle classes. Such a feeling is due primarily to the contradictions in power relationships in the Thai political economy which arise from the rapid process of materialistic capitalist development. A strong bureaucratic system still holds on to its power while the emerging middle classes find themselves relatively powerless. In these circumstances, they find it difficult to explain their social position rationally.

At present, most members of the new middle class tend to pay attention to their individual and material self-interests without any clear spiritual and moral values appropriate to their new position. Moreover, they usually take the moral values of family and community for granted. Many of them suffer from problems of emotional and mental disorder, as can be seen from the number that came to consult folk healers and spirit mediums. Most of the clients do not know the reason for their illnesses but, from their own reports to the healers, these often coincide with some kind of conflict with their relatives, employers and members of their community. The nature of the conflicts indicates that these clients are experiencing moral confusion in the relationship between their ideas of self, family and community. In facing the spiritual and moral crises in their lives, the new middle classes are free to look for sources of knowledge and power, without any constraints. Many of them increasingly resort to folk healers and spirit mediums just for their ritual knowledge rather than their expertise in herbal medicine (Anan 1992b).

In the case of folk healers, their relationship with their middle-class clients not only transforms their power and status but also helps in the construction of middle-class values by reformulating the complex relationships between the ideas of self, family, and community. This cultural reproduction is, in itself, a contradictory process. On one hand, the healers try to generate their moral power from more diverse sources of popular knowledge than in the past. On the other hand, some healers are also reinforcing Buddhist rationality, while at the same time learning about types of modern medicine. The emphasis, however, remains on complex ritual processes utilizing various concepts of power within the Thai moral system (Anan 1992a; Anan 1992b).

In relation to this, spirit mediumship is considered to be a multifaceted source of stability that enables newcomers to urban society to find their bearings and to recover their physical and mental equilibrium. As an object of modern consumption, spirit mediumship also allows the coexistence of contradictory values and aspirations. On the one hand, it reinforces a strong individual desire for material prosperity and the fantasy of gaining new status and fortune. But at the same time, it encourages subordination to the power represented by the tutelary spirit, embodied by the medium. In this sense, the modern consumption of spirit mediumship represents a process of constructing contradictory values, both of emancipation and subordination (Tanabe 1996).

Besides their rural background, a large majority of the urban middle class are of Chinese descent, especially the class of the newly rich. Although they are the leading force in economic development and able to enjoy the new material culture of affluence, they are for the most part spiritually confused. Being first, second, or third generation immigrants to Thailand, they are almost completely uprooted from their Chinese traditions and they preserve their past mainly as an individual rather than as a communal practice (Thongchai 1995: 116). Due to their shallow and ambiguous historical roots, the new Thai urban middle classes of Chinese descent tend to identify themselves increasingly with the Thai past as well as the Thai state.

One obvious example is seen in the case of the cult of Sadet Pho Ro Ha. As King Rama V is not only a symbol of modernity but also an image of the Thai nation-state, an identification with him and his cult allows the new middle classes access to the "benevolent" Thai state as an imagined community (cf. Anderson 1983). Nithi has suggested that this kind of identity is only possible through various cult rituals since, in reality, the new middle classes still have very limited power under the highly centralized and bureaucratic polity of the Thai state (Nithi 1993). In these circumstances, they can be consoled with a sense of security because their cult is devoid of an anti-state ideology, but rather identifies itself with modernity.

While the cult of Sadet Pho Ro Ha may be needed as a means for dealing with the problems of everyday life, the cult of Chao Mae Kuan Im is required in the development of new moral values. Thus, it can be seen as an attempt by the new middle classes to construct their own values outside Buddhism, which is increasingly under state control, and increasingly less able to meet their needs. Here, Nithi is also able to offer a sound analytical explanation. He suggests that most of the recent reforms in Buddhism have put more emphasis on rationalism as distinct from the magical elements which have always been an integral part of popular Buddhism. This leads to the alienation of the new middle classes from Buddhism because magic is considered an aspect of Buddhism which is associated very closely with various social values, such as justice and honesty (Nithi 1994). The cult of Chao Mae Kuan Im, on the other hand, helps strengthen the unity between magic and Buddhist moral values, especially kindness. In this sense, the cult, on one hand, helps in the construction of middle-class values against the global values of materialism and consumerism and, on the other hand, establishes moral control over the spreading obsession with magic.

In addition to the various cult movements, the construction of contradictory values can also be found in Buddhist reform movements. On the one hand, Thammakai utilizes "this-worldly" asceticism to construct the middle-class values of cleanliness, orderliness, and modernity which correspond very well with capitalist ethics. On the other hand, Santi Asok focuses on the less worldly values of asceticism which can be represented as an antimodernist and anticonsumerist ethos. Although the contradictory moral values propagated by the two Buddhist reform movements attract many middle-class followers, they also create widespread controversy. They have largely resulted from an ongoing process of value formation among the middle classes at a time when several alternatives are competing each other within the sphere of popular knowledge.

New middle-class values are mainly constructed through popular knowledge but, in the case of self-identification, the process usually begins with indigenization. The middle class, especially people of Chinese descent who have recently acquired a Thai identity, usually associate themselves with a Thai past. Thongchai has noticed that the middle-class demand for a Thai past has grown so rapidly that it is turning into a form of social nostalgia. Urban intellectuals, for instance, are very conscious about recollecting the past, not to in order to live in it but mainly for their spiritual enrichment (Thongchai 1995: 116–17). However, the forces of globalization have increasingly transformed this type of demand into the commodification of nostalgia through greater consumption. In such circumstances, the past is itemized, objectified and processed for sale in various forms (Thongchai 1995: 117). The process is clearly manifested in the case of the Thai popular magazine, *Sinlapa Wattanatham* (Arts and Culture), which increasingly promotes the commodification of culture to be consumed as a new form of middle-class identity (Hong 1996).

In the area of the mass media where the market forces of globalization are strongest, even Thai identity itself has been transformed into a commodity. In the process, Thai-ness becomes just a signifier that is free from the control of a specifically Thai national and ethnic essence. Thai people, in this sense, can be alienated from Thai-ness, which is evidently considered only as a thing to be consumed as self-identity. Kasian has pointed this out very clearly as follows:

> Since the exclusive power of Thainess as a signifier to refer to only Thai things is loosened, the signified of Thainess also changes from the supposed embodiment of the inherent essence of all things Thai into just one identity option among many others, national, ethnic or otherwise, which anyone can partake of and indulge in through the purchase and consumption of commodities as identity signs. To put it another way, the manifold freedom from barriers imposed by national or ethnic self-identity simultaneously allows Thai consumers the possibility to consume commodities as identity commodities, i.e. the consumption of consumer products not for their intrinsic use value or socioeconomic exchange value, but for their cultural value as signs of desired identity. (Kasian 1996)

In other words, Thai-ness has attained an universal status whereby anyone, no matter how remote they are from the Thai entity, can claim a Thai identity simply by the consumption of Thai-ness in the global market. At present, this is how most of the urban middle class who are of mixed descent acquire their Thai identity, by buying and consuming Thai-ness (which Kasian calls a form of "cultural schizophrenia") as an attempt to reconcile themselves to the overwhelming force of cultural globalization (Kasian 1996).

From Individual Rights to Collective Rights

The current stage of globalization allows the Thai state to strengthen its control over the population through its domination of the communications and education systems. In this context, some socioeconomic groups, especially those in urban centers, have managed to gain culturally by associating themselves with the state, as seen in the cases of the Sadet Pho Ro Ha cult and the Thammakai movement. The former has adopted the symbols of the modern Thai state as a form of identity while the latter always allies itself with the mainstream politicians in power. This is also true for most spirit medium cults which have increasingly adopted the spirits of various Thai kings into their pantheon. In contrast, Santi Asok is very critical of the state and even encourages its followers to participate fully in politics in an attempt to purify state corruption.

While some members of the urban middle class have opted for various forms of popular knowledge in their relations with the state and global culture, rural villagers seem to base their counterhegemonic ideology on the universal language of rights which has impinged on them through global-ization and the process of nation-building. In this sense, the global and national hegemonic ideologies can be a basis of both contradiction and con-flict at the same time. As mentioned above, the global market ideology has managed to transform some aspects of local culture into a commodity. But the concept of rights, on the other hand, provides rural villagers with a way to create a different kind of cultural space in their encounter with the impact of marginalization. This is clearly manifested in the intense competition over resources in which the state and global economic forces have increas-ingly encroached on local control.

In his study of Thai nation-building and peasant resistance, Vandergeest found that the construction of the nation state through increasing regulation is closely linked with the institutionalization of individual rights. Both regu-lations and universalistic rights can only be realized in the nation-state through the institution of citizenship. The Thai state considers its people as individual citizens for the purpose of regulation. This construction of the individual has been carried out through legal and educational systems which have produced both new boundaries and new forms of exclusion. Such insti-tutions have, in turn, opened up a space for dialogue between the state and its citizens who are excluded. For example, when the state tightens up regu-lation by forcing the public to adhere to the law, the villagers gain a new basis for their struggle against state officials who cheat and exploit them. Villagers will often take action or threaten to expose lawless practices, even if this does not result in court cases. Vandergeest argues that this kind of struggle is possible because the law has become a major theme in the hege-monic discourses of modernization and nationalism, an outcome of the popu-lar struggles of the 1970s, which may only be specific to the Thai case (Vandergeest 1993).

In addition to protecting their individual rights, rural villagers have also been struggling recently to gain collective control over common property. However, the transformation from individual to collective rights is not auto-matic but involves a complex confrontation between local and global knowl-edge as well as a debate over directions of development. Although individu-ally-based rights are at the same time collective institutions, the conscious-ness of collective rights, in the case of Thai rural society, is constructed through a long process of struggle for local control of resources. This began with a debate about the representation of village community by local NGOs and urban intellectuals in the 1980s, as seen in the case of the so-called "community culture" school of thought.

This school began its arguments by criticizing the course of develop-ment Thailand has been experiencing as contradictory to the Thai values found in rural villages. Intellectuals of this school have consistently shown through their research that villages are the "original" Thai community in contrast to the state which is merely the result of recent development (Anan 1993a; Thongchai 1995; Kitahara 1996). They encourage the local people to study the history and culture of their own community as consciousness-raising research. A leading scholar, Chatthip, explains the importance of such a study as follows:

> An analysis of community history can enable the people to recover the origin of their practices and rituals; make them realize their own values and identity; discover the independent consciousness of the community; recognize the value of communal organization; include a sense of history of their own common struggle and make them realize the threat of domination from external alien cultures aimed at exploiting the villagers. (Chatthip 1991: 120)

In this sense, the "community culture" school seems to put more emphasis on advocating a kind of populist discourse as a way to strengthen the villagers' influence in relation to outside powers. But the success of such a discourse is limited only to the promotion of the spirit of self-reliance of closed communities and is not yet able to bring about an awareness, or the reality, of a universal level of collective rights. The problem is that this kind of discourse is based mainly on an idealistic image of villages but ignores the dynamic context of rural communities (Anan 1993a).

By the late 1980s, the economic and cultural realities of rural villages had become so critical that a simple self-reliance strategy was almost irrelevant. The state and global economic forces have not only encroached on the local control of resources, but they have also marginalized rural communities to the extent that the latter no longer have a sufficient resource base to sustain themselves. Some of them are threatened and their inhabitants have actually been evicted from their land. The denial of these community rights by the state has led to a cultural crisis which is becoming clearly visible throughout Thailand. The most notable signs are the corruption of morality, the dissolution of rural society and the deterioration of the natural environment.

The results lead to conflict in the relations between the state and rural villages, especially those in marginal areas such as forest land. On one hand, large influxes of rural migrants into urban areas are more frequent. On the other hand, many other communities are joining the protest against the state policy of encroaching on natural resources by designating more areas for forest conservation, which, in many cases, overlap with the villagers' land and community forests.

During the last decade, these marginal villages have struggled to form various networks as well as allying themselves with local NGOs and urban intellectuals to argue for community rights over resources. They have based their advocacy largely on a knowledge of the customary practices of local organizations in the management of community forests, reflecting the conflict between national laws and local customs. In order to strengthen local control over resources, these networks have been campaigning for the recognition of community forests as common property (Anan 1993b). In their campaign, the cultural reproduction of local customs is always reinforced and this has become a widespread social phenomenon, especially in the north and northeast regions of Thailand. The government has recently been in the process of passing the community forest legislation which, hopefully, will legitimize community or collective rights. If this legislation is successful it will show that a universal concept of rights can play a considerable role in the transformation of local customs into national law.

Conclusion

During rapid economic development during the past decade, Thailand has experienced considerable cultural impact and social transformation as a result of globalization. The most notable effects can be seen in the changes in cultural understanding by various social groups in conflicting and contradictory relationships between self, family, and community on one hand and between the state and localities on the other.

Popular knowledge seems to be a dynamic form of local culture which is most frequently revitalized by those in the new urban environment, in an attempt to adjust themselves to such global values as individualism, consumerism, and materialism. Although popular knowledge allows the urban middle classes to construct new values and identities, the values and identities which result are mostly contradictory. Those values can result in both emancipation from, and subordination to, global values and state domination. This reflects the inherent capacity of globalization to strengthen state control as well as the commodification of values and identities. However, some forms of popular knowledge are dynamic enough to allow for the construction of alternative values and identities when they are critical of state and global domination. In these circumstances popular knowledge can put some limits on the power of globalization in the commodification of culture.

There are also contradictory aspects in some global values, such as universal concepts of rights and law, which can help villagers and localities in their struggles to adjust to their new relationship with the nation-state in specific ways, such as through organizing popular movements. Such a global hegemonic ideology, in many cases, does not only allow for the con-struction of a counter-hegemonic ideology but can also be utilized for the dynamic transformation of local custom into national law, or even into a universal concept, as was seen in the case of community rights. Thus, the dynamics of culture in Thailand clearly indicate that globalization is a con-tradictory process which can lead to the construction of different values and identities in addition to the adjustment of complex relationships between various forms of social existence based on both individualism and the col-lectivity.

References

Anan Ganjanapan 1992a. "Northern Thai rituals and beliefs: the reproduc-tion of morality," in *Proceedings of the First International Symposium to Present the Results of Projects Funded Under the Toyota Foundation's International Grant Program.* Tokyo: The Toyota Foundation.

Anan Ganjanapan 1992b. "The changing power and position of *Mo Muang* in Northern Thai healing rituals," paper presented at a workshop on "Popular Knowledge and Spirit Cults in Southeast Asia," National Mu-seum of Ethnology, Osaka, Japan. (Included as pp. 135–60 in *Anthro-pology of Practical Religion: The World of Theravada Buddhism, ed.* Shigeharu Tanabe. Kyoto: Kyoto University Press, 1993.)

Anan Ganjanapan 1993a. "The cultural dimension of development in Thai-land: a survey of alternative methodologies," in *Sub-Regional Meeting on Methodologies for Incorporating Cultural Factors into Development Projects and Planning.* Hanoi: Vietnam National Comminssion for UNESCO.

Anan Ganjanapan 1993b. "The reproduction of a sense of community: the case of community forestry in Northern Thailand," paper presented at the 5th International Conference on Thai Studies, School of Oriental and African Studies, University of London.

Anderson, Benedict. 1983. *Imagined Communities: Reflections on the Ori-gin and Spread of Nationalism.* London: Verso.

Apinya Feungfusakul. 1993. "Buddhist Reform Movements in Contempo-rary Thai Urban Context: Thammakai and Santi Asok." Ph.D. disser-tation, Bielefeld University.

Chatthip Nartsupha. 1991. "The community culture school of thought," pp. 118–141 in *Thai Constructions of Knowledge,* eds. Manas Chitkasem and Andrew Turton. London: School of Oriental and African Studies, University of London.

Friedman, Jonathan. 1990. "Being in the world: globalization and localiza-tion," *Theory Culture & Society* 7: 311–28.

Hong, Lysa. 1996. "Fifteen years of Sinlapa Watanatham: from fragmentation to commodification of Thai art and culture," *Proceedings of the 6th International Conference on Thai Studies*. Chiang Mai: Chiang Mai University.

Irvine, Walter. 1984. "Decline of village spirit cults and growth of urban spirit mediumship: the persistence of spirit beliefs, the position of women and modernization," *Mankind* 14: 315–24.

Kasian Tejapira. 1996. "The postmodernization of Thainess," *Proceedings of the 6th International Conference on Thai Studies*. Chiang Mai: Chiang Mai University.

Keyes, Charles F. 1989. "Buddhist politics and their revolutionary origins in Thailand," *International Political Science Review* 10: 121–42.

Kitahara, Atsushi. 1996. *The Thai Rural Community Reconsidered: Historical Community Formation and Contemporary Development Movements*. Bangkok: The Political Economy Centre, Faculty of Economics, Chulalongkorn University.

Nithi Aeusrivongse. 1993. "Lathi Phithi Sadet Pho Ro Ha," *Art and Culture Magazine* 14 (10): 76–98.

Nithi Aeusrivongse. 1994. "Lathi Phithi Chao Mae Kuan Im," *Art and Culture Magazine* 15 (10): 79–106.

Robertson, Roland. 1992. *Globalization: Social Theory and Global Culture*. London: Sage.

Tambiah, Stanley Jeyaraja. 1984. *The Buddhist Saints of the Forest and the Cult of Amulets*. Cambridge: Cambridge University Press.

Tanabe, Shigeharu 1991. "Spirits, power, and the discourse of female gender: the Phi Meng Cult in northern Thailand," pp. 183–212 in *Thai Constructions of Knowledge*, eds. Manas Chitakasem and Andrew Turton. London: School of Oriental and African Studies, University of London.

Thongchai Winichakul. 1995. "The changing landscape of the past: new histories in Thailand since 1973," *Journal of Southeast Asian Studies* 26: 99–120.

Vandergeest, Peter. 1993. "Constructing Thailand: regulation, everyday resistance, and citizenship," *Comparative Studies in Society and History* 35: 133–158.

Zehner, Edwin. 1990. "Reform symbolism of a Thai middle-class sect: the growth and appeal of the Thammakai Movement," *Journal of Southeast Asian Studies*, 21: 402–26.

Part III

The Periphery of Nation States

Chapter 9

"Center" and "Periphery" in Oral Historiography in a

Peripheral Area in Southeast Indonesia

Eriko AOKI

Introduction

> In the beginning, there was no land at all, but only sea everywhere. The
> only dry land was the summit of Mt. Lepembusu. The sky was an elbow
> high, the land was a span wide. There was a liana reaching the sky.
> Anakalo lived there. There were no other living human beings. And
> then Anakalo severed the vine of the liana. The sky flew high up, the sea
> withdrew far.

This short myth was narrated by a middle-aged man living in a mountainous area on Flores Island, eastern Indonesia.[1] It can be approached in various ways. It may be seen as a version of the "orphan stories" ("orphan"
being the literal meaning of Anakalo) which are widely distributed in eastern Indonesia. It can be analyzed as an example revealing the significance
of parallelism in this society, or it can be understood as an example of the
distribution of mythical knowledge in the society. In this paper, it will be
treated as a speech act. Since I was a foreigner, my presence often encouraged my informants' consciousness of their identity. They also told me about
the origin of the world, stressing that Mt. Lepembusu, a high mountain in
their area, was the center of the world.

This paper aims to point out that while Flores Island is usually treated as
part of the periphery in the hegemonic discourse of the "modern" world,
this perspective is not necessarily valid in two respects. First, southeast In-

donesia, where Flores is located, has been characterized throughout its history by busy traffic, which the hegemonic view has tended to disregard. Secondly, the population in a mountainous area in Flores insist that they themselves are at the "center" of the world.

The spatial metaphor of "center" and "periphery" has been adopted to express the hierarchical structure not only in "modern," but also in "traditional" world views. In many "traditional" societies in Indonesia, this metaphor plays an important role, and the center is associated with authority as it is in "modern" world views (Andaya 1993; Anderson 1972; Errington 1989, 1990; Traube 1986). This is one of the simplest metaphors for a hierarchical or asymmetric relationship.

The following section explicates how the hegemonic modern world view, which peripheralizes Flores and its people, is pervasive among us, although that view is only one of the possible frameworks for conceptualizing the world. The second section, by sketching the prehistoric and historical situation in eastern Indonesia, shows that southeast Indonesia has fostered a busy traffic, which has eluded both centralized control and the hegemonic modern world view. The third section turns to the specific situation in the mountainous area in central Flores in terms of its response to modern exogenous power. The fourth section then draws on oral historiography among the people in this area in which the themes of center and periphery play an important role. The last section points out that the oral historiography dealt in the fourth section can match written academic historiography in some respects, including the notion that both telling a "history" and writing a "history" are performative acts (Austin 1960).

Modern Historiography and its Foundations

The conceptual framework of "center" and "periphery" has a major role in discourses about the "modern" world (Wallerstein 1974).[2] In the 1930s, for example, some Japanese authors, such as Koyama and Kosaka, wrote that, even though until the mid-nineteenth century the whole habitable globe seemed to have been gradually deployed in a way which allowed the "West" to be seen as the sole "center," thereafter this discursive or political centralization of the West dissolved because of the independence of the non-West (Koyama 1940; summary in Sakai 1996: 25). No matter when the modern period is regarded as beginning or ending, most discussions of modernity posit it as a historical process in which people have been polarized between one pole conceptualized as the "West" or "the modern" and the other as the "non-Western" or the "premodern." In other words, those arguments centralize the former and peripheralize the latter. Sakai, for example, suggests that "modernity" is a mode of thinking which limits the possibility of seeing the world historically and geopolitically, and instead conceptualizes it with a specific type of polarization or distortion (1996: 5).

According to this kind of criticism, anthropology can be regarded not only as a product but also as a coproducer of this polarization. In response to this criticism, it has now become popular for anthropologists to refer to the people who would formerly have been referred to as "primitive" as either "peripheral" or "peripheralized."

We can regard, as Wallerstein does, the age of European maritime expansion when the perspective that "the world is the globe" began to pervade Europe as the beginning of the modern period (Wallerstein 1974). That age, which started with a search for the terra incognita, consequently ended up by denying its existence. The globe thus came to be recognized as the all-encompassing geographic space, and the places which the Europeans "discovered" were (re)named following their wishes. Except in philosophical, and probably theological, arguments, it was now taken for granted that the word, "world," as in "world economy," "world weather" and "world history," could be represented by a globe, supposedly a model of the world, or a world map, which is a two-dimensional version of a globe. This perspective thus came into existence through historical processes, and from then on it has become pervasive through modern education and the mass media as "common sense." Although we see a world map on television and in the newspapers every day as a representation of the "world," and though this conceptualization is so privileged that we regard it as though it were the only one, it is in fact only one of the numerous possible ways of conceptualizing the world as the most encompassing arena for human life. So what makes this conceptualization so privileged among us? One reason might be that it is attuned to a basic "modern" mode of thinking, which tends to constrain our conceptualization in every sphere of life. I refer to this mode as "popular scientism,"since it is based on the concept of "empty time and space" put forward by modern science.

Anderson explores the relation between the conceptualization of empty time and that of the world as follows. Discussing the profound fictiveness of newspapers, he observes that calendrical coincidence or the steady onward clocking of homogeneous empty time is one of the sources of the imagined linkage of otherwise arbitrarily juxtaposed articles such as stories about Soviet dissidents, famine in Mali, a gruesome murder, a coup in Iraq, the discovery of a rare fossil in Zimbabwe, and a speech by Mitterand (1983: 37). Within that time, "the world" ambles sturdily on. Although Anderson does not mention the spatial framework, geographical space as physical existence precisely represented by a globe or a world map is another source of the imagined linkage of the events. In other words events acquire their position by being pinned down in this empty geographical space and time, which may date back to the time of Galileo (Imamura 1994: 136).

By reading newspapers and watching television every day, we live in this "conceptualized world" and continually reconfirm this conceptualization embodied in the time on the clock and the space on the globe. The hegemonic historiographies peripheralizing eastern Indonesia, especially the mountainous area of central Flores, also entail this spatio-temporal framework.

The conceptualization of the "world" represented by a globe is reinforced by another fiction, that the "world" comprises – or is segmented into – nation-states. Modern world history is usually written as a history of the nation-states within a "West"-centered perspective (Imamura 1994: 205). According to this fiction, a nation-state is postulated as the most inclusive unit of agents sharing a collective subjectivity. It is then assumed that the array of these agents can be spatially projected onto a globe or a world map.

Since political institutions in the form of "nation-states" have prevailed since World War II, the topography of hegemony of "the world" has been transformed in two respects. First, at least in principle, the oppressive relationship between the colonizers and the colonized was dissolved, and the colonized also acquired a politically independent status as nation-states. The polarization between the colonizers and the colonized, however, was replaced with another asymmetric polarization between the developed and the developing. Secondly, because of the establishment of new nation-states, the polarization of "center" and "periphery" within a nation-state has become further articulated administratively, politically and economically. Within this context, the mountainous areas of central Flores have been peripheralized in a number of ways: in terms of the polarization between the developed and the developing nations; in terms of the Indonesian nation-state; and in terms of the differentiation between urban and rural areas.

Because of the pervasiveness of historiographies based on "popular scientism" and the nation-state, all the discourses which ignore them tend to be disregarded as "noise." However, it may be worthwhile listening to the "noise," such as oral histories by people of societies thus peripheralized by the hegemonic discourse, in order to objectify the hegemonic modern world view and the fictiveness of nation-states. I am not arguing that we should return to the anthropological fallacy that a "primitive" or "premodern" society is closed, static and confined to one locality. Whether or not it is "primitive" or "premodern," no society has ever been completely closed or unchanged.

Prehistoric, linguistic and historical data point to the fact that the people in the Indonesian archipelago have long been highly mobile. Innumerable oral traditions in the archipelago contain the motifs of ancestral migration.

While this does not necessarily mean, in a positivistic sense, that the ancestors migrated exactly as those oral traditions suggest, it may be an indication of the fact that the people in the archipelago regard migration as an integral part of the foundation of their society. The next section describes how migration and free traffic have long histories in the Indonesian archipelago, and how southeast Indonesia, especially Flores, escaped the political control which generally characterized that area.

A Pre-Historic and Historical Sketch of Southeast Indonesia

Little archaeological research has been done in southeast Indonesia. Knowledge about its prehistory is restricted to only a general outline. Almost all the languages in southeast Indonesia belong to the Austronesian family, which originated from the south coast of China and/or Taiwan, and then spread widely over a period of six to seven thousand years (Fox 1993: 2; Shaffer 1996: 7). According to Bellwood, part of these Austronesian-speaking people reached southeast Indonesia by about 2500 B.C. (Bellwood 1985: 233).

Bellwood maintains that some contact between India and eastern Indonesia can be traced back to 200 B.C. or even earlier (1985: 307). He also suggests that there was indigenous cultural development and exchange within the Indonesian archipelago, independent from Indian influence, from the later part of the first millennium B.C. (Bellwood 1985: 316–317). Leur (1955) also assumes that Indian trade had already reached as far as the Indonesian archipelago by about the beginning of the Christian era, and it might also have reached southeast Indonesia (Ormeling 1956: 94). Archaeological and linguistic studies thus indicate that southeast Indonesia was open to the outside world and influenced by trade and migration over a long period of time. The wide distribution of the Austronesians and the remains of their trade point to their maritime techniques. Only in the thirteenth century did southeast Indonesia appear in historical documents. The Chinese inspector of overseas trade, Chau Ju-Kua, refers in 1225 to Tiwu (Timor) as being rich in sandalwood and owing allegiance to the Hindu-Javanese realm of Kadiri (Krom 1926; Ormeling 1956). A Chinese "Description of the Barbarians of the Isles," dated 1349, mentions ports on the coast of Timor, where silver, iron, porcelain, and cloth were traded for sandalwood (Hamilton 1994: 29–30; Rockhill 1915: 257–58). The *Nagarakertagama*, a Majapahit chronicle from the middle of the fourteenth century, contains a list of dependencies of Majapahit, which refers to some islands of southeast Indonesia such as Sumba, Timor, and an island called Solot, which might be Solor, Lembata or the general area including Flores (Barnes 1982).

As early as 1400, and possibly earlier, southeast Indonesia was regularly visited by traders from the harbors of eastern Java, where Muslim traders from India settled and made their way into the already existing sea lanes (Ormeling 1956). The import of *patola*, double-ikat silks from Gujarat, was part of the Timor sandalwood trade and is believed to have predated the arrival of the Europeans in southeast Indonesia (Hamilton 1994: 31).

With the rise of Islam in the Java Sea and throughout the archipelago, the Majapahit state collapsed. Hamilton maintains that, in the fifteenth century and until 1511 when the Islamic sultanate of Malacca on the Malay peninsula fell to the Portuguese, the extensive trading system based at Malacca encompassed Sumba and Timor, and that sandalwood from Timor was exchanged for textiles of Indian and Javanese manufacture (Hamilton 1994: 30). In the eastern part of the archipelago the rise of Islam led to the establishment of the Islamic sultanates of Goa in southern Sulawesi and of Ternate and Tidore in the northern Moluccas. A maritime code of the kingdom of Malacca, dating from about the middle of the fifteenth century, mentions traders from south Sulawesi sailing to Sumbawa, Singapore, Johore, Malacca, Perak, Aceh, and Timor (Andaya 1981).

Early in the sixteenth century the Portuguese found their way to the Moluccas and southeast Indonesia by following local and Chinese traders (Hamilton 1994: 31; Ormeling 1956). While the main purpose of their visit to southeast Indonesia was the trade in sandalwood in Timor, they also visited various coastal regions in southeast Indonesia. As is apparent from the fact that the *Victoria*, the first Spanish vessel to traverse the Flores Sea, was guided by two Timorese pilots (Barnes 1982: 408–409; 1987), European maritime activity in the archipelago was not an innovation but followed an existing indigenous system, especially in terms of the sea lanes (Shaffer 1996).

In the Moluccas, two local sultanates, Tidore and Ternate, and two European powers, Portugal and Spain, were drawn into a four-way struggle in the sixteenth century. It is not surprising that the Portuguese activity did not remain unchallenged in southeast Indonesia. Portuguese enterprise in southeast Indonesia was continually threatened by other powers such as Javanese Muslims, Ternate, Goa/Macassar, Buton, pirates and the Dutch (Barnes 1987; Metzner 1982: 67; Prior 1988: 7).

After their arrival in southeast Indonesia in 1613, the Dutch gradually took over the position of the Portuguese in most parts of southeast Indonesia, while East Timor remained a Portuguese territory until 1975. While the Dutch government made efforts to establish its authority over southeast Indonesia by making use of the "traditional" political structures, the local people seem to have manipulated their relations with the Dutch government in order to increase their own benefits and power (Fox 1977).

Southeast Indonesia is possibly the only area of the Indonesian archipelago where Christianity preceded the coming of Islam. By 1556 the Dominicans claimed their first converts on Flores and Timor. In 1566, to protect local converts, the Portuguese erected a fortress incorporating a church and garrison on Solor, an island to the east of Flores (Prior 1988; Barnes 1987). The Portuguese-speaking *mestizo* population, identifying themselves as "Portuguese" and known as the Topasses or "Black Portuguese," eventually established themselves on Timor and Flores. They became an independent power allied with local rulers and resisted both Dutch incursions into their territory and "official" Portuguese attempts at controlling them (Fox 1977; 1980; 1982b; 1985).

In 1613, the Dutch besieged the Portuguese fortress and removed its population to Larantuka, a place in eastern Flores. In 1653 the Dutch moved their garrison to Kupang at the western end of Timor. Unlike the Portuguese, the Dutch did not encourage people to convert (Fox 1977; 1982b). In 1851 the Portuguese Governor in Dili ceded all Portuguese claims to eastern Flores and its nearby islands in return for an immediate payment of eighty thousand florins. One essential stipulation of the negotiations between the Portuguese and the Dutch was that the territories relinquished by the Portuguese were to remain Catholic. Consequently Dutch priests began to replace the Portuguese priests. The whole of the Flores and Timor mission was assigned to the Jesuits, who remained for fifty years, until 1913, when they turned it over to the Society of the Divine Word (Fox 1980). The present distribution and concentration of the Catholic population of southeast Indonesia stems from the Dutch designation of the entire island of Flores, and much of central and eastern Timor, as Catholic mission territory.

Southeast Indonesia remained in the backwaters of European colonialism. Within a century of the arrival of the first Portuguese traders, the supply of sandalwood from Timor had been so depleted that this trade offered little attraction to the Dutch. Southeast Indonesia has had few products worth exploiting and consequently they have never experienced the massive intervention that characterized other areas of Indonesia. This area was administered at an economic loss by the Dutch colonial government (Fox 1977: 3, 73). The fact that Sukarno, one of the leaders of the independence movement as well as the first president, was exiled by the Dutch government to Ende in Flores shows that the island and its vicinity were regarded as too remote a place for him to engage in any anticolonial activities.

In 1942 the Japanese army arrived in Kupang and began the military occupation, which ended in 1945. The Japanese government used the Dutch colonial administrative system, only changing the names of the administrative units and the titles of their heads (Winokan 1960). At least until the traumatic national events of 1965, the power of the Indonesian government was known only in limited areas of southeast Indonesia. Today it is still registered as loss making area (*daerah minus*) economically.

Thanks to being politically as well as economically insignificant, most areas of southeast Indonesia have been relatively independent not only of colonial but also of Indonesian state control, and have enjoyed free traffic. Today a number of Floresian men, for example, move in and out of Malaysia as illegal, or semi-legal laborers on plantations. It is also reported that some of the maritime populations in southeast Indonesia regularly sail to Australia in their small boats.

The description above suggests that the hegemony of the West and the Indonesian state had not penetrated southeast Indonesia to the same extent as in the other regions of the country. In the following section, let me characterize the response to exogenous power by the people in the mountainous areas of central Flores, whose historiography I draw on later, compared with the people in other areas of southeast Indonesia.

The Response to Exogenous Powers in the Mountainous Area of Central Flores

Each society in southeast Indonesia responded differently, and at different times, to the presence of European and other exogenous powers. People in Solor, for example, were involved in the struggles against exogenous powers such as the "official" Portuguese, the Black Portuguese, Muslims, and the Dutch (Barnes 1987; Fox 1980). In Larantuka, which has been a stronghold of the Catholics since the beginning of the seventeenth century, people have fostered a local Catholicism. It is reported that the indigenous population in the hinterland of Larantuka resisted the Dutch colonial government and the Catholic missionaries, and they have since been struggling for their autonomy against the Catholic Church and the Indonesian government (Graham 1993; 1994).

Generally speaking, the people of Roti have been one of the most enterprising of the peoples in southeast Indonesia in relation to exogenous powers. By assimilating exogenous knowledge and technology, especially Christian knowledge and Malay writing, they have adapted to changing political situations to their own advantage. As allies of the Dutch, they sought to become Christians. In 1679, a few of Roti's local rulers began to study Malay at the behest of the Dutch East India Company. By the early eighteenth century the conversion of Roti's ruling elites had begun. In 1735 a Rotinese Christian ruler opened the first local Malay school in his domain (*nusak*), which, in turn, prompted rivalry among the other rulers of Roti to establish schools in their domains. By 1781, these schools – staffed with Rotinese teachers – had become nearly self-sustaining and remained so throughout the first half of the nineteenth century. While in some other areas in the Indonesian archipelago Malay is associated with Islam, in Roti Malay came to be regarded as the language of Christianity. Here the acceptance of Christianity preceded the arrival of Dutch missionaries by nearly one hundred years, and by the late nineteenth century Rotinese congregations had sufficient confidence and sophistication to reject and expel a newly arrived Dutch missionary who attempted to introduce "deviant" interpretations of Christianity based on the latest European biblical scholarship. The Rotinese have produced versions of the scriptures using appropriate Rotinese oral idioms. Christ, for example, is indicated by a couplet, "a banana with copper blossom / a sugar cane with golden sheath," and his death and resurrection are metaphorically linked to the growth cycle of the "yam and taro." The process of conversion in Roti was gradual and only completed after 1966 (Fox 1977; 1980; 1982a; 1982b; 1983; 1988; 1991).

In contrast with Eastern Flores and Roti, the mountainous area of central Flores, where I did my fieldwork, is one of the areas where the Dutch government did not start to intervene at all before the start of the twentieth century. The inland areas of central Flores were not known to the Dutch until 1890 and this state of knowledge did not change until August 1907, when pacification by a Dutch military force started throughout the island (Suchtelen 1921; Winokan 1960: 11–13). In October 1907, two men from the mountainous areas attacked the Dutch headquarters on the coast. (Suchtelen 1921: 13). This was the first incident which involved people from the mountains, and suggests that, although the Dutch were ignorant about the mountains, the people there knew about the Dutch headquarters and the pacification expedition. It also indicates that there were social networks through which that information was conveyed; the two men were able to walk safely for more than forty kilometers passing through a number of villages to reach the town where the Dutch headquarters were located. Even after the establishment of colonial administration over the mountain areas, the Dutch colonial government was much annoyed by the indigenous leaders who abused the privileges given them by the Dutch colonial government (Bruyne 1947).

In 1917 the Dutch government started to bring the mountainous areas of central Flores under its administration. That area initially comprised two rajahdoms, Ndona and Tana Kunu Lima. In 1924 these were combined into a single rajahdom, Lio. The colonial government appointed an indigenous chief for each rajahdom, though both documents and the local situation indicate that there was no overarching indigenous authority in this area (Shuchtelen 1921; Bruyne 1947). The chiefs were chosen by the colonial government mainly because of their ability to communicate with it. The expectations of the Dutch notwithstanding, the chiefs were difficult to control. Not only did the colonial government distrust them, but also many of the indigenous people seemed to deny their authority.

Catholic missionaries of the Society of the Divine Word were not sent to the area before military pacification. However, by 1970 most people in the area had converted to Catholicism, perhaps as a result of the traumatic events of 1965. Compared with the strict doctrines of Protestantism, the Catholicism of the Society of the Divine Word is elaborately ritualized (Hoskins 1994). While the Protestant missionaries in Timor forced converts to abandon their traditional beliefs and rituals, the Catholic missionaries in Flores have not forced the converts to do so (Munanjar, personal communication). It seems that among Catholic missionaries there has been a view that regards the local ancestral beliefs as analogous to the biblical Old Testament (see Graham 1994). The catechism in Lionese contains many parallels with the indigenous myth of origin, which is one of the most significant examples of their oral literature (Ende Bishopric 1977). For the people of this part of Flores, Catholicism and the ancestral beliefs are not opposed as they are in other societies such as Anakalang in Sumba (Keane 1995b).

The people in Larantuka, like the Rotinese, have made some basic ideas originating from Christianity or colonial rule central to their social life, through their long and close association with these exogenous sources of knowledge and power (Fox 1977; Graham 1993; 1994). By contrast, the peoples in the mountainous areas of central Flores have not integrated any exogenous idioms into their social lives, but seem to keep their distance from them. Instead they have emphasized their "tradition," as did some of the people in Sumba (Keane 1995a). Accordingly, they often regard the Indonesian government as having taken over the position of previous foreign powers such as the Portuguese, the Dutch, and the Japanese (Cunningham 1965; cf. Grimes 1990). One man, for example, expressed this perspective as follows: "First the Portuguese came. The Dutch came next. Then the Japanese came. After that the Javanese came and have stayed on until now." The Indonesian government is equated with the Javanese and is seen as being as foreign as the Dutch and the Japanese colonial government. Most of the population have never felt themselves as members of the "imagined community" of the Indonesian nation state (or at least not until the end of 1984).

However, it does not follow that these people have disregarded the presence of the Indonesian government or other foreign powers such as the Dutch and Japanese. Rather, they feel deep fear and anxiety because they see these powers as agents of violence, and they tell stories about them. In these stories Dutch violence is usually equated with gunfire, and Japanese violence with beating with a big stick called "number 9" (*nomor sembilan*). I frequently heard, for example, the following story:

When the Japanese were here, they beat us up very often for one reason or another. They beat us up because we had fights with each other, because we stole their property, or even for reasons we did not know. Before the beating, the Japanese usually told us to choose one of the sticks they had prepared. These sticks had numbers. The biggest one was "number 9." If we chose the smallest one, they took the biggest, "number 9" and beat us up. If we chose the biggest one, they praised our bravery and used the smallest one.

The stories about Indonesian state violence concern the traumatic nation-wide incidents in 1965 and 1966. It seems that there was no bloodshed in the mountainous area in central Flores, yet it is not unusual for people to tell horrifying stories about those incidents. In the face of this latent fear, the people seem to be struggling to maintain or restore their autonomy. In the next section, we turn finally to indigenous historiography, in which the people themselves are at the center, and compare it with conventional modern historiography.

"Center" and "Periphery" in the Historiography of a Mountainous Area of Central Flores

I did my fieldwork among people inhabiting a mountainous area in central Flores, in southeast Indonesia. They speak a dialect of the Lio language of the Sumba-Bima group of the Austronesian family, which I call West Lio. Wet-rice cultivation was introduced in the area in the late 1930s and the number of wet-rice fields increased in the 1960s and 1970s. Before the introduction of wet-rice cultivation, people practiced swidden agriculture and additional husbandry of animals such as water buffaloes, goats, pigs, and chickens. The introduction of wet-rice cultivation has transformed the people's lives in various respects. It is said that people tended to inhabit the village of the traditional authority and the hamlets surrounding it in the past except during certain seasons, while most people now live near their own wet-rice fields and come back to the village only for ritual occasions. While the economic importance of wet-rice cultivation has been increasing, especially in relation to the cash economy, "traditional" swidden agriculture remains significant in terms of indigenous metaphysics, especially in terms of the relationships between people and land.

Not only the Dutch colonial government, but also the Indonesian nation-state and the Catholic missionaries, which people regard as exogenous, seem to have influenced peoples' lives. Narratives about the colonial era

155

often suggest that the men who were given administrative titles took advantage of, or abused, their status. Becoming a civil servant, Catholic priest or an officer is still thought to be a good way to gain access to a stable cash income as well as links to the outside world, although it is extremely difficult to achieve. While people assert that their customary law does not basically allow personal ownership of land, they are keen to acquire certificates of personal ownership of wet-rice fields issued by the local government in order to establish their ownership. However, Catholic doctrine or the principles of the nation-state, such as *pancasila* (the national principles) and *pembagunan* (development), have not been integrated into the principles which constitute the basis of the people's own identity and prestige.

Cash is sought for but it is not regarded as representing prosperity, which is usually represented by an abundant harvest, lots of descendants, animals, and gold items. On the one hand, people by and large try to gain access to, or take advantage of, exogenous resources such as cash, modern technology and knowledge, manufactured goods, and the authority given by Catholicism or the nation-state to secure their position. On the other hand, people give indigenous resources central significance and peripheralize exogenous resources in relation to identity and prestige.

As long as the people feel that their prestige is not threatened by the exogenous powers, they can become absorbed in their game of gaining access to exogenous resources. Once they are conscious that their prestige is at stake they tend to tell stories highlighting their superiority over others. They live at the foot of Mt. Lepembusu, which is the highest mountain in central Flores and is asserted to be the center of the world. Their "histories" are attuned to this spatial metaphor about the structure of the world.

In addition to stories about the origin of the world as presented at the beginning of this paper, stories are also told which explain the transformation and development of the human world as follows. Human beings slid down from Mt. Lepembusu. Prior to that, no human beings lived on the world except on Mt. Lepembusu. The dispersal is depicted as a centrifugal movement from the "navel" or center of the world. Some people spread further across the sea. Because the people in the mountainous areas of central Flores who tell these narratives are the legitimate successors to the first human ancestors, they are the "source" of all other peoples in the world today, and so can influence all other peoples' lives and well-being. In the past, powerful protagonists from outside, including the Dutch and the Japanese, "came back" to this area. However, since they ignored the truth that the people there were the direct descendants of their own original ancestors, in the end they lost their power, and many Japanese in particular died miserably.

Within this historiographical framework common to almost everyone, a middle-aged man, for example, located the Dutch invasion by describing the following "historical" events.

> Once upon a time there were seven villages on Mt. Lepembusu. The rest of the world was covered by water. There lived Goa people, Tidhu people, Buto people, Melaka people, Java people and other peoples lived in their respective villages. When the Buto people felled the *buto* tree, the water withdrew. The people dispersed. In separating from each other at Watuwatawanda, those seven peoples made an alliance treaty (*pore jaji*) by slaughtering a tiny male buffalo and a tiny male pig. But the white people forgot the alliance treaty and attacked us. When they first attacked us, we defeated them by making the following war chant (*kadha*) against them.

> Once upon a time we lived together
> here on Mt. Lepembusu at the same place
> then we separated and divided
> you, white people, overseas
> we remained here
> you make gunpowder, mold bullets
> we cultivate the fields, clear the forest to be replete
> you overseas down there
> we remained here
> we separated from each other down there at Watuwatawanda
> we cut a tiny male buffalo, our alliance not to be broken
> we slaughtered a tiny male pig, our treaty not to be infringed
> now you are looking for us again
> you do not ask
> you do not recognize
> take apart the houses
> break the nest
> our roaring makes you scared
> our threatening makes you fearful
> may the bullet hit you.

A gun was fired after this war chant. Though only one bullet was shot, it killed a white soldier and made all the Dutch flee with fear. Although the Dutch fired, the bullets never hit us. For three years the Dutch could not invade us.

This narrative exemplifies how the people of Flores peripheralize exogenous powers. These people narrate very proudly that the white people, or the Dutch, finally withdrew because they ignored the "truth" that the Flores people were the source or progenitors of the Dutch/whites, or because they ignored the alliance treaty. These people assert that they are the source of all foreign peoples, because all human beings originated from Mt. Lepembusu, and therefore all foreign peoples owe the people of Flores their lives and well-being. The concept of "source" is represented by the words, *pu'u* (trunk, base, stem) and *ine ame* (forebear). The idea that the "source" influences the lives and well-being of the people who originated from it holds also for relations between individuals.

In the West Lio historiography about the "world," which also depicts the process of "globalization" in its own way, the spatial metaphor of "center" and "periphery" is used to represent the hierarchical relationships of the peoples in the world. It would be easy from a positivistic point of view to dismiss this as only a mythical account, which does not deserve the name of "history." However, a brief reflection upon modern historiography may make us suspend this judgment, as shown in the final section.

Conclusion

Modern historiographies presume the framework of clock time and empty space, which is supposedly free from any subjectivity. As a number of historians maintain, history is always written not for the past but for the present, and it involves selection of past "facts." Carr writes about this that:

> History ... is a process of selection in terms of historical significance. To borrow Talcott Parsons' phrase once more, history is "a selective system" not only of cognitive, but of causal, orientations to reality. Just as from the infinite ocean of facts the historian selects those which are significant for his purpose, so from the multiplicity of sequences of cause and effect he extracts those, and only those, which are historically significant; and the standard of historical significance is his ability to fit them into his pattern of rational explanation and interpretation. Other sequences of cause and effect have to be rejected as accidental, not because the relation between cause and effect is different, but because the sequence itself is irrelevant. (1964: 105)

While Carr believes that rationality shapes the historical selection of facts, White regards history as similar to literature, in which rationality plays a less important role (White 1978). According to White, lack of objectivity in history is exemplified by differing conceptions of the same sets of events in various historical narratives. Comparing several types of histories about the same sets of events with one another, White maintains: "The consistent elaboration of a number of equally comprehensive and plausible, yet apparently mutually exclusive, conceptions of the same sets of events was enough to undermine confidence in history's claim to 'objectivity,' 'scientificity,' and 'realism'" (1973: 41).

Under the guise of objectivity based on clock time and empty space, modern historiographies select facts for each purpose. A nationalistic history selects and arrays "facts," first of all, in order to present the nation as a continuous natural subject of the history. Academic historians cannot avoid being selective in dealing with "facts" so that they may be consistent in terms of causality. In other words, "facts" are teleologically selected and arrayed so as to fit the framework of causal consistency. Furthermore it is almost impossible even for academic historians to be free from hegemonic discourse. The following statement by Parmentier may also hold in the case of scholarly historians. He writes that history is "a universal cultural category manifested differently in different in societies, in which the relationship between past, present and future states of a society is expressed by signs in various media which are organized by locally valorised schemes of classification" (1987: 4–5).

Dening, in a metaphorical tone, writes about the same account that "the relics of the past are always cargo to the present. Things that cross cultural boundaries lose the meaning encapsulated in them and are reconstituted in meaning by the cultures that receive them" (1991: 354). While we should take precautions against his cultural determinism, the point he makes reminds us that the same objects or even the same events can be given different meanings by different cultures, as Sahlins exemplified using the case of Captain Cook's death (1981).

By arguing thus, I am not intending to posit scholarly historiography as being completely equivalent to the West Lio historiography. On the contrary, I agree that the spatio-temporal framework of the West Lio historiography cannot be a better alternative to that of scholarly historiography, and that the latter has been, so far, the only available framework through which millions of people of different languages and different cultures can come to a consensus. However West Lio and modern historiographies do have in common such features as a lack of complete objectivity and selectivity, and the fact that they are influenced by a society's culture or hegemonic discourse.

In addition to these, they also share the following feature. Telling or writing history is a performative rather than constative act (Austin 1960).

There is not only an epistemological issue but also an issue relating to speech acts. People tell or write history about something in order to influence others, or in order to acquire their agreement. In Austin's terms, telling or writing histories is a "perlocutional" act, while according to Ricoeur it is an "interlocutional" act (Austin 1960; Ricoeur 1969). While the text of history, once written, can be detached from the act, oral history always accompanies the act of production. These West Lio speaking people tell histories about the "true" and "right" relationship between outsiders and themselves to others within and outside their society. Even though people in this area have never experienced the same degree of control by exogenous powers as people in other areas of Indonesia, they always fear the possibility of overwhelming violence by the exogenous powers. Taking their fear into consideration, the act of telling histories can be understood as a peaceful struggle for complete autonomy in relation to exogenous powers. In a sense, their act of telling histories may have some similarity to ritual millenarianistic movements.

This understanding is supported by various stories about their experiences which West Lio people liked to tell me. Some people, for example, proudly told me the following story. A Catholic priest visited them in order to write a book, which became very famous because he asked them to talk as his *ine ame* (forebears). By the same token, I was accepted by West Lio people very warmly once they understood that I came to them in order to ask them to make me successful, that is to say, I respected them as my "source." They referred to me tenderly as "child who has come back" or "grandchild who has returned to us."

There are no obvious resistance movements such as millenarian cults, cargo cults, or violent struggles for autonomy against the exogenous powers in the mountainous area in central Flores. It can be said, however, the people there have been steadily waging a peaceful battle against them by telling their histories to others within and outside their society. If we find their historiography unconvincing and that their performative act fails, it is mainly because we do not share their fundamental spatio-temporal framework for historiography, and because we are caught up with the hegemonic modern world view, rather than because West Lio historiography is not as ideologically free as modern historiography.

In southeast Indonesia, migration and social change as results of migration seem always to have been an integral part of life. Conflicts, negotiations, and the integration of orthodoxy and heterodoxy or contested cultural ideologies are processes which must take place in every society. In these contexts, lived cultures must often have been objectified by the people living within them and restructured, even before the contact with the Europeans and without the imposition of external perspectives such as state policies, tourism, and so on (see Acciaioli 1985; Forth 1994; Yamashita 1994). Recently the situation in the mountainous area of central Flores in terms of its relation to the Indonesian state has changed. A special subsidy was allocated to the local government in that area. Younger educated men have been chosen as the heads of the administrative villages. A person who has been in hiding in Java since the events of 1965 recently sent a statue to a Catholic congregation in that area. While the West Lio people have long kept themselves apart from exogenous values in insisting on their prestige and autonomy, the way in which they insist on it may be transformed in accordance with the changing situation. Further fieldwork should be carried out to follow up on what is happening at present.

Notes

1 Fieldwork in 1982-1984 was funded by the INPEX foundation, under the auspices of the Indonesian Institute of Sciences (LIPI) and Universita Nusa Cendana, Kupang. I also revisited Flores in 1987, 1990, 1992 and 1998.
2 Postmodern world views also seem to rely on this metaphor, since they postulate the postmodern world as decentered, that is to say, it must presuppose that the modern world should be polarized between "center" and "periphery."

References

Acciaioli, Greg. 1985. "Culture as art," *Canberra Anthropology* 8: 148–72.
Anderson, Benedict. 1972. "The idea of power in Javanese culture," pp. 1–69 in *Culture and Politics in Indonesia*, ed. C. Holt. Ithaca and London: Cornell University Press,.
Anderson, Benedict. 1983. *Imagined Communities.* London: Verso.
Andaya, L.Y. 1981. *The Heritage of Arung Pallaka.* The Hague: Martinus Nijhoff.
Andaya, L.Y. 1993. *The World of Maluku.* Honolulu: University of Hawaii Press.
Austin, J.L. 1960. *How to Do Things with Words.* Oxford: Oxford University Press.
Barnes, R.H. 1982. "The Majapahit dependency of Galiyao," *Bijdragen tot de Taal-, Land- en Volkenkunde* 138: 407–12.
Barnes, R.H. 1987. "Avarice and inquity at the Solor Fort," *Bijtragen tot de Taal-, Land- en Volkenkunde,* 142: 208–36.
Bellwood, Peter 1985. *The Pre-History of the Indo-Malaysian Archipelago.*

Sydney: Academic Press.

Carr, E.H. 1964. *What is History?* Harmondsworth: Penguin Books.

Cunningham, E. Clark. 1965. "Order and change in Atoni diarchy," *South-western Journal of Anthropology* 21: 359–83.

Dening, Greg. 1991. "A poetic for histories," pp. 348–80 in *Clio in Oceania*, ed. A. Biersack. Washington D.C. and London: Smithsonian Institute Press.

Ende Bishopric. 1977. *Katekismus Lio.* Ende: Arnoldus.

Errington, Shelly. 1989. *Meaning and Power in a Southeast Asian Realm.* Princeton, NJ: Princeton University Press.

Errington, Shelly. 1990. "Recasting sex, gender, and power," in *Power and Difference*, ed. J.M. Atkinson and S. Errington. Stanford: Stanford University Press.

Forth, Gregory. 1994. "Post-modernism: issues of meaning, cultural objectification and national-local distinctions in an eastern Indonesian community," *Social Analysis* 35: 144–64.

Fox, James J. 1977. *Harvest of the Palm.* Cambridge, Mass.: Harvard University Press.

Fox, James J. 1980a. "The 'Movement of the Spirit' in the Timor area: Christian traditions and ethnic identities," pp. 235–46 in *Indonesia: The Making of a Culture*, ed. J.J. Fox. Canberra: Research School of Pacific Studies, The Australian National University.

Fox, James J. 1980b. "The Great Lord rests at the centre," *Canberra Anthropology* 5: 22–23.

Fox, James J. 1982. "The Rotinese Chotbah as a linguistic performance," pp. 311–18 in *Accent on Variety, Vol.3: Papers from the Third International Conference on Austraonesian Linguistics*, ed. A. Halim et al. Canberra: Pacific Linguistics,.

Fox, James J. 1983. "Adam and Eve on the island of Roti: a conflation of oral and written traditions," *Indonesia* 36: 15–23.

Fox, James J. 1988. "A historical consequence of changing patterns of livelihood on Timor," in *Contemporary Issues in Development*, ed. Deborah Wade-Marshall and Peter Loveday. Darwin: Australian National University, North Australia Research.

Fox, James J. 1991. "Bound to the core, held locked in all our hearts: prayers and invocations among the Rotinese," *Canberra Anthropology* 14(2): 30–48.

Fox, James J. 1993. "Comparative perspectives on Austronesian houses: an introductory essay," pp. 1–29 in *Inside Houses*, ed. J.J. Fox. Canberra: Department of Anthropology, Research School of Pacific Studies, Australian National University.

Graham, Penelope. 1993. "Appropriating the Virgin: icons of authority and relations of power in an eastern Indonesian setting." Paper presented to the Association of Social Anthropologists Decennial Conference on "The Use of Knowledge: Global and Local Relations," Oxford.

Graham, Penelope (1994) "Rhetorics of consensus, politics of diversity: church, state and local identity in eastern Indonesia," *Social Analysis* 35: 122–43.

Grimes, B.D. 1990. "The Return of the Bride." M.A. dissertation, Australian National University, Canberra.

Hamilton, R.W. 1994. *Gift of the Cotton Maiden*. Los Angeles: Fowler Museum of Cultural History.

Hoskins, Janet. 1993. *The Play of Time: Kodi Perspective on Calendars, History and Exchange*. Berkeley: University of California Press.

Imamura, Hitoshi. 1994. *Kindaisei no kôzô* [The structure of modernity]. Tokyo: Kôdansha.

Keane, Webb. 1995a. "The spoken house: text, act, and object in eastern Indonesia," *American Ethnologist* 22 (1): 102–24.

Keane, Webb 1995b. "Religious change and historical reflection in Anakalang, West Sumba, Indonesia," *Journal of Southeast Asian Studies* 26 (2): 289–306.

Koyama, I. 1940. "Sekaishi no rinen" [Theory of world history], *Shisô* 215: 1-21; 216:1-32.

Krom, N.J. 1926. *Hindoe-Javaansche Geschiedenis*. The Hague: Martinus Nijhoff.

Leur, J.C. van (1955 [1934]) *Indonesian Trade and Society*. Trans. J.S. Homes and A. van Marle. The Hague: Nijhoff.

Metzner, J.K. 1982. *Agriculture and Population Presssure in Sikka, Isle of Flores*. Canberra: Australian National University.

Ormeling, F.J. 1957. *The Timor Problem*. The Hague: Martinus Hijhoff.

Parmentier, R.J. 1987. *The Sacred Remains*. Chicago and London: University of Chicago Press.

Prior, J.M. 1988. *Church and Marriage in an Indonesian Village*. Frankfurt am Main: Peter Lang.

Ricoeur, P. 1969. *Le Conflit des Interprétations*. Paris: Sueil.

Rockhill, W.W. 1915. "Notes on the relations and trade of China with the Eastern Archipelago and the coast of the Indian Ocean during the fourteenth century, Part 2," *T'oung Pao* 16: 36–76.

Sakai, Naoki. 1996. *Shizan sareru nihongo, nihonjin*. [The still-born Japanese language and people]. Tokyo: Shinyôsha.

Sahlins, Marshall 1981. *Historical Metaphor and Mythical Reality*. Ann Arbor: University of Michigan Press.

Eriko Aoki

Shaffer, L. N. 1996. *Maritime Southeast Asia to 1500*. Armonk, New York: M.E. Sharpe.

Suchtelen, B.C.C.M.M. van. 1921. "Endeh (Flores)" Mededeelingen van het Bureauvoor de Bestuurszaken der Buitengewesten, Bewerkt door het Encyclopaedisch Bureau, Aflevering XXVI.

Traube, E. 1986. *Obligation to the Source*. Chicago: University of Chicago Press.

White, H.V. 1973. *Metahistory*. Baltimore: Johns Hopkins University Press.

Winokan. 1960. "Sedjarah Singkat dari Bekas Daerah Flores" [A Brief History of the Former Flores Province]. Unpublished ms.

Wallerstein, Immanuel. 1974. *The Modern World System*. New York: Academic Press.

Yamashita, Shinji. 1994. "Manipulating ethnic tradition: the funeral ceremony, tourism, and television among the Toraja of Sulawesi," *Indonesia* 58: 69–83.

Chapter 10

Transformation of Shamanic Rituals among the Sama of

Tabawan Island, Sulu Archipelago, Southern Philippines

Ikuya TOKORO

Introduction

The Muslim society of Sulu

The Muslim society of Sulu in the southern Philippines holds a unique position, not only for its geographical proximity to both the Malaysian and Indonesian borders, but also for its cultural peculiarity of being a Muslim minority community in the predominantly Christian Philippine nation-state. One purpose of this paper is to analyze aspects of change and the process of transformation of indigenous shamanic rituals in a Sama-speaking group in the Sulu archipelago from the viewpoint of the dynamics of local, national, and transnational cultures. Comparisons with similar cases in other areas, especially in Indonesia, will also be made.

It has been pointed out for a long time that one of the main tasks of ethnographic studies of religion in contemporary Southeast Asia, as in cultural anthropology in general, is to understand the transformation or reorganization of local traditions within the macro-level complex settings of the nation-state or the modern world system.[1] In the case of Indonesia, there are already quite a few ethnographic accounts on this subject, ranging from the pioneering work by Geertz (1957, 1964) to accounts such as that of Atkinson in an anthology edited by Kipp and Rodgers entitled *Indonesian Religions*

Ikuya TOKORO

in Transition (1987). In these studies, it has been argued that there exists an interplay between local religious practice and the national framework of the Indonesian state/government, and these authors have described how the former has responded to, and been reorganized by, the latter.

The Muslim peoples of the Sulu archipelago in the extreme south of the Philippines share many cultural similarities with Indonesia at the present because of both geographical proximity and long-term historical links through maritime trade in the region.[2] It therefore makes sense to treat the descriptions of this subject in the Indonesian ethnographies as a comparative frame of reference for the Sulu case. As a matter of fact, phenomena similar to those described for Indonesia are also very visible in Sulu society. However, the final object of this paper is to clarify a subtle but undeniable difference between the two cases rather than just to show the common characteristics.

Ethnographic studies of Sulu religious practice

Unlike the situation for Indonesia, the number of ethnographic studies of these types of religious issues in the Sulu area are very limited. It can be pointed out that the main conceptual framework of those who have studied Muslim religious traditions in Sulu is based on the so-called "folk Islam" model (e.g. Casino 1974; Kiefer 1985). In these kinds of analyses, religious beliefs and practices in Mindanao and Sulu have been described as an amalgam which has emerged through a process of mixture or "syncretism" between the "authentic" Islamic tradition of Middle Eastern origin and the local "pre-Islamic" indigenous beliefs. At first sight, this folk Islam model might seem adequate as a general approximation.

These arguments, however, should be further elaborated in relation to two points. First, in this model the religious traditions of folk Islam are assumed to be static, so that often it seems that they constitute a seamless fabric or a coherent system. As a consequence, the issue of internal differences or tension between the local elements and more orthodox Islam is hardly examined. The second point, which is relatively undeveloped in the folk Islam argument, is the relationship between local religious practice and the macro-level political setting such as the nation-state. So far, most of the anthropological studies on Filipino Muslims in Sulu have concentrated on micro-level description of local belief and religious practices.

This paper will therefore examine the dynamism and internal differences within folk-Islamic practices in the area and try to understand the transformations taking place as a result of this dynamism. In other words the main focus here is on the politics of religious practice in Sulu. In particular, the shamanism of the Sama people of Tabawan island in Tawi Tawi province of the Sulu archipelago will be examined in detail.[3]

Shamanism in Tabawan

Tabawan Island

Tabawan is a tiny tropical island of about eight thousand residents. It belongs to Tawi Tawi province which encompasses the southern half of the Sulu archipelago. Except for a few Chinese and Christian Filipino migrants from the Visaya region, most of the residents are Sama-speaking people. Economically, most of them are engaged in either small-scale fishing or coconut farming. However, as a consequence of fierce armed conflict between Muslim secessionist rebels and the Philippine government since the 1970s, there has been an evident socioeconomic decline in the Sulu area. Because of this decline, huge numbers of Muslims from the area, including Tabawan, have sought asylum in Sabah, the Malaysian part of northern Borneo, either as refugees or as "illegal immigrant workers."[4] Significant numbers of migrants from Tabawan are working in Sabah as construction workers, workers on oil palm plantations, and so on.

The Sama-speaking people in Tabawan are without exception Muslims and they make up one group of the so-called "Moro" or Muslim Filipino population. Although they are Muslims, they are also known for their strong adherence to "folk" or "pre-Islamic" elements in their religious practices. The shamanic beliefs of the people on Tabawan island are particularly famous, even in comparison with other Sama-speaking groups on neighboring islands in Tawi Tawi or in Sulu. Traditionally, shamanism in Tabawan is based on the belief in spirits called *duwata*.[5] A shaman or spirit medium, called *papagan* locally, is a person who can communicate with the *duwata*, cure a sick person or perform divination when they are possessed by these spirits. Most female shamans can also serve as midwives. Usually, most shamans begin to acquire their abilities after recovering from a serious illness or after having a mystical vision in their dreams.

This belief in *duwata* has a strong connection with the traditional cosmology in Tabawan. For example, there is a deep well called the "*duwata* well" on the island and it is regarded by locals as "the origin of the world" (*awwal junia*). According to local belief, Tabawan island itself is "the center of the world" (*ponsodd junia*).[6] It is also regarded as a place where mystical grace (*barakat*) was bestowed by God and the spirits. Stories like the one below illustrate the traditional cosmology in Tabawan.

Text 1

> The well (in Tabawan) is the origin of the world. At the bottom of the
> well, there resides a black snake, a "snake of the earth" (*sowa ettom*). In
> possessing this well, Tabawan island is a "land beloved by God" (*lahatt
> kinalasahan heh Tuhan*) as well as the "navel of the world."
>
> Once upon a time, when there was a strong storm, people saved their
> lives by escaping to the inland of Tabawan. Besides this, whenever pi-
> rates attack here, the *duwata* spirits can predict the attack, so that people
> can defend this island. (Male informant aged about 50, husband of a
> *papagan*)

The crisis of shamanism in Tabawan

Though it was once very influential, shamanism in Tabawan now seems to
be on the verge of a crisis. Symptoms of this crisis have become more visible, especially since the 1980s, as is shown by the fact that both the number
of villagers joining in shamanic rituals and the amount of donations (*sadakka*)
are decreasing. The shamans themselves clearly recognize these tendencies.
During my stay on the island, several shamanic rituals were canceled because of the lack of donations to cover the cost. In addition the number of
shamans itself is now decreasing more sharply than ever.

An interesting development is that changes in both the form and content
of the shamanic beliefs can be seen in confronting this crisis. One of these
changes is that, nowadays, shamans are beginning to emphasize the idea of
"punishment by God and the spirits" which was not given such a central
importance in the past. This change may signal that shamans have begun to
emphasize this idea so as to prevent their followers from abandoning their
faith. It is often said that people may be punished by the supernatural if they
abandon their traditional way of life: traditional clothing, food and – most
importantly – traditional rituals.

The background to this crisis of shamanism in Tabawan is complex, and
multiple factors are intertwined. The first important factor is the effects of
the activities of the modern medical sector on the island, centered on a free
clinic which was established by the government ten years ago. Since then, a
doctor and three nurses have been actively engaged in medical and health
care programs. Since one of the sources of the shamans' social prestige had
been based on their abilities as healers and midwives, it is easy to assume
that the introduction of effective alternatives in the form of modern medi-

cine is a serious threat to the folk medical practices of the shamans. Indeed, some shamans criticize those who prefer to go to the modern medical clinic for their treatment. One shaman even hinted that those who relied more on the modern clinic than the shamans' seances would be cursed by the spirits.

However, if one examines the case in more detail, the relationship between shamanism and the modern medical sector is not necessarily either incompatible or hostile. For example, the staff of the clinic have persuaded some of the shamans to undertake medical training programs, for instance in sterilizing methods, so that the traditional midwife-shamans can play a role which complements and supports that of the modern clinic. So far, ten shamans have taken the course. In the long run, however, one cannot deny that the penetration of modern medicine may damage the social basis of shamanism.

The Impact of Islamic Resurgence

The background to Islamic resurgence in the southern Philippines

The second and the more profound factor in the crisis of shamanism is the impact of Islamic resurgence in the Philippines. Since there is no room here to describe the whole history of this resurgence, I will touch briefly only on the background.

Though over 90 percent of the population in the Philippines are Christians, there are approximately six million Muslims in the Mindanao and Sulu areas. Historically speaking, unlike the colonized Christian majority in the north, the Muslims in the southern Philippines once formed their own sultanates and Islamic kingdoms and, by so doing, maintained their respective cultures and distinctive identities, while fiercely resisting colonization by the Spanish. But, beginning with colonization by the United States in the early twentieth century, Muslim society in the south in what was known as Moro province gradually began to be incorporated into the colonial framework. After the Second World War, this Muslim area was totally incorporated in the newly independent Republic of the Philippines.

This was not an entirely happy ending, at least for the Muslims. Facing a massive in-migration of Christian farmers to Mindanao, also known as the "land of promise," the Muslims in Mindanao and Sulu began to feel that they were becoming more and more marginalized and increasingly a minority in their own homeland. Finally during the second half of the 1960s, land disputes between Christian migrants and Muslim locals gradually led to sporadic armed confrontation. In 1968, Datu Matalam, a traditional Muslim politician in Mindanao, declared the start of the Mindanao Independence Movement (MIM). In the first half of the 1970s, the armed conflict between the Armed Forces of the Philippines and the Moro National Liberation Front (MNLF), led by a Sulu-born Muslim intellectual, Professor Nur Misuari, escalated almost to the level of conventional warfare. The city of Jolo, the capital city and political center of Sulu province, was totally destroyed in 1974 as a result of heavy fighting. This Mindanao conflict has exerted a profound influence on many fields of life in the Philippines up to this day.[7]

One of the most salient features which has accompanied the progress of this Muslim secessionist movement is the deepening sense of Islamic consciousness in the area (Che Man 1990: 57–59). Although it is misleading to say that the Mindanao conflict is just a "religious" conflict because its origins are so complex, it has been seen as such in various quarters. Indeed, the secessionist cause holds a strong appeal for ordinary Muslims because it has been presented as a kind of "Jihad" (Islamic Holy War) aimed at defending the ancestral Muslim homeland against "land grabbing" by Christian settlers and government forces of whom the majority are Christians. As a matter of fact, both Muslim identity and the position of Islam as its spiritual core have been consolidated through the confrontation with the Christian-dominated armed forces of the Philippines.

Another important point is that Philippine Muslims' strong consciousness of belonging to global Islamic community or *ummah* has been drastically intensified. This is because at the height of the Mindanao conflict the MNLF and other Muslim rebels in the Philippines were strongly supported, both morally and materially, by other Islamic countries such as Libya, Saudi Arabia, Malaysia, and Pakistan. To sum up, with the Mindanao conflict as the turning point, the Islamic resurgence and consciousness of Islamic identity have both developed into significant social phenomena in the Muslim areas of Mindanao and Sulu.

Islamic resurgence and local practice in Sulu

As concrete examples of Islamic resurgence in Sulu we might mention phenomena such as an increase in the numbers of mosques and *madrasa* (religious schools), increasing numbers of Islamic seminars and Koranic reading contests, and the popularity of Islamic practices such as strict abstinence from forbidden foods (*halam*), and the wearing of veils by women. In particular proselytizing activities such as Islamic seminars in *madrasa* aimed at the propagation of purer, more orthodox and "more correct" forms of Islam (*dawwah* or *dakwah*) are currently becoming increasingly visible in the region.

One distinctive feature of these *dawwah* movements is their strong connection with foreign *dawwah* groups or movements in other Islamic countries. In Sulu most of the activities of local *dawwah* groups have been performed in coordination with foreign *dawwah* groups in Pakistan, Egypt, or Iran. The main areas of their influence are the relatively urbanized areas like the city of Jolo in Sulu province and the city of Bongao in Tawi Tawi province. Both of them are provincial capitals, and they are the political and economic centers of their respective provinces. The *madrasa* teachers, generally called *ustadz*, are among the most active members of the *dawwah* movement in Sulu. Their main activity is to propagate "true Islam" among the local people. To fulfil this purpose, they usually furiously criticize the local customs and practices which are perceived by them as "un-Islamic" or "against orthodox Islam." The following statements are drawn from the answers to my questions while interviewing in one *madrasa* in Bongao, the provincial capital of Tawi Tawi.

Text 2

The purpose of the activity in this *madrasa* is to teach people about the true Islam. There are still a lot of un-Islamic customs in Tawi Tawi. One of the examples is that a lot of women are still not wearing a veil over their faces." (Male, twenty years old, a *madrasa* student)

Text 3.

There are many un-Islamic customs and traditions in Tawi Tawi. We are trying to change these un-Islamic traditions so that people can live in a truly Islamic way. One of these un-Islamic practices is praying at a sacred place like a graveyard in the mountain. Many people do this when their child becomes sick. (Male, thirty-six years old, *ustadz*)

And when I asked about the belief in spirits such as *duwata* or *jinn*, the answer from the same speaker was as follows;

Text 4

It's true that the *jinn* or *saitan* exist even in the teaching of Islam. But the power of those spirits is so weak. Therefore, it is wrong to believe in their power. And it is against Islam if Muslims give offerings to anyone other than Allah.

As shown above, beliefs in the power of the spirits and offerings to them are criticized by the *ustadz* on the grounds that the doctrine of *tauhid* or the Oneness of God will be threatened. In recent years, tension between the *ustadz* and the practitioners of local beliefs has become much higher than in the past. The reason for this tension is that the strength of the Muslim *dawwah* movements in the area is increasing remarkably, as a result of strong support by, and strong linkages with, Islamic *dawwah* organizations. Even in Tabawan, several foreign *ustadz*, most of them Pakistan nationals, are actively engaged in *dawwah* activity. Another important factor is that a considerable numbers of Tabawan migrant returnees from Malaysia have become familiar with more "authentic" forms of Islam there. Some of them have become strong supporters of the *dawwah* movement since their return to Tabawan.

Compared with the effects of modern medicine, the consequences of criticism by the *dawwah* movement are more serious and far-reaching for local shamans. This is because in the case of modern medicine it is possible for shamans to coexist with doctors in the clinic where shamanic seances perform a complementary role to modern medicine, as discussed above. However in the case of the *dawwah* movement there is no room for shamanism to coexist. This is because for the *ustadz* the shamanic seance or ritual itself is defined as an act "against Islam" which should thus be abandoned.

It is in this context that drastic transformations of shamanic rituals are taking place in Tabawan at present. It seems that the traditional shamanic ritual is becoming an arena of informal political struggle between the *dawwah* movement led by the *ustadz* on the one hand and the local shamans on the other.

The Transformation of Shamanic Ritual in Tabawan

I will now examine more concretely the process of the transformation of shamanic ritual in Tabawan. The ritual examined here is called Pai Bahau in the local dialect, which means literally "new unhulled rice." This is celebrated annually and according to some locals the purpose of the ritual is to express gratitude for the harvest. Usually, this ritual is performed in the house of a shaman, and villagers bring plates of offerings made of yellow rice to the house at the time of ritual. These are placed in the middle of the shaman's house.

Traditionally, the essential part of the Pai Bahau ritual is when the spirit-possessed shaman smells the offering. The meaning of this is the symbolic acceptance of the offering by the shaman, who then makes the other people eat the offerings. In some cases, the shamans hold additional dancing sessions for several days.

An interesting development is that the recent Pai Bahau rituals have gradually taken on a new form never observed before. As will be shown later, the new tendency is for the ritual speech of the shaman to be prolonged and emphasized as an essential part of the ritual process. In the traditional form of the Pai Bahau, the shaman's speech is neither a necessary nor an essential part of the ritual. The speech consists of either a dialogue between the shaman and the villagers or a long monologue by the shaman. A monologue by a shaman at the Pai Bahau ritual in September 1993 will be examined here as a typical example. This speech was made by a male shaman named Astarani in front of about forty villagers.[8]

Text 5

(1) You, people! You commit a sin against customs. You commit a sin against *agama* (religion), because you are accommodating the *ustadz*! … By them, you are made to believe that the *jinn* are *saitan* (devils) …

(2) I am not a *saitan*! I am an *awliya* (i.e. an Islamic holy man). If you don't believe in *jinn* or *saitan*, I can accept (them) because there is (such a thing as) *jinn saitan* (*jinn* which are devils). But there is (such a thing as) a *jinn islam* (an Islamic spirit), too! … The *jinn* here are Muslims! So, why don't you join the ritual? You will be cursed because of this! … You are cursed because you don't join the ritual anymore. The *jinn* are Muslims. They are not *saitan*.

(3) Many people now follow *ustadz*, saying that "*jinn* are *saitan*." But *jinn* are not *saitan* … It is wrong to think that if you do pray (i.e. follow Islam), you can enter Heaven … You don't have to depend on praying in the mosque.

(4) Many people still believe that you can enter heaven after death as long as you pray (in the mosque). But this is wrong! Praying is only an obligation to Allah! … Even if you don't pray, you can enter heaven if you are good and kind to your neighbor …

(5) If any *ustadz* wants to debate this matter with me, I accept the challenge!

We have to examine the particular context and situation of this ambiguous speech so that we can grasp its real meaning. First of all, Astarani (the shaman who gave the speech) appeared in front of the villagers wearing a white long-sleeved coat, with a white turban on his head. This is the typical clothing worn by pious Muslims for praying in the mosque, or by religious officials, the most visible of which are the *ustadz*. The monologue style in front of many followers is itself very similar to that of a religious sermon (*hutbah*) by an *ustadz*, either at a *madrasa* or at the Friday prayers in the mosque. From this it can be inferred that this shaman was highly conscious of looking and acting like an *ustadz*. Since this kind of monologue used to be rare at rituals but is now becoming distinctive of the shamans in Tabawan, it is reasonable to suppose that it is a new innovation resulting from imitation of the *ustadz* style. By imitating the style of the *ustadz*, the shaman tries to be seen by the villagers not as anti-Islamic, according to the criticism of the *ustadz*, but as being in line with Islam. However the question remains: why do the shamans try to imitate their toughest opponents, namely the *ustadz*? This can be answered by analyzing the content of the speech.

In the first section of the speech, Astarani criticizes both the *ustadz* and the people who accept him as their teacher, saying that the people are committing a "sin against religion." In the second section, Astarani tries to justify the practice of shamanism as being in line with Islam. The reason he uses for this justification is that the *jinn* in Tabawan island are not satanic *jinn* but Muslim *jinn*.

In the third and fourth sections, the shaman tries to challenge the teachings of the *ustadz* who are, in general, eager to emphasize the importance of praying five times a day as an essential part of Islam. The interesting point here is that though Astarani tries to present himself as a pious Muslim by imitating the style of the *ustadz*, he also tries to change and manipulate the definition of Islamic identity in his speech. In other words, he attempts to prevent Islamic identity, an important form of symbolic capital, from being monopolized by the *ustadz*. This is done both through strategies of imitation (through using the speech style of the *ustadz*) and differentiation (through presenting teachings different from those of the *ustadz*). This is an example of the "politics of meaning" in relation to the definition of Islamic identity. As already mentioned, both the *ustadz* and the shamans criticize each other as being opposed to "real Islam." In this sense, the *ustadz* and the shamans are competitors in a game to acquire followers by demonstrating their religious authenticity. Both of them are trying to redefine the meaning of Islam. In this context, it is not unreasonable to recognize that the principle of mimesis underlies the strategy of the shaman in Tabawan. As Michael Taussig remarks in his *Mimesis and Alterity* (1993), one can gain part of the power and authenticity of the other through mimesis, by imitating the original. In the case of Tabawan, shamans are trying to gain authenticity in relation to Islam by imitating the appearance and/or the speech style of the *ustadz*.

The important point here is that the Pai Bahau ritual now appears to be becoming an arena of tacit political struggle. This transformation of the ritual is a direct result of the tension between the shamans and the *ustadz* at the village level in Tabawan. However, it is also obvious that this tension itself reflects the impact of the Islamic resurgence and its rapid spread since the start of armed confrontation between the Muslim secessionist movement and the Philippine state.

Concluding Remarks

As mentioned in the introduction, there already exist many ethnographic studies of religions in Indonesia which deal with the dynamics of the relationship between local and national cultures. Generally speaking, as is often pointed out in these studies, the role of the national government or the framework of the Indonesian nation state has been emphasized in the process of the transformation of local cultures and/or religious practices. As is clearly shown in the cases of Balinese Hinduism or the Kahaligan religion in Kalimantan, many local beliefs and practices have been transformed and reorganized so as to fit into the official definition of religion in the *pancasila* ideology of the Indonesian government. In the politics of religion in Indonesia, the national government occupies a privileged position in reorganizing and redefining local religious practices, so that the interplay of the local and national sectors is clearly visible in the process of transformation of religious practice within the country.

In contrast to the Indonesian case, the national government of the Philippines is not such a privileged or paramount agent in the politics of religion for several reasons. First of all, the official ideology of the Philippines as a secular state is based on the principle of the separation of church and state, so that, in principle at least, the state cannot officially intervene in religious affairs or regulate them. In the case of Indonesia, there are state institutions concerned with religious affairs like the Ministry of Religion and the position and definition of the various religions are strongly controlled and regulated by either state policy or official state ideologies such as the *pancasila*. Besides being a secular state, the Philippines, which has sometimes been described as a "weak" state, lacks a strong official national ideology comparable to the *pancasila* in Indonesia.

Generally speaking, national consciousness or the sense of belonging to the Philippine state has so far been relatively weak, especially in Muslim-dominated Sulu because of the secessionist movement. Under these circumstances, it is not unreasonable to argue that the position of the Philippine state is, unlike Indonesia, not necessarily that of a privileged agent in the politics of religion, nor even the most important player in Sulu.

175

In the political dynamics of religion in Sulu, we have to take into consideration another important factor, namely the transnational, or even global, network of the Islamic resurgence movement. This is important because most Islamic resurgence movements in Sulu originate in foreign Islamic countries and are strongly supported by foreign Islamic organizations or governments. In addition, a significant number of the founding members of these movements are either Middle Eastern-educated Muslim intellectuals like the *ustadz* or *ulammah*, or people who are close to them. Among them, it is possible to recognize the emergence of a sense of belonging to the global Muslim community (*ummah*).

Therefore the significant dynamics of religious transformation in Sulu are not limited only to the local and the national. As is shown in the case of Tabawan, the transformation of shamanic ritual is a result of a complex interplay between the local shamans, the staff of the medical clinic organized by the Philippine government, and the *ustadz* supported by transnational Islamic networks. As this case shows, we have to take note of the complex interplay of local, national, and transnational cultures. There have already been numerous analyses of the interplay between local and global culture in the field of cultural studies. It now seems to be a cliché to say that the consequence of globalization is not necessarily a loss of local cultural traditions, but that rather, in many cases, local cultural practices and identities are paradoxically strengthened through the modern globalization process. A further significant result of this globalization process which has been noted is the relative weakening of the "national." As Rob Wilson and Wimal Dissanayake write:

> Within these spaces of uneven modernity, we are witnessing not so much the death and burial of "local cultural originality," as Fanon once feared within residually colonial structures of national modernity, as their rehabilitation, affirmation, and renewal in disjunctive phases and reassertions ... The nation-state, in effect, having been shaped into an "imagined community" of coherent modern identity through warfare, religion, blood, patriotic symbology, and language, is being undone by this fast imploding heteroglossic interface of the global with the local: what we would here diversely theorize as the global/local nexus. (Wilson and Dissanayake 1996: 3)

It is not difficult to discern that this "global/local nexus" is playing a decisive role in the case of religious transformation which we have analyzed here. But, another implication which we can draw from the Tabawan case in particular is that "the global" is not necessarily equivalent to "the West" and that "globalization" is not necessarily "Westernization." As we have shown in this paper, the most formidable adversary for indigenous shamanism in Tabawan is, paradoxically, not so much "secularization" in the form of modern Western medicine as "religious revivalism" in the form of the Islamic resurgence movement. And, as is sometimes pointed out, religious revivalism of this sort is itself a reaction to – or a rejection of – rapid Westernization or the challenge of Western modernity in one form or another. It is therefore too simple to represent the cultural dynamics in the Tabawan case as those of a simple dichotomy between global modernity and local shamanism, since the word "global" here does not have a single unambiguous meaning.

In sum, in examining this kind of very complex cultural interplay between the global and the local, it is also necessary to pay full attention to diversity or, to use Arjun Appadurai's words, the "disjunctions and differences" within each "global" or "local" version of cultural production.

Notes

1   Chapter 3 of Marcus and Fischer's *Anthropology as Cultural Critique* (1986: 77–110) examines the problematics of how to deal with these larger political/economical systems like nation-states or the "modern world system" in ethnographic representations.
2   James Warren (1981) describes this historical linkage through maritime trade between Sulu and other regions in maritime Southeast Asia very vividly.
3   The data on which this study is based was collected during my field research in the Sulu Archipelago from June 1992 to February 1995. The shamanic ritual which is examined in this paper was held in September 1993.
4   According to one estimate, these Filipinos in Sabah number as many as half a million.
5   In some Sama-speaking groups in other islands in Sulu, these spirits are called *jinn* (from the Arabic word) instead of *duwata*.
6   The word *ponsodd* literally means "navel."
7   The historical description and political analysis of Mindanao conflict and the Moro secessionist movement in this section is based on the study by W.K. Che Man (1990).
8   The names presented in this paper are pseudonyms. The speeches were originally given in Sinama (the Sama dialect).

Ikuya TOKORO

References

Atkinson, Jane Monnig. 1987. "Religions in dialogue: the construction of an Indonesian Minority Religion," pp.171–86 in *Indonesian Religions in Transition*, eds. Ritaq Smith Kipp and Susan Rodgers. Tucson: University of Arizona Press.

Casino, Eric. 1974. "Folk-Islam in the life cycle of the Jama Mapun," pp. 165–81 in *The Muslim Filipinos*, eds. Peter Going and Robert McAmis. Manila: Solidaridad Publishing House.

Che Man, W.K. 1990. *Muslim Separatism: The Moros of Southern Philippines and the Malays of Southern Thailand*. Oxford: Oxford University Press.

Geertz, Clifford. 1957. "Ritual and social change: a Javanese example," *American Anthropologist* 59: 32–54.

Geertz, Clifford. 1964. "Internal conversion in contemporary Bali," pp. 282–302 in *Malayan and Indonesian Studies Presented to Sir Richard Winstedt*, eds. J. Bastin and R. Roolvink. Oxford: Oxford University Press.

Kiefer, Thomas M. 1985. "Folk Islam and the supernatural," pp. 323–25 in *Readings on Islam in Southeast Asia*, eds. Ahmad Ibrahim and Sharon Iddique. Singapore: Institute of Southeast Asian Studies.

Kipp, Ritaq Smith and Susan Rodgers eds. 1987. *Indonesian Religions in Transition*. Tucson: University of Arizona Press.

Marcus, George E. and Michael M.J. Fischer. 1986. *Anthropology as Cultural Critique*. Chicago: The University of Chicago Press.

Taussig, Michael. 1993. *Mimesis and Alterity: A Particular History of the Senses*. New York: Routledge.

Warren, James Francis. 1981. *The Sulu Zone, 1768–1898: The Dynamics of External Trade, Slavery, and Ethnicity in the Transformation of a Southeast Asian Maritime State*. Singapore: Singapore University Press.

Wilson, Rob and Wimal Dissanayake eds. 1996. *Global/Local*. Durham, North Carolina: Duke University Press.

Chapter 11

Diaspora and Ethnic Awakening:

The Formation of Cultural Consciousness among the Ayta

of Mt. Pinatubo after the Eruption of 1991

Hiromu SHIMIZU

This paper focuses on the process of the emergence of ethnic awareness and cultural consciousness among the Ayta (also spelled Aeta), amid their struggle for survival after the Mt. Pinatubo eruption. Through the experience of diaspora (exodus, suffering, and resettlement and rehabilitation in new places), and especially through exposure to the lowland communities and through negotiations with journalists, government officials, and NGO workers, the Ayta have greatly enhanced their consciousness of being an indigenous people with a distinctive cultural heritage.

In terms of material culture and lifestyle, the lives of most of the Ayta victims and refugees are now greatly influenced by the Christian lowlanders with whom they have superficially assimilated. The sense of a shared similar experience of hardship and the effort of establishing solidarity among scattered groups, however, made the Ayta victims/refugees feel strongly that they belong to one and the same ethnic community. It is not too much to say that a new ethnic identity, that of the pan-Pinatubo Ayta, has arisen for the first time due to the eruption.

Eruption, Exodus and Sufferings

In scale, the eruption of Mt. Pinatubo in June 1991 was the largest of its kind in the twentieth century. The extent of the damage caused by the volcanic explosions and falling ash at the time of the eruption, as well as by rampaging landslides of wet volcanic debris during the successive rainy seasons, was astronomical and extended over five provinces. In addition to the 40,000 houses which were totally destroyed, another 110,000 were damaged. Well over a million people suffered the damage or loss of their properties. Over 100,000 people were forced to live in evacuation centers or tent cities temporarily, and were then later moved to twenty resettlement sites provided by the government: of these, eleven were for lowlanders, and nine for highlanders, including the Ayta.

The Ayta, who originally lived on the slopes and foots of Mt. Pinatubo, were the group most seriously affected by the disastrous eruption. In appearance they are Asian negritos with physical features such as short stature, kinky hair and very dark brown complexions. They are considered to be the descendants of the first migrants to the Philippines during the last glacial period, about 25,000 years ago, when the sea level sank and land bridges appeared. They were gradually forced to retreat to mountainous areas because of the pressure from later migrations of Indonesian and Malay peoples.

At present they are scattered over particular areas of the Philippines, and the Pinatubo Ayta are the largest group, with a population of 40-50,000, including people of mixed blood. I conducted twenty months of fieldwork in the late 1970s among the Ayta living in and around Kakilingan village in the southwestern part of the Mt. Pinatubo region, and have visited the area repeatedly since then.

The population of the southwestern Pinatubo Ayta at that time was only a few thousand, and they had retained their indigenous culture rather well compared to other groups of Pinatubo Ayta. To some extent they preferred to isolate themselves in the mountains and had little contact with lowland merchants. Their subsistence economy was based on the shifting cultivation of root crops (sweet potatoes, taros, and cassavas), together with others such as rice, corn, and beans. They also hunted, mainly birds and bats, using bows and arrows; they caught fish, eel and shrimp using *angtoko* (water goggles) and *biste* (short iron spears propelled by rubber bands); and they collected wild vegetables.

In addition to the southwestern Pinatubo Ayta who had preserved their indigenous culture, there were the more advanced or acculturated Ayta living on the lower part of the mountain slopes who had begun to try wet-rice cultivation in narrow swamps along the river by using *carabaos*. Even these "advanced" Ayta, however, maintained shifting cultivation as their basic means of livelihood. Whenever they went to the mountains to work on their swidden fields, they never failed to carry bows and arrows in case they had a chance to hunt.

The southwestern Pinatubo Ayta did not change completely from hunting and gathering to shifting cultivation or wet-rice agriculture. Acceptance of a new means of livelihood or new innovations in food acquisition did not necessarily eliminate the previous systems, but only added further alternatives to the existing variations. Depending on the situation, the Ayta have several options for acquiring food in the most effective manner. Many so-called "developmental stages," usually thought of as sequential, exist side by side in Ayta culture (for details of Ayta life before the eruption, see Shimizu 1989).

Because of this, the Ayta before the eruption were an example of what Sahlins (1972) described as "the original affluent society." Brosius, who conducted research among the Ayta living on the southwestern slopes in the early 1980s, concluded his report as follows:

> The degree to which the Negritos within the research area are nutrition-
> ally self-sufficient is remarkable. Self-sufficiency can be maintained al-
> most indefinitely. It is the source of their strength, independence and
> persistence. Their days are not "numbered" as perhaps are the days of
> other less independent Philippine Negrito groups. (Brosius 1984: 144–
> 45)

In short, life among the Ayta before the eruption was almost entirely eco-nomically self-sufficient and socially autonomous. A high value was placed on mutual support, while generosity, sharing and mutual help were also highly valued.

Everything, however, was suddenly changed by the eruption. The Ayta were driven away from the land that nourished them and were forced to live in overcrowded evacuation centers or tent cities with insufficient support systems. It was during this period that almost every Ayta became sick, and many of them died, the death toll reaching a thousand.[1] The direct causes of their deaths were measles, bronchial pneumonia and dehydration caused by severe diarrhea. Most of the victims were from the groups that lived in the highlands of Mt. Pinatubo who had led a traditional way of life with few contacts with lowland peoples.

Strategies for Survival

In March, 1996, nearly five years after the eruption, I made my fifth visit to the region to carry out research on the situation in the Pinatubo area and some of the resettlement sites. This visit confirmed that the members of each Ayta group were still struggling to establish secure and stable lives, as well as to enhance their standard of living, despite a variety of constraints. In almost all the resettlement sites the farm plot allocated to each family was so small, rocky, and barren that family sustenance by means of agriculture was not possible. This meant they had to find other means of livelihood outside their resettlement sites. Roughly speaking, there were three divergent strategies for the Ayta to follow. The first was to go back to the mountains to resume a lifestyle similar to that before the eruption. The second was to remain in the assigned resettlement site but go out to nearby villages, towns, and even big cities to work as laborers. The third was to find larger farms where they could resettle and develop them by themselves.

The first strategy was selected by those conservative Ayta who had had fewer contacts with lowlanders before the eruption, and also by those lucky Ayta whose former villages and farms were saved from severe damage simply because of their distance from the eruption. The nearer a village was to the summit of Mt. Pinatubo, the more serious was the damage from the falling ash and pebbles which accumulated there. However, on the mountain slopes several kilometers away from the summit, the accumulated ash has been washed away by heavy rainfall, and the vegetation has recovered sufficiently for swidden agriculture. Of course, as these areas are still rather small in size and limited in number, not all Ayta victims who wish to return can go back there.

The second strategy was selected by the comparatively acculturated Ayta. For example, of the hundred or so Ayta families who had lived in Villar, the central village in the western part of the Mt. Pinatubo region, and who had been relocated to the Loob-bunga resettlement site near Botolan town, more than half of the male household heads now stay on a construction site in Manila. They work as laborers with wages of 120 pesos per day, and they come back home once every few weeks. As the air is hot, humid, and polluted in Manila, these Ayta workers are having a hard time there and often become sick. They do not want to work in Manila, but feel that they cannot do otherwise. The whole village and all the farms of old Villar are now completely buried under thick lava, and there are few farms to cultivate and few opportunities for work in Loob-bunga. The other Ayta, who had not been so accustomed to the lowland ways as the Villar Ayta, prefer working in nearby villages and towns as rice planters and harvesters, as construction workers, or as mere laborers.

Nearly half of the Kakilingan Ayta of southwestern Pinatubo, among whom I conducted my first fieldwork in the late 1970s, had settled at the Iram resettlement site located in the suburbs of Olongapo City. They prefer staying there because of the many advantages and conveniences available, such as hospitals, education, and job opportunities. Some of them work inside the former U.S. naval base, Subic, which is now being transformed into an industrial, commercial, and trade zone.

The third strategy was followed by the other half of the Kakilingan Ayta. After the first rainy season was over in early 1992, they moved from Iram to Kanaynayan, which is located on the other side of the small mountains separating it from Kakilingan. As they can see Kakilingan and Mt. Pinatubo from the mountain ridges, they feel at home and close to their motherland. Although the mountain slopes and rolling hills there are covered with ash twenty to thirty centimeters deep, they can still plant root crops and bananas, if not upland rice. Moreover the stream running through the valley there does not originate from Mt. Pinatubo but from a different mountain, and therefore the lava slides during the rainy season are not so severe, making it a safer place for them to live.

The land at Kanaynayan belongs to the government. In order to get permission to develop land there for themselves as an "alternative resettlement site" (as they call it), more than 250 Ayta chartered buses and held a rally in front of the office of the DENR (Department of Environment and Natural Resources) in Quezon City in January 1992. They met with Secretary Fulgencio of the department to present their petition directly, and they received a verbal promise that 1,400 hectares of government land would be leased to them in the form of a community forest stewardship so that they could settle. After coming back from Manila, they began to build a new Ayta village in Kanaynayan with strong financial support in the form of an annual budget of three million pesos for several years from HEKS, a Swiss NGO operating in the Philippines.

Old Kakilingan was established at the southwestern foot of Mt. Pinatubo in 1975 by a local NGO, the Ecumenical Foundation for Minority Development (EFMD), as part of an eight-year project designed to persuade the Ayta in the hinterland to come down to settle. The project aimed to provide, first, the necessary technology and equipment for plow agriculture, and, second, a combination of elementary education for Ayta children and literacy classes for the adults. Unfortunately, however, EFMD failed to achieve its goals within eight years. It revised and extended its program several times and remained in operation until the Pinatubo eruption.

Aware of the difficulties for the Ayta in operating any kind of project unilaterally, EFMD encouraged the Ayta leaders to organize themselves and then helped them to establish the ADA (Aeta Development Association) in 1985. ADA is a nonprofit organization of local people, whose overall goal is to "uplift the social and economic conditions of the Aytas and to protect their human and ancestral land rights."

In the beginning ADA was a rather passive affiliate of the EFMD. It was the crisis of Ayta survival that strengthened the role of the ADA as the body for organizing rehabilitation, and ironically it also revived the EFMD, which at that time was in the very final phase of its withdrawal, this time with the help of large emergency funding from supporting NGOs, and especially HEKS. The size of the funds, however, led to corruption on the part of several members of the board (which consisted of non-Ayta), who spent much of the money on their own allowances, honoraria, and traveling and lodging expenses – 100,000 pesos for the latter half of 1991 and 250,000 pesos for the first half of 1992.

HEKS became angry with the EFMD board members: threatening withdrawal of its financial support, it demanded structural changes in the EFMD to clean up the corruption. The confrontation of the EFMD board members with HEKS led to the abolition of the EFMD. The director of EFMD, a man called Tima from Kalinga in northern Luzon who was himself a member of an indigenous ethnic minority and who had been trusted by both Ayta and HEKS transferred to ADA as its executive director, and transformed it into an institution for planning and implementing a variety of rehabilitation and development projects. Although all the board members of ADA are now Ayta, Director Tima is still influential.

After the eruption, ADA conducted various projects to establish a new community based on agriculture (both swidden and plow) in Kanaynayan. With an annual budget of three million pesos and more than ten members of staff, it built houses along with other facilities such as an elementary school building, demonstration farms, wet rice fields, an access road from a nearby village, and a water supply system.

Emerging Organizations and Solidarity

Not only the ADA members but also many other Ayta were encouraged to organize themselves and to strengthen their ethnic identity through negotiating with lowlanders, journalists, government officers and NGO workers amid the sufferings, difficulties, and struggles for survival and rehabilitation.

One good example of the ethnically awakened Ayta is the establishment of a people's organization known as PINATUBO, standing for Pinagsamasamang Aeta na Tutulong Para Umunlad ang Botolan (Aeta Cooperative Association for the Development of the Botolan Area). For a year or so after the eruption, Ayta evacuees were passive receivers of relief supplies or working as laborers in food-for-work projects run by the DSWD (Department of Social Welfare and Development) and the NGOs, because of the severe physical and psychological damage caused by the drastic changes in all areas of life. As the life in resettlement sites became more stable, despite its minimal level, the Ayta leaders, at first with the encouragement of some NGOs, started to organize their fellow Ayta residents. This was in order to establish an autonomous body to plan a subsistence project, apply for funds from the DTI (Department of Trades and Industries) and the NGOs, and then implement it by themselves. They clearly understood that the time for emergency support was over and that it was already becoming hard to secure funds for projects without a responsible organization of Ayta residents.

PINATUBO was born out LAKAS (Lubos na Alyansa ng maga Katutubong Ayta ng Sambales). This had been established in 1987 as the result of a literacy class and consciousness-raising program devotedly carried out by Catholic sisters working first among the Ayta living in Yamot, and then in several adjacent villages on the western slopes of Mt. Pinatubo.

After the eruption, Mr. Paylot Cabalic, one of the leaders of LAKAS, wanted to become independent from the guidance and intervention of the charitable sisters. So he left the group to establish a new Ayta organization with encouragement and support from some NGOs. He went around the two resettlement sites of Loob-bunga and Baquilan near Botolan town, and succeeded in persuading the leaders of each ward of the old village to establish their own people's organizations. He then established PINATUBO as an umbrella organization for these newly established groups. In 1993 PINATUBO received nearly one million pesos and purchased a passenger vehicle for transportation between the two resettlement sites and the town of Botolan, as well as several sets of transceivers for communication among the leaders. It also purchased one hectare of land and rented several other hectares for agricultural projects.

PINATUBO and ADA formed the CLAA (Central Luzon Ayta Association) in late 1991 together with other umbrella organizations of Ayta in different areas in the four provinces, namely Zambales, Bataan, Pampanga and Tarlac. The establishment of the CLAA was a program jointly initiated by OXFAM-UK-Ireland and SENTRO which sponsored a seminar workshop of representatives from nine Ayta associations in Central Luzon on 24 and 25 October that year to share their experiences and opinions. They discussed living conditions, problems and the necessary solutions, and future plans and projects. Thanks to this opportunity and to the continuous encouragement of the sponsoring NGOs and volunteer workers, these Ayta representatives and leaders organized the CLAA.

Since then CLAA has engaged in such activities as seminars, sharing experiences and problems, rallies, cultural activities enhancing Ayta consciousness and pride, and demonstrations and press conferences in Manila demanding more adequate subsistence projects, especially more land for cultivation. The following is the translation of the statement issued by CLAA on the first anniversary of the major eruption on 15 June 1992.

THE AYTA OF PINATUBO: A STORY OF ABANDONMENT AND EXPLOITATION

We are indigenous Ayta – quiet, generous and peace loving – these positive characters became the means which others took advantage of. Many times we were driven away from our own land when the U.S. military bases were built. Many times we were driven away from our own land when ranches and plantations invaded to occupy our own land. We were driven away from our home when the volcano erupted.

One year has passed. Slowly and swiftly.

Slowly. The promises were slowly fulfilled. Medicines and food were slowly delivered. Rescue slowly reached us.

Swiftly. Children and elders got easily sick. Mr. Death was swiftly running after anybody. We were soon forgotten – and our problems were quickly passed from one government agency to another.

Five months we stayed at an evacuation center before we were transferred to where they declared resettlement sites. During that period, 487 Ayta quickly died. Most of them were child-victims of epidemic diseases and measles.

It was the buildings of DSWD and clusters of toilets that were made of cement in the resettlement site, the place where they brought us. Our new house has an area of fifty-six square feet. And was made of sawali, cogon and coco lumber. According to Mr. Carague, they spent 197.2 million pesos to build these houses. From the 344.7 million pesos of funds that was intended for us, the government promised that they will provide pigs, goats, chicken and carabao for our livelihood. Also they promised to build an electric deep-well pump for water supply, electricity, children's playground, public market, kind doctors and intelligent teachers. It has been a year now, where are those promises?

The flow of supplies of sardines became less when news agencies lost their interest to tell our stories. And later, rice was rarely supplied. But we did not lose hope, instead, we strive harder. For us, it is better to die while we work than to die while depending on others' mercy. We extract everything from what was left at Mt. Pinatubo – we make and sell charcoal, we mowed cogon, we sold our strength of labor.

One whole year filled with anxiety, fear, hunger, illness and death is more than enough to be a reason for us to end our meekness and silence. If there is anything in us that was improved, it was not our livelihood but our mind. If there is anything in us that was changed, it was not our miserable life but our timid heart. Through our experiences of these hardships we are simply appealing: We were abandoned before, and currently exploited. We are continually forced to bear sufferings so that others may live in prosperity. We are continually forced to live like the dumb so that they can use us unfairly.

On this day, by way of meditating on the one year adversity, we will try to divert the Ayta history. They must give us the privilege to avail of real prosperity that only Ayta can settle. In this land we have lived, and will continuously live. As our prime objective to prosper, we ask them to give us the land and the assurance of our freedom, that has been robbed from us. We are earnestly asking this to all who are concerned.

LET US DECLARE THAT THE PINATUBO AREA IS THE ANCESTRAL LAND OF THE AYTA!

LET THOSE WHO STOLE THE FUNDS WHICH WAS INTENDED FOR US ANSWER!

WE DEMAND AN AMENDMENT OF THE OLD POLICIES CONCERNING AYTA AND ALL THE INDIGENOUS PEOPLE OF THE COUNTRY!

One thing we learned from the Mt. Pinatubo adversity, and should always keep in mind: A silent person is more furious and extremely destructive from his anger.

Central Luzon Ayta Association (CLAA)
Kalipunan ng mga Katutubong Mamamayan ng Pilipingas (KAMP) in cooperation with:
Asian Volunteers' Network for Human Rights (AVN)
Tunay na Alyansa ng Bayan Alay sa Katutubo (TABAK)
Sentro ng Ganap na Pamayanan (SENTRO)

Through the sufferings and difficulties after the eruption, the Ayta living in and around the Pinatubo area came to realize that they shared the same experiences of hardship and that they should be united in order to secure their human and indigenous rights. Just as when the American bases were driven away from the Philippines, the Mt. Pinatubo eruption created solidarity and cooperation among the Ayta through the networking and organizing efforts of those people whose consciousness of being Ayta had been greatly strengthened.

CLAA soon joined KAMP (Kalipunan ng mga Katutubong Mamamayan ng Pilipinas), the umbrella association for indigenous communities in the Philippines. Each Ayta person in the government resettlement sites and other places is thus linked in a tree-like structure through their respective grassroots organizations to the overall Pinatubo Ayta association, and then to the Pan-Filipino association of indigenous communities. Of course this is still at the initial stage of institutionalization, but it will become involved in various activities in the future.

The Discovery of "Culture" and the Birth of Indigenous Consciousness

Mr. Cabalic, the founder and the core leader of PINATUBO, received tremendous encouragement and inspiration for raising the Ayta consciousness of their indigenous status during his travels in Australia for three months in 1989. He traveled extensively and visited all the major cities on the continent to attend seminars, conferences, and meetings as a guest speaker. He also had meetings with aborigines to share experiences and opinions. He was very much impressed by those aborigines who had been engaged in movements and struggles for securing ancestral lands and human rights, and realized that the Ayta also had to awaken and organize themselves. The text of a speech which he delivered at these meetings was published in the book published by LAKAS after the eruption, of which the following is an excerpt.

> Due to foreign conquest, we suffered continuous displacement from our lands and subsequent destruction of our culture. Unlike the Igorots of Nothern Cordillera and the Lumads of Southern Mindanao, our tribe lost its ancestral lands and, with it, our culture. The wanderings and the scatterings of our tribe were not inherent to our culture. Rather, we were driven into it by the necessity of looking for food.
>
> Sad to say, in the Philippines, the indigenous people are called the cultural minorities or the "little natives." This nomenclature came from the

Spaniards. Under the Spanish government, the natives who refused to be baptized were marginalized and classified as the cultural minority, a name deemed unworthy of the baptized Christians. The term "minority" was reserved in a derogatory fashion for the "pagans," the unbelievers, the untutored and the illiterate, the voiceless and the powerless.

Most of our indigenous people have a low self-image in spite of the fact that we were the original inhabitants of the Philippines. This is the result of a long history of oppression. We have been victims of various types of exploitation and have been driven from our lands countless times … We live by the produce of our farms, but many of us still survive by hunting wild boar, deer, birds, and also by fishing in the rivers. We have a council of elders who settle in the village.

In our place, 95 percent are illiterate … Learning to read and write enhanced our self-confidence. Now we are no longer subject to the deceptions of the middlemen and the military. We now control the prices of our products. Gradually we are moving from the barter system to cash economy. Slowly we are being liberated from the clutches of middlemen and from the pitfall of eternal debts. We are now in the direction of self-development where before our destiny was in the hands of unscrupulous middlemen.

In the literacy program we were awakened to the reality of human dignity. We came to know that we have rights and that we are destined for justice, freedom and peace. We have broken the culture of silence that had long imprisoned us.

It is not only education that will empower our people. We also need to organize. We know there is power in organized groups. We started organizing our villages. Now we have seven village groups which are under an umbrella organization named LAKAS, literally meaning power … The binding force of LAKAS derives from its commitment to such important concerns as self-determination, ancestral domain, human rights and sovereignty …

We have learned to take pride in our cultural heritage and we have committed ourselves to the service of our people. We are moving towards the enhancement and the promotion of our culture. We also share our culture with other peoples for mutual enrichment. (LAKAS 1991: 16–19)

This text may have been written by Mr. Cabalic in cooperation with Sister Mengay who accompanied him in his travels, or the sister herself might have written the draft for him. Regardless of the writing process, this explanation of the historical background and the present situation was the most important text yet to appear in creating an understanding for himself as well as for the whole Ayta community. Moreover the sisters' devotion to the empowerment of the Ayta bore fruit in the fact that Mr. Cabalic and some other young leaders left LAKAS in order to be independent and to establish PINATUBO after the eruption.

For Mr. Cabalic, the culture in which the Ayta had lived with their nomadic and scattered lifestyle, as well as their silence and timidity, was not inherited from their ancestors, but was forced on them by aggressive and oppressive lowlanders encroaching on lands in the Ayta ancestral domain. It was therefore a false culture. According to his statements, the original and authentic culture of the Ayta had been almost destroyed when they were driven out of, and deprived of, their ancestral lands. That is why the recovery of the ancestral lands had to go side by side with the recovery and the promotion of the Ayta cultural heritage, in order to retain self-determination, the ancestral domain, human rights, and sovereignty.

The Zambal word for culture, *kultura*, is the same as the equivalent word in the Filipino national language. Before the eruption, however, I rarely heard the Ayta use that word. The frequent reference to the Ayta culture in Mr. Cabalic's speech text is rather exceptional for that time. He was able to speak about it because of his consciousness as leader and the chairman of LAKAS at that time. He addressed his Australian audiences not only as a representative of the Pinatubo, but also of the whole Ayta community in the Philippines. For him, it was not their physical features but a cultural heritage which had yet to be revived which was the basis of an identity in which the Ayta could take pride.

In the daily conversation of ordinary people before the eruption, they commonly used the word *ogali* instead of *kultura*. The meaning of *ogali* is wide, ranging from personal dispositions and character to the unique behavior patterns of a family, or to the ways of life, manners, and customs of a certain group. When people paid special attention to the particular behavior of a person, a family, or a group, either to praise or to criticize it, they often explained that "it is their *ogali*, so it's natural."

Before the eruption, *ogali* was sometimes used in referring to some features of Ayta culture in general, such as their marriage procedures with the payment of bridewealth, their unique ways of childrearing, their lifestyle which depended heavily on hunting and gathering, and the rituals accompanying these activities together with shifting cultivation. On these occasions, when they talked about the *ogali* of the Ayta, the contrast in the speakers' minds was that between the "straight-haired" peoples (*unat*) and the townsfolk (*bawobanowa*), as opposed to the Ayta as curly-haired mountainfolk.

Soon after the eruption, however, the word *kultura* came to be used frequently instead of *ogali*. In such cases *kultura* did not refer to a certain individual nor to a particular group, but was used in the context of demanding special assistance and consideration for the whole Pinatubo Ayta community sharing the same cultural heritage.

Pinatubo Ayta society before the eruption, however, was not culturally and linguistically homogeneous nor well-integrated. According to Brosius, "four or five sub-dialects are presently spoken by Ayta within the Zambales area, each with perhaps 1,000 speakers, in an area of approximately 100 sq. kilometers" (1983: 85–86). Moreover, there were the more "advanced" Ayta living on the lower slopes of the mountains or even in lowland villages leading almost the same life style as the Zambal, Ilocano and Tagalog lowlanders. Ayta society was already fairly diversified in lifestyle, and accordingly so was ethnic consciousness. This diversification has been widening between those who have gone back to the mountains to resume the "traditional" life based on swidden cultivation and those who have settled in the lowlands and become politicized, although the majority are located somewhere between these two extreme poles.

At first after the eruption, the word *kultura* came to be used often, first by the Ayta leaders and the most politicized figures, and then by their friends and followers. Once they started to refer to "Ayta culture," the existence of the Pinatubo Ayta community as a whole became real and concrete and was supported by the fact of sharing the same heritage and fate. They emphasized the value of Ayta culture within the context of demanding special assistance and consideration, especially land for the Ayta community to cultivate in order to survive in Philippine society with dignity and security.

The content of "Ayta culture," however, is different depending on the context and according to the speaker. In tape-recorded free narratives of memories of their lives before and after the eruption, some informants like Mr. Cabalic explained Ayta culture as the complex of beliefs and practices of *manganito* (possession seance), while others emphasized features such as bridewealth transactions at marriage, language and its related world views, or the slash and burn agriculture system supplemented with hunting and gathering activities.

Mr. Rudy Bulatao, who was previously one of the leaders of LAKAS but who led a splinter group to resettle on government land near Botolan soon after the eruption, gave the following account. "One feature of our culture is not to live together with lowlanders, because they might oppress us. We have our own culture which is different from the lowlanders'. A person's food is shared with all. For example, if I have a deer, I would divide it into pieces so that everybody can eat. For example, if somebody wants to build a house, we all help each other."

Other Ayta evacuees repeatedly described the Ayta community in the same way as Mr. Bulatao, as being closely united by a spirit of fraternity, and also sustained by the sharing of food and cooperation in work. Life before the eruption was always remembered and described to me in retrospect as free, affluent, and happy, with people strongly attached to their homes and eager to return there. The memories and narratives of individual Ayta, however, were not real but idealized, as were projections of the future. Both were total reversals of the present situation. Real life before the eruption was not one of paradise on earth but was often troubled by sickness, intragroup and intergroup conflicts, and food shortages, especially during the latter part of the rainy season.

It is true that group hunting was the embodiment of cooperation and the symbol of unity, but it had not been practiced since the 1960s when the deforestation of the Pinatubo area due to commercial logging decreased the number of deer and wild pigs drastically. The Ayta leaders, however, put forward an image of themselves as hunters when they try to claim the uniqueness of being Ayta in relation to non-Ayta. This is the case with PINATUBO. The symbol used to represent the organization is an Ayta man with a bow and an arrow standing with the rising sun and the smoking Mt. Pinatubo in the background. This design is used on their headed notepaper as well as on the front and side of the passenger vehicle the organization purchased. Mr. Cabalic who went to Australia in 1989 in his second term as chairman of LAKAS designed it. For the benefit of paternalistic and benevolent foreign philanthropists, the most "acculturated" and politically aware Ayta make strategic use of bows and arrows (symbolizing hunting) and g-strings (symbolizing indigenousness) as the symbols of Ayta-ness.

Leaders of ADA, LAKAS, PINATUBO and other Ayta organizations usually present traditional dances performed by men wearing g-strings with bows and arrows together with modern dances performed by schoolchildren when they give parties for important guests from supporting NGOs. These symbols are used, not because hunting plays an important role in the subsistence economy or in religious ceremonies, but because they are the best expressions of Ayta cultural identity as different from that of the lowlanders and other indigenous peoples who define themselves as shifting cultivators or rice-terrace cultivators. It is also an effective way to get maximum benefits by attracting foreign and domestic philanthropists fascinated by the exotic images of "noble savages" or "primitive" hunter-gatherers. They feel annoyed and hurt, however, when philanthropists or people from the NGOs strongly ask, or even sometimes force, them to pose in this attire for a photo session before or after the ceremonial donation of relief supplies. Here they encounter the painful and degrading experience of being pigeonholed as helpless and impotent hunter-gatherers lost in a totally alien society. There is a big difference between these two situations, the crucial point being the subjective feelings of the Ayta and whether or not they can manipulate and determine for themselves how their image is presented.

A Case for Begging

Among those Ayta who decided to settle down in the government resettlement sites, some go to nearby towns or cities to beg along the roads once in a while, whenever their food or money runs out. Many Ayta go in groups to Olongapo City or even to Manila to beg, especially during the Christmas season, and this has attracted the attention and concern of other people and the mass media. Before the eruption, no Ayta were engaged in begging. The basic reason why they started was insufficient support on the part of the government and/or its failure to provide them with enough farm land to cultivate. The blame therefore lies not with the Ayta but with the government.

When the mass media, however, printed reports about Ayta beggars on the roads and the streets of Manila, they failed to present this viewpoint. Newspaper reports during the 1995 Christmas season described the Ayta in Manila not as fellow Filipino citizens but as more like aliens from another planet. For example, Avendano of the *Philippine Daily Inquirer* started his report with the headline "Aetas will have a dark Xmas: Bright lights, big city not for them, say officials" and followed this with the following account (emphasis added): "Close to 600 Aeta families have *invaded* Metro Manila streets to beg for Christmas alms but officials said they would be hauled back starting today" (21 December 1995: 22). After a week, an anonymous report appeared, in the same newspaper as follows, again using the word "invade" (emphasis added):

Yesterday, a day after Christmas, government authorities resumed operations to bring back home to Central Luzon the rest of the 2,500 Aetas who recently *invaded* Metro Manila streets to beg for alms ... A 1978 law prohibited begging in the streets. The Aeta beggars have started trekking to Metro Manila in 1991, the year following the eruption of Mt. Pinatubo. They would come during the Christmas holidays and leave later. But their numbers proved alarming this Christmas season, prompting officials to do something about the unusual exodus. (27 December 1995: 20)

According to the dictionary, the word "invade" means 1) to enter forcefully as an enemy, 2) to enter like an enemy, 3) to enter as if to take possession, 4) to enter and affect injuriously or destructively, as disease, etc. (*Random House Dictionary*, 1987). As the Ayta's presence in Manila was felt like an "invasion," it was logical for the government to try to "beat them back," i.e. to take them back by force to the resettlement areas. It seemed to have become a criminal offense for Ayta to stay in Manila. Ayta loitering along the streets were seen as somehow contaminating the city and disturbing its order and harmony. Moreover, taking them back home by bus or truck was presented as an act of generosity, carried out from a humanitarian point of view. It was also suggested that a crime syndicate might have organized these begging groups to a get rake-off from them, and that sending them back home was an act of salvation.

It is hard and painful for the Ayta to beg around the hot, dusty, and overcrowded streets of Manila amid the curious and scornful eyes of the lowlanders. Sleeping under a bus shelter or in a porch of a building is totally different from life in the mountains or even life in resettlement sites. However, it is worth tolerating such mental anguish and physical hardship, because they can make a fairly large amount of money from begging.

My old friend Pichay from my first fieldwork days, who now resides in Iram, was involved in begging at the Victory Bus Liner terminal in Caloocan City, Metro Manila, over the New Year holiday. As a reward for working hard for two whole days and nights she earned nearly fifteen hundred pesos. Comparing this with the average daily wage of one hundred pesos for a construction worker and fifty or sixty pesos for an agricultural laborer, one can easily understand the profitability of begging as a sideline during the Christmas and New Year holiday season.

With the fifteen hundred pesos Pichay bought a radio cassette recorder in Olongapo City. As her husband had found a job several months before at Subic Base as a carpenter and helper, and as she herself kept a small *sari-sari* store (in the past she worked as a laundry woman), she did not have to use this windfall income to meet a deficit in the family budget. Having experienced working as a house maid for a family living in the *poblacion* of San Marcelino town for more than a year, she did not have any fear or hesitation about going to Manila to beg. With kinky hair and a dark brown complexion, she looks just like any other typical Ayta woman, though she actually belongs to the most acculturated group of Ayta who have assimilated to the lowlanders.

Her friend, who had recently given birth, earned three thousand pesos on Christmas Eve, the highest record for a single day. Seeing her with her newborn baby begging around the Victory Bus Liner terminal, a kind security guard took her to the entrance gate which was better for soliciting alms from the passengers. Her case was rather exceptional, as the average earnings from a day's begging are only between three hundred and five hundred pesos. Begging is not a permanent means of livelihood for most of these Ayta but a special option which they can utilize. Pichay's father stayed in Manila straight from Christmas to New Year, also to beg.

Among those Ayta living in and around Kakilingan village before the eruption, those who were engaged in begging during the Christmas season were not the conservative or traditional Ayta. The most conservative ones (there were around one hundred of them) refused to come down from their villages (mainly Maage-age and Lomboy) during the eruption, even after repeated warnings and persuasion. They evacuated to the caves in the mountains where they were helpless and were burned to death. The Ayta beggars from the Iram resettlement site are rather the "advanced and acculturated" Ayta, who were the ones living on the lower part of the mountains and who maintained frequent contacts with the lowlanders before the eruption. Begging is, of course, the product of the experience of severe hardship after the eruption. At the same time, however, it is also an active and aggressive tactic which can be used by the Ayta to exploit the prejudiced perceptions of lowlanders that they are hunter-gatherers or forest nomads made helpless as miserable victims of the eruption. They clearly understand that the Christmas season offers the best opportunity to appeal to the charitable instincts of the lowlanders in order to make money rather easily by presenting a suitable image of poor and shabby Ayta victims.

Some of these Ayta, once in a while, make bows and arrows which they sell to NGO staff, government employees and visitors to their areas, as well as to drivers and passengers waiting at stoplights or to pedestrians in Olongapo City or even in Manila. The price is three hundred pesos per set for foreigners and between one and two hundred pesos for Filipinos. They do not feel intimidated riding a bus to Manila, walking around the city and negotiating with lowlanders or even foreigners. It is interesting to note that the most advanced and acculturated Ayta, who had already abandoned the traditional way of life in the mountains based on swidden cultivation with hunting-gathering, are the most successful at exploiting the cultural symbols of the Pinatubo Ayta.

For those Ayta who get extra income from manipulating the fixed ideas of "Ayta-ness" held by lowlanders by selling bows and arrows or by begging and soliciting money, the essence of exotic Ayta-ness is anything that is different from the lowlanders' way of life, especially the image of hunter-gatherers or nomads in the forests. While anything to do with "Ayta-ness" is in one context the target of lowlanders' contempt and discrimination, in another context it can be the object of their curiosity and charity once their sense of superiority is transformed into sympathy and compassion. Those Ayta who decided not to go back to the mountains but to live among lowlanders are constantly renegotiating their identities through interaction with lowlanders. Their strategic presentation of an image for the sake of their own gain is based on calculation and manipulation, but as a side effect it also strengthens the stereotypes of lowlanders about the Ayta.

The government officials who prohibited the Ayta from begging in Manila and ordered them to go back to their homes did not see the Ayta tactics as the rational strategies of equal human beings, nor could they imagine the hardships of life in the resettlement areas. They were surprised to find so many Ayta in the center of the capital, and they took the line that compulsory repatriation was the most humanitarian course of action for the Ayta's welfare, out of what they presented as goodwill and pity for the beggars.

Behind this surface consideration, however, the real reason for the hard line taken against the Ayta staying in Manila until the New Year could easily be seen. The biggest concern was not for the Ayta's hardship in Manila, but because these seemingly depressed people cast a dark shadow in the midst of the Christmas season which should have been a time for pleasant celebration. Moreover the presence of the Ayta in Manila itself raised tacit objections and radical questions about the present social order which the middle class citizens take for granted. As the definition of the Ayta in Philippine society and the relationship with them causes uneasiness among the "haves" and the middle classes, not only the government officials and the media personnel but also ordinary citizens wanted to drive the Ayta away from Manila so that they could erase them from their visible world as well as from their consciousness.

In short, it is not because the Ayta do not have the capacity to adjust themselves to survival in the urban environment, but because they do not have the right to live in the capital as Filipino citizens. In other words the Ayta were not allowed to stay in Manila during the Christmas season because they were not considered fellow Filipinos with full rights of citizenship.

For the lowlander Filipinos, especially intellectuals, the Ayta raise the very basic question of who are the "proper Filipinos," and force them to reconsider their definitions. With their short stature, dark brown complexions and kinky hair, the Ayta symbolize values and aesthetics opposite to those which have prevailed since the era of Spanish and American colonization. Can such "uncivilized" people really be fellow citizens along with ordinary Filipinos of Malayan stock? If so, then who are the real or authentic Filipinos? That is the question raised by the Ayta in Manila, and it irritates the paternalistic Filipinos in their attempts to be charitable towards the Ayta.

Professor Randy David of the University of the Philippines took up this issue in his column in a newspaper as follows;

> If angels are real, then this year they came to us in the form of the Aeta ... By their mere presence in the streets of Manila during these holidays, the Aetas have challenged us to rethink our notions of family, Church, community and nation.
>
> The fate of the Aetas, this archipelago's first modern settlers, is an issue that our society does not seem prepared to address. This is why their presence in our midst is very disturbing to many. Do we consider them part of us? Are they entitled to partake of the feasts that we have prepared for our family and friends? ... When will the Church open its doors to them? Will the guards ever allow them inside the megamalls? Is Philippines 2000 also for them?
>
> We are sending them back where they came from because we are not prepared to answer these questions. In fact, we have almost forgotten that they still exist ...
>
> All they asked today is to let them stay in the city till after the New Year. But the police and government social workers have started to round them up to send them back to the mountains where they can live and die without assaulting our consciences. The sight of them darkly huddled in front of gleaming shopping centers and well-lit churches is just too powerful to behold. They bring up the past. They interrogate our values. And their mute presence comes as a question: Who owns this country? (*Philippine Daily Inquirer*, 24 December 1995).

Because of the influences of Spanish and American domination, Christianity and the English language represent the positive values of "civilization." The Spanish as well as the Americans who are tall and "good-looking" with white complexions and long noses once monopolized power, wealth and the refined lifestyle, and still occupy the most sought after positions on the scale of values. In contrast to them, the ethnic minorities in the remote mountains, as well as Muslims in southern Mindanao, are thought to have been left behind in the march toward progress and development.

Among these peoples, the Ayta are thought to be the most "primitive" and "backward," occupying the lowest point on the scale of values. Most of the Ayta are not Christians, receive little or no school education, and cannot speak English. Every characteristic of the Ayta is associated with undesirable values which ordinary Filipinos try to deny and exclude. The more, therefore, the lowlanders look up to the whites and feel an inferiority complex in relation to them, the more they look down with a superiority complex on the short, dark-skinned Ayta.

Before the eruption, however, most of the lowlander Filipinos, except for those living in the towns near Mt. Pinatubo, were not conscious at all of the presence of the Ayta. In this sense the Ayta were invisible and did not exist. Although schoolchildren learned that the Ayta were the first migrants to this archipelago, they easily forgot it and never remembered or imagined that these people existed in contemporary society. The eruption of Mt. Pinatubo suddenly turned a spotlight on the Ayta, and their subsequent sufferings attracted the nationwide attention and concern of the general public through the mass media.

Concluding Remarks: Exodus and Ayta Consciousness

Before the eruption, Pinatubo Ayta society was not culturally homogeneous. Individual Ayta were located on a gradual continuum between the two ideal types of "culturally pure" Ayta living on the higher parts of Mt. Pinatubo on the one hand and the Christian lowlanders on the other hand. After the eruption this diversity has widened much further. In general, the Ayta who maintain the "traditional" way of life by practicing swidden cultivation are becoming fewer in number. Even though individuals may maintain a strong identity of being Ayta, they may still be strongly influenced by the lowlanders. In terms of material culture and life style, the Pinatubo Ayta will, on the whole, move step by step closer to the Christian lowlanders' way of life.

Contrary to my worries about their ethnic and cultural survival after the eruption, their consciousness of being Ayta has been strongly enhanced through interaction and negotiations with lowlanders, government employees, and NGO staff, and even with foreign journalists and philanthropists. From their mixed feelings of depression and revulsion against the lowlanders' scornful attitudes, they have been led to realize that they are discriminated against because of being Ayta. At the same time, however, they also understand that they are being given special aid and consideration by support agencies also because of being Ayta.

They are keenly aware of the fact that they were the people who suffered most violently from the eruption, not only from the deaths of close relatives but also from the hardship of life both in the evacuation centers and resettlement sites. They feel that all the Pinatubo Ayta share this fate equally.

Moreover, a couple of years after the eruption, Ayta residents in each resettlement site started to establish small grass-roots organizations among themselves according to residential and factional subdivisions in order to qualify as beneficiaries of government or NGO projects, and to apply for funds for their own subsistence projects. These small grass-roots organizations have formed in turn regional umbrella organizations such as PINATUBO in the IBA-Botolan area, ADA in the Subic-Olongapo area, and, at the widest level, CLAA, the Central Luzon Ayta Association. Because of the eruption, through their exodus and suffering, and through their exposure to and struggles in lowland society, the Pinatubo Ayta have strengthened their ethnic identity and, more importantly, have established solidarity among themselves.

They have been facing the same problems as other indigenous people like the Tasaday in Mindanao (Headland 1992), the Batak in Palawan (Eder 1987) and the Agta in the Sierra Madre of Northeastern Luzon (Rai 1990). The common problem of these groups is how to secure a geographical space in which to make a living as well as a sociopolitical position in which they can enhance their human, civil, and ancestral rights, given that they can no longer live in the isolation from the outside world nor maintain the basic resources necessary for their livelihood. The urgent issue for them is to find a way to avoid being absorbed totally and helplessly within the political and economic system of the modern world, at the very bottom of the hierarchical social order.

The Tasaday, for example, are caught in a dilemma. If they are a true "Stone Age" people, they are not allowed to live as our contemporaries and citizens with equal status, but are excluded as an exotic and confined to cultural preservation schemes resembling human zoos. But if they are not "Stone Age," they become a mere ethnic minority with no legitimate claim to cultural uniqueness or special rights as a group (Bodly 1992).

When the leaders of the Ayta groups recognized this same dilemma and decided to try and survive with dignity in lowland society, demanding their rights as indigenous people as well as Filipino citizens, they started to use the term *kultura nin Ayta* (culture of Ayta) frequently. When they apply for funds for subsistence and other projects, they usually explain the urgency and the necessity of a project as being indispensable for the restoration and maintenance of the Ayta community with its distinctive culture. Consciousness raising and the frequent use of Ayta culture is, in one sense, an appropriation of the tactics of the NGOs. They explain that special assistance to the Ayta has priority over that to lowlander refugees by emphasizing the importance of the Ayta cultural heritage for the sake of the continuity, integration, and development of the community.

It is interesting to note that the Ayta utilize bows and arrows as the symbol of their indigenousness. They follow a seemingly contradictory strategy of describing themselves as hunters so as to recover the Clark Air Base and other ancestral lands in order to become self-reliant farmers, besides getting other special assistance. Bows and arrows represent not primitiveness but their indigenous status and aggressiveness in fighting for their rights and dignity.[2] Although this kind of self-representation runs the risk of strengthening the stereotypes and prejudices of the general public through the media reports – which often call them ironically "our ancestors" with mixed feeling of contempt and respect – it is still effective in their cultural politics thanks to strong support from foreign and domestic NGOs, as well as from progressive urban intellectuals.

Notes

1 According to the Department of Health record, 483 people died in evacuation centers within four months from the eruption to 11 October and more than 90 percent of them were Ayta. If we count those whose deaths were not reported or who died outside the centers, the total toll would be far more than one thousand. The LAKAS group of western Pinatubo, which was most functionally organized and well-supported by foreign funding agencies, recorded sixty deaths among 240 families in a population of one thousand (Koshida, 1993: 256). If the overall mortality rate was 6 percent, the total number of deaths among the Ayta would have been around two thousand.

2 Such a strategy of cultural politics is neither unique nor isolated, and the Kayapo of the Brazilian Amazon, for example, present another illuminating case. Turner reports that "In 1986–87, and even more in 1989, it was common to hear Kayapo leaders and ordinary men and women speaking about continuing to follow their cultural way of life and defending it against assimilative or destructive pressures from the national society as the animating purpose of their political struggle" (1991: 304).

References

Bodley, John. 1992. "The Tasaday debate and indigenous people," in *The Tasaday Controversy*, ed. Thomas Headland. Washington D.C.: American Anthropological Association.

Brosius, Peter. 1983. "The Zambales Negritos: swidden agriculture and environmental change," *Philippine Quarterly of Culture and Society* 2 (1–2).

Eder, James. 1987. *On the Road to Tribal Extinction*. Berkeley: University of California Press.

Headland, Thomas. 1992. "The Tasaday: a hoax or not?" in *The Tasaday Controversy*, ed. Thomas Headland. Washington, D.C.: American Anthropological Association.

Koshida, Takashi. 1993. "Jiritsu e no mosaku" [Groping towards autonomy], *Hokkaidô Daigaku Kyôikugakubu Kiyô* 60.

LAKAS. 1991. *Eruption and Exodus: Mt. Pinatubo and the Ayta of Zambales.* Quezon City, Claretian Publications.

Rai, Navin. 1990. *Living in a Lean-to: Philippine Negrito Foragers in Transition.* Ann Arbor: The Regents of the University of Michigan.

Sahlins, Marshall. 1972. *Stone Age Economics.* Chicago: Aldine Publishing Co.

Shimizu, Hiromu. 1989. *Pinatubo Ayta: Continuity and Change.* Quezon City; Ateneo de Manila University Press.

Turner, Terence. 1991. "Representing, resisting, rethinking: historical transformations of Kayapo culture and anthropological consciousness," in *Colonial Situations*, ed. G. Stocking, Jr. Madison: University of Wisconsin Press.

Chapter 12

Cultural and Religious Identities in Okinawa Today:

A Case Study of Seventh-Day Adventist Proselytization

in a Northern Okinawan Village

Bachtiar ALAM

A homogeneous population, as Kelly (1991: 416) has aptly put it, has been one of the ideological homilies of cultural nationalism in twentieth-century Japan. It is true, that while Japan is unusual in having a two-millennium history in which ethnic, political, and linguistic boundaries have been largely coterminous, it remains a dangerous fallacy to conflate boundary isomorphism with internal homogeneity. Because homogeneity has been one of the most salient ideological preoccupations of the modern Japanese nation, the presence of ethnic minorities and other marginals in Japan – the Ainu, the *burakumin*, the Koreans, the Okinawans, etc. – poses an intricate problem, both conceptual and political.

In addressing the issue of the dynamics of local and national culture in Southeast Asia, this paper examines the cultural and religious identities of the Okinawans, the ethnic minorities inhabiting the southern end of the Japanese archipelago. Having developed an indigenous Okinawan culture and language varying from those of the rest of Japan, the Okinawans have long been stigmatized as disadvantaged marginals whose distinctive ethnicity nevertheless presents a powerful argument against the myth of Japanese homogeneity. This inimitable position of Okinawan society offers a valuable vantage point for the analysis of the relationship between local and national culture, a dissenting perspective that is particularly useful to understand better the contested and cooptive nature of ethnic diversity and national unity in Southeast Asia. This study focuses on one particular aspect of cultural processes going on in Okinawa today, i.e. the proselytization by a particular Christian sect, namely Seventh-Day Adventism, in a northern Okinawan village. The subject was chosen for its potential to shed light on the multiplicity of cultural and religious identities in Okinawa today.[1]

Okuma: A Profile

Okuma, a small village in northern Okinawa where the fieldwork for this study was conducted from 1992 to 1993, lies on the eastern coast of Kunigami – a district located in the northern extremities of the island – where much of the land is mountainous and there are only a few isolated valley areas with marginal fields between the steep hills and the sea.

A three-hour drive from Naha, the capital of Okinawa prefecture, Okuma, like most of the other villages or *shima* (literally "island" in standard Japanese), displays a tightly nucleated settlement pattern whose spatial form is determined by the surrounding hills and open fields. With a population of 547 as of December 1992, Okuma has a village council hall (*koominkan*), an elementary school, a village cooperative (*kyoodooten*), and a number of sacred places, including an *utaki* (a sacred grove), a Taoist monument, and a Buddhist shrine, as well as a religious building that is somewhat unusual in Okinawa, a Seventh-Day Adventist Church.

Traditionally, the northern part of Okinawa where Okuma is situated is referred to as Yanbaru (literally, "plain on a mountain"), a term that is slightly derogatory, connoting the supposedly backward and uncultivated life style of the north as opposed to the refined and cosmopolitan culture of Shuri, the former capital of the Ryukyu kingdom. Okuma, however, is one of a few villages in the north that claim strong historical (and mythical) ties with the Shuri court.

Okinawan Religion: An Overview

Religious practices in Okinawa are traditionally centered around two distinct but interrelated ritual complexes, i.e. agrarian rites and ancestor worship, with two major religious specialists representing each of them, namely the priestess (*noro*) and her cult organization who officiates at all the agricultural rites, and the female shaman (*yuta*) who performs all the rituals related to death. As is evident in the case of priestesses and female shamans, ritual leadership in Okinawa is monopolized by females, which is a manifestation of a distinctively Okinawan notion of the spiritual predominance of females over males.

While the majority of agrarian rites in Okinawa pertain to the cultivation of rice, wheat, and sweet potatoes, ancestor worship is focused on death rites such as funerals and memorial services which are normally considered "impure" and therefore cannot be performed by the priestesses. Further, in contrast to the village priestess's office that is passed along a specific patrilineal line in the village, with the eldest daughter of a stem family being the most likely successor, a female shaman's status has to be acquired, most often through spirit possession and recognition by another shaman.

Closely related to the role of female shaman is the concept of *sadaka* or the gift of a high degree of spiritual power (*sa* means "spiritual power" and *daka* means "high"). As stated earlier, in Okinawa women are generally regarded as having potentially great spiritual power, but certain individuals, normally women but also men in some cases, are regarded as being gifted with extraordinarily strong supernatural power which enables them to communicate with spirits, notably with the spirits of the dead as well as *kami* or divine spirits. Traditionally, such people would eventually become shamans but nowadays there are many who claim to be *sadaka* without becoming professional shamans. This qualification, *sadaka*, is not something that one can acquire, nor can one reject it. Those who are gifted with such supernatural power are normally unaware of their spiritual capacity until they eventually realize it through certain supernatural indications such as disturbing dreams, auditory and visual hallucinations, and various mental and physical disorders including physical debility or illness, loss of appetite, vomiting, nausea, dizziness, delusions, insomnia, and so forth. When such symptoms persist, the family members will suspect that these sufferings may be due to the person's spiritual qualities and consult a shaman. Whether or not one is *sadaka* has to be recognized by a shaman, who will subsequently instruct the person in becoming a shaman if she so wishes, until she identifies her own tutelary deity (*chijist*).

Despite such differences between the priestess and the female shaman, the hitherto available anthropological literature on Okinawan religion (e.g. Itoh 1980, Kreiner 1968, Lebra 1966) has emphasized a unique complementarity between agrarian rites and shamanism as being two interrelated facets of Okinawan religion. Such a "traditional" form of religious practice, however, has been significantly disturbed by recent social changes. The shift in Okinawan agriculture from the rice farm to the sugarcane and pineapple plantation has severed the conceptual ties between agriculture and the communal rituals performed by priestesses. Agrarian rites, which were once numerous and diverse, have therefore been reduced and simplified, and in most parts of Okinawa the simplification of agrarian rites is accompanied by the vacancy of the office of the priestess. But on the other

hand, ancestor worship in each household and kin group has been reinvigo-
rated – seemingly in inverse proportion to the decline of communal religion
– and at the same time people's reliance on shamanism in all the matters
concerned with death and ancestor worship has increased, resulting in the
consolidation of the formerly ambiguous patrilineal system of Okinawa. Further, the agricultural shift in Okinawa has brought about a thorough integration of the island into the larger capitalist market of Japan, one of the
inevitable consequences of which is the influx of world religions, especially
Buddhism, Taoism and Christianity, into Okinawan rural communities.

Christianity in Okinawa

Beyond the Buddhist and the Taoist influences in the distant past, Okinawan
society has been exposed to the influences of other foreign religions in more
recent times. The most evident among these is Christianity, a particular sect
of which called Seventh-Day Adventism has left an indelible mark on the
religious scene of Okuma.

Christian missionaries began to appear in Okinawa in the sixteenth century when the burgeoning Western powers sought to gain access to East
Asian shores, but for several centuries they were unable to achieve any significant results due to the severe persecution of Christians by the Japanese
military rulers who conquered Okinawa in 1609.

More vigorous proselytization in Okinawa was achieved under the American occupation. Following the complete devastation of the Battle of Okinawa
in which 150,000 civilians are said to have perished, Okinawans in general
were severely bewildered and traumatized by their war experiences, and the
Christian missionaries found fertile ground for their evangelism in this war-
stricken island. As may be readily supposed, most of the missionary work
during this period was carried out by American evangelists. Catholic
proselytization was undertaken in 1947 by two Franciscan priests who had
been working in Guam. Protestant evangelism was initially promoted by
American military chaplains, but later in 1947 a non-denominational
Okinawan Christian Association (Okinawa Kirisuto Renmei) was founded
under the leadership of local ministers. The association was subsequently
developed into an ecumenical body called the United Church of Christ in
Okinawa (Okinawa Kirisuto Kyôdan), modeled after the Japanese counter-
part. Since then this Protestant non-denominational organization has been
particularly articulate in voicing its pacifist stance throughout the turbulent
years of Okinawan politics evolving around the issue of the removal of American military installations.

Figure 1. Christian Believers and Organizations in Japan by Prefecture

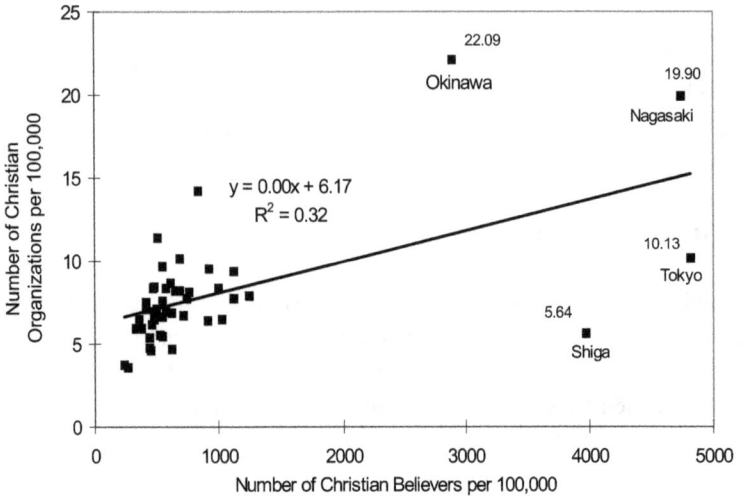

Source: Data on the number of Christian believers and organizations from Shukyo Nenkan (Annual Statistics of Religion), 1993; data on population from 1990 Population Census of Japan.

As a result of such missionary work, the number of Christian organizations and believers in Okinawa has steadily increased, giving the prefecture one of the highest concentrations of Christian believers and organizations in Japan.[2] Figure 1 shows the figures per 100,000 people, compared to other prefectures in Japan. It is evident that at 22.09 per 100,000, Okinawa has the highest concentration of Christian organizations in the country, exceeding that of Nagasaki, the historical center of Japanese Catholicism, and nearly twice as high as the national average of 12.86. In terms of the concentration of Christian believers, Okinawa ranks fourth highest after Tokyo, Nagasaki and Shiga,[3] with nearly 2,900 per 100,000. The high concentration of Christian organizations in Okinawa clearly indicates the peculiar characteristics of Christian movements in the island, which are marked by the profusion of small, independent churches and sects.

Such a distinctive development of Christianity in Okinawa notwithstanding, the subject of Christian propagation has been largely ignored in conventional Okinawan studies which have been overwhelmingly preoccupied with "traditional" Okinawan culture and religion. Notable exceptions to this general trend can be found in such non-standard areas of Okinawan studies as Takaishi's work (1984) on folk beliefs and mental health, which discusses the cases of mental disorders related to conversion to religions of foreign origin; Anzai's pioneering works (1976; 1984) on the propagation of Catholicism and sectarian new religions; and Ikegami's innovative monographs (1991; 1993) on a charismatic Christian church. In accounting for the limited scholarly attention accorded to Christian proselytization, Ikegami (1991: 14–15) struck a particularly insightful note when he pointed out that Christianity in Okinawa has been the subject of academic consideration only from two highly parochial perspectives. The first is represented by a few reports written from the missionary point of view, which discuss the relationship between Christianity and Okinawan culture insofar as it throws light on evangelical strategies for overcoming the indigenous magical beliefs and ancestor worship. The second is the perspective often found among students of "traditional" Okinawan culture and social organization, which views the evangelical Christian movement in Okinawa as a disruptive alien influence contributing to the destruction of indigenous social life. But neither of these perspectives, understandable though they are, examine Okinawan Christianity and its relationship to the local culture as a subject for research in its own right. It is only in recent innovative works that such an issue begins to figure prominently, with the result that Ikegami (1993: 75) unequivocally concludes that we "cannot ignore the close relationship" between charismatic Christianity and the indigenous spirit world of folk shamanism.

In what follows we shall examine a specific example of the local experience of Christianity in Okuma, and the distinctive form it has taken in the Christian movement known as Seventh-Day Adventism.

Seventh-Day Adventism: An Overview

In order to understand how this Christian movement that originated in the nineteenth-century millenarian revival in the eastern United States has come to take root in a small village in Okinawa, it will be necessary first to sketch the movement's formative development and the basic contours of its doctrine.

As is well known, the American Revolution and the formation of the Republic in the struggle against Britain were viewed in unambiguously millenarian terms, and the resulting civil millenarianism was soon transformed into Christian revivalism in the early nineteenth century (Bull 1989: 179–180). Thus when a former army officer named William Miller began preaching as a Baptist minister, he did so within a religious milieu marked by fervent anticipation that the millennium was imminent. He prophesied on the basis of the apocalyptic books of Daniel and Revelation – and especially on the basis of the verse in Daniel 8, "Unto two thousand and three hundred days; then shall the sanctuary be cleansed" – that the second coming of Christ would take place around the year 1843. His teachings drew a large number of followers who came to be known as Adventists or Millerites, and after a number of attempts, they eventually settled on 22 October 1844, as the date for Christ's coming, i.e. the Day of Atonement falling on the tenth day of the seventh month in the Jewish calendar.

The uneventful passing of the day, however, brought about the "Great Disappointment" among the Millerites, who subsequently splintered into several factions. The majority, including Miller, admitted their exegetical fallacy but adamantly continued to expect Christ's return without setting a new date. This group eventually coalesced into the Advent Christian churches. A handful of other Adventists, however, refused to renounce the significance of the prediction in the Book of Daniel, and they adopted the view that only the event, not the date, had been wrong: "that instead of our High Priest coming out of the Most Holy of the heavenly sanctuary to come to this earth on the tenth day of the seventh month, at the end of the 2,300 days, he for the first time entered on that day the second apartment of that sanctuary and that he had a work to perform in the Most Holy before coming to this earth" (quoted in Butler and Numbers 1987: 180). This group of staunch Adventists soon espoused a doctrine that the observance of Saturday as the Sabbath as required by the Ten Commandments, instead of Sunday, was essential to facilitate Christ's second advent. Hence, they later came to be known as the "Seventh-Day Adventists."

Among such early fundamentalists was Ellen Gould Harmon, a sickly, introverted adolescent ecstatic from Portland, Maine. Harmon was born in 1827, raised as a Methodist, and when she was nine an angry schoolmate hit her in the face with rock, knocking her unconscious for three weeks, during which "she fell senseless, hemorrhaging profusely, and … remained in a stupor" (Butler 1991: 6). But these profound physical and spiritual ordeals transformed her into an intensely religious person, who soon began to have numerous visionary experiences confirming the Millerites' interpretation of the 1844 incident and the importance of the observation of the Sabbath on Saturday. She subsequently married James White, the group's leading theologian and biblical exegete, and decided to take up a prophetic career. Ellen White, as she was later to be better known, along with her husband, built up the Seventh-Day Adventists (the name officially adopted in 1860) as a church. In this, James White served as organizer and entrepreneur while Ellen played the role of exhorter and visionary (Butler and Numbers 1987: 180).

What is most illuminating in Ellen White's life history as summed up above is the striking resemblance of her prophetic initiation to the general pattern of the shamanic career. Like so many shamans in the non-Christian religious traditions, her early life was characterized by extreme physical and psychological torments which eventually led her to see them as "divine afflictions" urging her to yield and assent to her calling. After her initial trance experiences, she too, like neophyte shamans, was reluctant to take up a prophetic role until she learned that her hesitation only aggravated her already impaired health. And even after embarking on her prophetic career, she conceded that she was "led by no one but the 'angel messenger' who appeared in each of her visions, whom she referred to variously as 'the angel,' 'my guide,' 'my instructor,' or 'the young man'" (Butler 1991: 15), suggesting her special relationship with an angel similar to the tutelary deity in shamanism. So suggestive are these commonalities that Butler, who studied Ellen White's early life, refers to Lewis's work on shamanism *Ecstatic Religion* (1977) and compares her passage to her prophetic role with shamanic initiation in which shamans "are badgered with afflictions and adversity until they relent and accept their vocation" (Butler 1991: 13).

The preponderance of shamanic characteristics in Ellen White's charismatic life may lead one to believe that such commonalities would certainly establish a powerful affinity between the teachings of Seventh-Day Adventism and the religious practices prevalent in Okinawa, but that is in fact not the case. The irony of the development of Seventh-Day Adventism, as has been pointed out by many (cf. Bull 1989: 177–78; Theobald 1985: 121), is that, despite its charismatic origin as exemplified in Ellen White's personality, the movement's doctrines in the course of its development became increasingly legalistic and biblicistic ("*sola scriptura* biblicism" according to Butler and Numbers, 1987: 180). This eventually led to internal conflict and tension as well as ambiguity in its doctrinal identity. Attempts to steer Adventism back to mainstream Protestantism, which cannot be elaborated here, occasioned a permanent rift between the "evangelists," who sought reconciliation with mainstream Protestantism, and the "traditionalists," who wanted to stick to the group's charismatic identity. The movement has now evolved from its distinctively charismatic origin into an plurality that embraces various shades of religious orientation and theological persuasion,[4] characterized by a curious combination of cult-like origin and sect-like ideology (Bull 1989: 178). An example that best illustrates this contradiction is that, although Ellen White as a prophetess and cofounder of the movement clearly demonstrated charismatic – or even shamanic – characteristics, Seventh-Day Adventism throughout its development has been "emphatically not Pentecostal" (Theobald 1985: 125–6). It claims that Pentecostal revivalism is a "counterfeit spiritual movement enacted by Satan who tries to confuse it with the genuine work of the Holy Spirit" (Chinen 1970: 32–39; White 1911 [1888]: 464). Consequently, the suppression of Adventism's charismatic heritage in the course of its attempt at rapprochement with mainstream Protestantism has occasioned a considerable ambiguity in its doctrinal identity.[5] Thus when Seventh-Day Adventism was first introduced to Okinawa in the 1950s, while the general attitude of the church leaders was favorably disposed to the rapprochement with evangelical Protestantism, the movement's doctrinal ambiguity provided ample possibilities for the development of a unique religious movement through its encounter with local religious orientations.

Seventh-Day Adventism in Okuma[6]

The circumstances surrounding the development of the Seventh-Day Adventist mission work in Okuma are reconstructed here based on the information gathered from the church members in 1992 and 1993. The evangelical work of Seventh-Day Adventism in Okinawa was pioneered by a repatriate from Hawaii named Yabiku Mokichi. A well-to-do entrepreneur, Yabiku established a soft-drink company called "Best Soda" in Okinawa soon after his return. His large household was in need of a housemaid, and in the early 1950s he hired a woman named Yamakawa Ushi,[7] who was an Okuma native and who happened to be spiritually gifted (*sadaka*). Ushi somehow became interested in the large volume of Christian literature found in the Yabiku household, and two particular books especially attracted her attention: the Japanese translations of Ellen White's *Great Controversy* (1888) and *Patriarchs and Prophets* (1890), which respectively represent the initial and the final stages in the Adventists' eschatological world view as illuminated by White's mystical revelations. Without obtaining permission from her employer, Ushi then brought back these books to Okuma when she returned home for her days off. She showed the books to her neighbors, young female high-school students who were full of curiosity, not only because they were young but also because the impoverished life in Okinawa at the time lacked any sort of distraction. As the number of young students gathering at Ushi's house grew, she began showing them the Adventist evangelical pamphlet *Yogen no koe* (the Voice of Prophecy), and she asked her employer Yabiku to arrange to send Adventist evangelists to Okuma to instruct prospective believers.

With Ushi as an intermediary, religious meetings began to be held regularly with the ministers from Shuri visiting the village monthly, and other Okuma residents who had been attending Methodist Christian meetings became interested in Adventism as well. But having introduced Adventism to Okuma, Ushi herself was not converted to Christianity. Throughout her life she maintained a good relationship with the Christian converts in the village, especially with the Adventist ministers who later took up residence in Okuma after the completion of the church in 1958. But she never became a regular attender of the church services and died tragically by drowning in the mid-1960s. She nevertheless left an indelible impression in the memories of many Okuma residents, which also had something to do with the fact that she in many ways epitomized the charismatic personality as sanctioned by the Okinawan concept of *sadaka*.

Ushi came from a kin group named Ota, which as described earlier, was also the kin group of the female shaman, Ota Haru, and she was known as possessing an extreme sensitivity to spiritual phenomena. She was married to a man from the Yamakawa clan, a small kin group in Okuma, and had twin children. Her family was said to be very poor, which was part of the reason she had to take up a job as a housemaid in Naha. Those close to her invariably remembered her as an unusually sharp-eyed, sensitive person with an inexplicable air of ethereality, whose often unexpected appearance at the church, an Adventist minister later recalled, "could somehow send chills down the spine." While she was unmistakably recognized by the fellow villagers as a *sadaka* individual who could hear and see spirits, she did not perform a shamanic role of any sort. One of the most respected Seventh-Day Adventist members in the village, Oshiro Kama, who was formerly the president of the women's association in the district, recalled that Ushi once prophesied three things: first, that of the two groves surrounding Okuma, one would be demolished; second, that the long-forsaken folk dance called *ushidoku* would be revived; and third, that something symbolized by three numbers (3-6-3) would happen to Kama's husband, who was the education secretary (*kyôikuchô*) of the district This referred to the new school system that would be adopted in the future, consisting of six-year elementary, three-year junior high, and three-year high schools. All these predictions, she acknowledged, later came true. Oshiro Kama is a devout Adventist, who entirely disavows the efficacy of any shamanic prophecy, but her admiration of Ushi's augury does seem to indicate the latter's unusual charismatic quality.

Despite the high regard accorded to Ushi, some other villagers noted that she nevertheless suffered a great deal from mental disorders caused by her spiritual sensitivity. Her husband's younger brother recalled that when she was spiritually disturbed, she would roam around the village in delirium; and one of her nephews remembered that toward the end of her life she was especially unstable and demonstrated deranged behavior such as throwing a stone at the ancestral altar and breaking dishes at midnight. The female shaman in the village, Ota Haru, who was also a patrilineal relative, was of the opinion that Ushi became deranged because she did not worship her tutelary spirit due to her attraction to Christianity. One day in the mid-1960s, Ushi was found dead in a river near Okuma, presumably because she fell into it while wandering around in delirium. Further details of her life and death could not be obtained at the time of the fieldwork as her husband and children had left the village after her death, but she was clearly remembered by many villagers as a person of great spiritual sensitivity, and as the person who introduced Seventh-Day Adventism to Okuma.

A number of Okuma youngsters who were first introduced to Christianity at Ushi's house later continued their education at the Seventh-Day Adventist mission college in mainland Japan and became ordained ministers and nurses. Other than these juveniles, many of the first Okuma residents who became interested in Seventh-day Adventism were *sadaka* individuals. One such individual was Sakihara Yasuo, who was one of the first Okuma residents baptized by the Adventist minister. Mr. Sakihara, who was born in 1928, had a life characteristic of a *sadaka* individual. He was of a fragile constitution as a child and able to see and hear spirits from the time when he was very young. In order to improve his health, however, he began praying at various sacred places in and around the village under the tutelage of the most influential female shaman in the area, who eventually revealed to him that his tutelary deities were *Misama nu kami*, the three Okinawan deities of heaven, earth and sea. As he discovered his own tutelary deities, he realized that he had to make use of his spiritual power for the benefit of others; thus while his main livelihood was agriculture, he decided to learn acupuncture as a way to engage in humanitarian causes, and opened a folk therapy practice at home. That sort of folk practice was in fact not entirely alien to him for many of his ancestors were engaged in midwifery and folk medicine. It was under such circumstances that an Okuma woman known as a *sadaka* individual, Miyagi Hatsu, invited him to a Christian discussion meeting held in the nearby town of Hentona. Hatsu had also been very sensitive to spiritual phenomena since she was very young, and was introduced to Christianity before the war when she was working for a cotton mill in mainland Japan. Later her husband died in the war and she started to practice Christianity seriously, and when she returned to Okuma she learned that a Methodist congregation met regularly in Hentona, and she decided to join.

After espousing Adventism, Mr. Sakihara came to a realization that his tutelary deities, *Misama nu kami* or the tripartite Okinawan gods, were actually the equivalent of the concept of the trinity in Christianity, and that the sacred grove of the village, Amangushiku, was in fact the temple of God the Creator. Having been enlightened as to the fundamental compatibility between Okinawan religiosity and Christianity, Mr. Sakihara along with Mrs. Miyagi embarked on coordinated efforts to propagate Adventism among fellow Okinawans, especially to those gifted with spiritual sensitivity. Soon another *sadaka* individual in the village, Matsuda Shinsei, who had often suffered an extremely intense state of *kamidari* (divine affliction) as though he was being electrocuted, joined the congregation, followed by other villagers.

The growth of the Adventist organization in the village and its appeal to many *sadaka* individuals understandably upset the "traditional" religious specialists. A person who was especially agitated was in fact Mr. Sakihara's former mentor, a prominent female shaman of the village, who explicitly chastised her protégé as disregarding "traditional" Okinawan religion. But shortly after Mr. Sakihara's baptism, the female shaman had a dream of a white angel with large wings descending by her bedside. According to her later recollection to Mr. Sakihara, the angel in her dream first addressed her as *ushiri*, "the woman born in the year of the cow," following the way religious specialists normally introduced themselves to *kami* (deities) in their prayers, and asked her a question in Okinawan, "gakumun yt nu chiji shomuchi shomushtsami?" ("could you uphold the spiritual power [*chiji*] of the era of knowledge [*gakumun yt*]?" She answered deferentially, "gakumun ya uruka, muchtsabiran," ("being an illiterate, I can't possibly uphold such a deity"). The angel then reportedly advised her, "wakati ukuringwa tu kukuru ittin ni shi, kami chiji muchiagirytni," ("work with young shamans [*ukukringwa*] with one accord, and uphold the spirit of the *kami* [*kami chiji*]"). She interpreted this dream as a revelation urging her support for Christian evangelism in the village, but she could not actually fulfill that command during her lifetime. On her deathbed, therefore, she expressed her remorse to another *sadaka* woman who became a Christian, Sakima Haru. "Kami [the childhood name of Sakima Haru]," she said, "I only worshipped my tutelary deity (*chijist*) in my life because I thought it was the right thing to do, but will I face a terrible fate after my death [for not following the angel's counsel]?" Hearing this remorseful confession, Hatsu's heart went out to the old female shaman, and she did her best to console her: "*Chane arando, oba; nt aransa*" ("Don't worry grandma; nothing of the sort will ever happen to you").

The implication of all these episodes, which are still remembered by Mr. Sakihara and other villagers, was that in the early stages of its propagation, Adventism attracted the attention of quite a few *sadaka* individuals in the village, which in turn somehow affected the religious discourses of the female shamans who were not interested in Christianity itself. The major social event that was taking place at that time, the start of the American occupation, might also have had a profound effect on the female shamans' perception of Adventism as a religion of American origin that would probably be dominant in Okinawa from then on. But in any case, these singular circumstances paved the way for further development of Adventism in the village. Another *sadaka* woman in the village also had a dream of an angel descending onto the land owned by her family, and in fact the Adventist church would later be built on that piece of land in 1958.

Interestingly, no severe objections from Okuma residents were encountered during this initial stage of Adventist missionary work. The only notable incident was the problem of the Saturday Sabbath observance. As stated earlier, a few youngsters were involved in the early Adventist congregation, and as they grew confident of the Adventist doctrines some of them decided to observe the Sabbath, which meant they would not go to school on Saturdays and instead attended the Adventist religious service. The fact that a number of junior high school students were absent from school and attending the Adventist gathering became known to their teachers, who reprimanded both the students and the parents. Since most of the parents were not converted to Adventism themselves, their children were severely chastised, resulting, in some cases, in domestic violence. The issue also attracted media attention and was publicized in the Okinawan newspapers in early 1954, becoming known as the *ansokunichi mondai* (the Sabbath day problem). The Adventist officials tried to solve the problem amicably by inviting the American Adventist educator, R.S. Moore, to give an explanation to the education department of the Ryukyu government,[8] but to no avail. The regional educational committee was not willing to make any exceptions for the Adventist students, and local high schools refused to give pass grades to those who skipped class on Saturdays. Consequently, some of the Adventist students had to be transferred to the church's mission school in mainland Japan so that they could obtain their high school diploma.

Aside from such a relatively minor confrontation with the state and the local authorities, in the 1950s the Adventist missionary work in Okuma progressed steadily, gaining unexpected support from *sadaka* individuals in the area. In the early 1960s, however, the church was confronted with an unprecedented predicament that was occasioned precisely by the participation of *sadaka* individuals in the congregation. This series of incidents, which took place in the summer of 1961, will be reconstructed here based on a number of interviews with the Okuma residents and the church officials, but especially by drawing on the diary of the minister's wife who witnessed it firsthand. The Adventist minister at the time, Rev. Nakamura Katusmi, a native of Shuri, was stationed in Okuma from 1960 to 1962, and his wife, Hisako, an Okuma native, was one of the young students who had initially heard about the Adventist teachings from Yamakawa Ushi.

The incidents unfolded around one particular church attendant named Ota Yoshio, an intensely *sadaka* individual from the Ota clan, who had been attending the church meetings for nearly a year under the tutelage of Mr. Sakihara. On 15 July 1961, there was a Bible study meeting at the Okuma church, and when the attendants were praying after the meeting, Yoshio fell into trance. He was attacked by a fit of shivering, and Mr. Sakihara led him out from the church to the parking lot, but Yoshio's condition remained critical; he continued to shiver and perspire profusely. The minister's wife, Hisako, who had been trained as a nurse, first suspected that he might be having an epileptic seizure, but she soon noticed that Yoshio was still conscious. Deeply concerned about this novitiate church member, Mr. Sakihara asked the minister, Pastor Nakamura, who was still in the church building, to take a look at Yoshio. A young pastor in his late twenties who had graduated from the University of the Ryukyus and the Adventist seminary in mainland Japan, Rev. Nakamura had never encountered a phenomenon like this. The only thing he could do was to pray with him to try to alleviate his sufferings, and it worked; immediately after the minister offered a prayer, Yoshio's condition returned to normal.

After this first incident, however, Yoshio began to fall into trances with increasing frequency. The next day, on 16 July 1961, he fell unconscious during the church prayers, and on 18 July, at around 2 a.m. he was found lying unconscious in front of Mr. Sakihara's house. Rev. Nakamura was called in by Yoshio's father to look after him, and after the minister offered a prayer on the site Yoshio immediately regained his consciousness. On 18 July, Yoshio came to the church accompanied by two *sadaka* individuals, Mr. Sakihara and Mrs. Miyagi; no sooner had they arrived at the church than Yoshio began praying by holding the minister's hand, and he started speaking in tongues, sounding like a prophet, counseling the minister: "The Father speaks through the eldest son of the Otas. You already understand everything in your mind," which Rev. Nakamura and his wife interpreted as an admonition against their inclination to understand Christian doctrines intellectually.

Due to this series of uncanny incidents, the attendance at the next Bible study meeting on 20 July suddenly increased, and all the participants were engrossed in fervent prayer. Having encountered successive occurrences of preternatural events, the newly ordained minister was at a loss as to what to make of them. On the night of 20 July he examined the scriptures, fervently attempting to find a biblical justification, but the psychological burden was too much for him and he developed a high fever, in which he was repeatedly reminded of Ellen White's mystical experiences. He concluded, after this ordeal, that while he was uncertain whether Yoshio's experiences were the work of the Holy Spirit or Satan, he should be supportive of Yoshio without being judgmental. The next morning, Yoshio and Mr. Sakihara appeared at the church early, and they told the minister that they knew he suffered a great deal the previous night.

All such incidents were soon known by the villagers in and around Okuma. On the next Sabbath religious service on Saturday 22 July, the church was inundated by an unprecedented gathering of around a hundred people. By then Rev. Nakamura and his wife had become convinced that the string of incidents which had developed around Yoshio was of religious significance. Over the weekend, therefore, they visited other Adventist churches in Shuri and Koza to share their recent experiences. Adventist ministers and officials, however, were entirely skeptical of the authenticity of such occurrences. The Nakamuras nevertheless continued to preach the significance of the recent incidents and to give impassioned testimonies on the imminence of Christ's second coming.[9] It was not long before the Adventist officials in Shuri decided to take action to correct what they perceived to be Rev. Nakamura's unwarranted approval and endorsement of a believer's spiritual possession. The argument put forth by one of the officials was that the trance experiences of Ota Yoshio were definitely not occasioned by the Holy Spirit, for while it would be understandable if an ordained minister had such a spiritual experience, it was entirely inconceivable that a lay believer, let alone one who had not been baptized, could have had such an revelation. This view evidently suggested that Yoshio's experiences were the work of an evil spirit.

While some Adventist believers from other areas who attended meetings in Okuma to witness Yoshio's trance were convinced that they heard the "moan of Christ" in his utterances, the same phenomenon appeared as a heretical farce to the Adventist officials. One female evangelist recalled that when she visited the Okuma church during that period, the atmosphere was unmistakably peculiar, with a number of people experiencing spiritual possession and displaying strange behavior such as jumping out of the church window. In the following week, therefore, a tract was printed at the Shuri church warning the church believers of the fake prophet appearing in Okuma. By then it had become clear to Rev. Nakamura and his wife that none of the church officials accepted the religious significance of Yoshio's experiences. They were nevertheless not discouraged and adhered to their view that, rather than judging Yoshio's experience as heretical or evil, they should respect it and tried to guide him to the correct path of Adventist beliefs.

But in the meantime, the church officials' disapproval of Yoshio heightened. On 1 August, Yoshio visited the Shuri church to pray in front of the altar, but while he was praying one of the ministers reportedly approached him and asked him to leave the room because he was possessed by Satan. Yoshio, however, tried to be friendly and tried to shake the minister's hand only to be rebuffed by the latter. Rev. Nakamura arrived at the church right after this incident and he somehow consoled Yoshio and returned to Okuma with him.

After these incidents, Yoshio's mental disorder became aggravated, and his parents eventually felt that their son's spiritual sensitivity could cause considerable harm to their neighbors. They thereby decided to make the difficult decision to have him undergo psychiatric treatment. Yoshio was then confined to a mental hospital in Naha for a few months beginning on 24 August 1961. Yoshio's hospitalization practically ended his involvement with Christianity, but the predicament of Rev. Nakamura and his wife persisted. Having learned that the main evildoer had been confined to a mental hospital, the church officials became even more confident that the series of preternatural occurrences that had taken place in Okuma were the work of Satan. A number of church officials from Shuri including some American ministers were then dispatched to Okuma to reform and remedy the "straying" faith of the villagers. Particularly difficult for the Nakamuras at this juncture was the church officials' demand that they should admit that the Yoshio incident was the work of Satan. Rev. Nakamura and his wife, however, refused to do so, and their intransigence further instigated the ire of the local church officials. Coincidentally the president of the General Conference, the church's main governing body, was visiting Okinawa at the time, and the church officials in Shuri tried to seize upon this opportunity to have the visiting dignitary reprimand Rev. Nakamura for his deviation. The visiting church leader, however, was mindful of creating any rift within the burgeoning Okinawan mission, and thus assumed a more conciliatory stance. Rev. Nakamura therefore was not subjected to any official rebuke and was allowed to continue his missionary work at the Okuma church.

As for Yoshio, after being discharged from the mental hospital he gave up Christianity and continues to live in the village as a *sadaka* individual helping other people with similar problems. He conceded in 1993 that he still suffered a great deal from spirit possession; he could not, for instance, attend a funeral or visit a tomb for he would be possessed by the spirit of the dead and suffer from a high fever and hives. He noted with exasperation that the people from his kin group, the Ota, are particularly vulnerable to spiritual possession, a fact he attributed to the ritual violation of his kin group's tomb which is also shared by an unrelated kin group. Asked about the reason he abandoned Christianity, he maintained that while he had tried to find ways to cure *kamidari* (divine afflictions), the church was unable to help him.

The Adventist church in Okuma continued to increase in membership after these incidents, but the high concentration of *sadaka* individuals in the church congregation was a phenomenon peculiar to the 1950s and early 1960s. The church's attraction to *sadaka* individuals during this period was so salient that the church was once known among the locals as *furimun kyôkai* (the lunatic church), a designation which no longer reflects the situation at present although the core members of the Okuma church are still those who joined it in the 1950s and early 1960s. Mr. Sakihara and Mrs. Miyagi, for instance, are still active members of the church, although the latter has recently been confined to a nursing home due to her fragile health. Today, while there are no longer such dramatic incidents as the ones just described, the *sadaka* individuals belonging to the church still believe that their spiritual sensitivity is vital for furthering their Christian faith. One *sadaka* female believer who was still undergoing psychiatric treatment for her frequent hallucinations acknowledged that the best way to cope with the symptoms was to listen to hymns. One of the female pioneer believers in the area conceded that she had received numerous biblical revelations through her dreams, in which specific passages were highlighted for her. As stated earlier, as the Adventist movement has attempted a rapprochement with mainstream Protestantism, such mystical experiences by no means represent a mode of religious practice sanctioned by the church today. They therefore rarely surface in the official discourse of the church congregations, but many believers in Okuma continue to have such experiences. Reflecting on the incidents concerning Yoshio that happened thirty years ago, Rev. Nakamura, who is currently the minister of the Adventist church in Naha, commented that they had proved a turning point for his faith in the sense that they had taught him the importance of spiritual as opposed to intellectual understanding. He believes that this revelation further convinced him that a profound understanding of spiritual phenomena is indispensable for furthering the Christian faith because all spiritual phenomena are basically of the same nature. "Many evangelists who fanatically condemn *yuta* or female shamans," he said, "often do not have a deep understanding of the holy spirit." But such a view is perhaps not a largely accepted one in today's Seventh-day Adventism. And yet, there is no doubt that the local religiosity as represented in the concept of *sadaka* did play a major role in the propagation of Seventh-Day Adventism in Okuma as is evident by its impact on Rev. Nakamura's revised spiritual view.

Religious Process as Social Practice

Through a detailed account of the religious experiences of the *sadaka* individuals involved in the introduction and propagation of Adventism in Okuma in the 1950s and 1960s, this paper has tried to demonstrate that in the experiences of these spiritually sensitive individuals who at one point became keenly interested in Christianity but were eventually not converted to it, one can discern a paradigmatic case of what I call "religious process," i.e. a process of continuous interactions between individual subjects and the religious symbols, whereby the former articulate and appropriate the latter as part of their cultural strategy and project in a given social context. This model of religious process, informed by the evolving body of practice theories as exemplified by Bourdieu (1977), Moore (1987), Ortner (1984) and, most recently, Ohnuki-Tierney (1995), is specifically designed to capture the historicity of cultural change and reproduction in a unified analytical matrix.

This processual approach seems particularly effective in addressing such questions as to why in the 1950s and early 1960s a host of *sadaka* (spiritually sensitive) individuals in Okuma became preoccupied with Adventism to the point where even the female shamans who were not attending church meetings received a number of revelations relevant to Christianity. The string of events which unfolded during this formative period of the Adventist church in Okuma – a *sadaka* woman bringing Adventist study material from Naha, a few female shamans having visionary experiences of Christianity despite their opposition to it, a *sadaka* man falling into a trance in church meetings uttering biblical truths, etc. – can hardly be adequately accounted for by a conventional model of religious change or conversion. They are best illuminated by the concept of practice, which underscores the role of individual subjects while acknowledging a generative mechanism of practice that is not entirely conscious to the actors.

A case in point is the divine revelations experienced by two female shamans in Okuma. These female shamans were by no means sympathetic to the Christian cause; on the contrary, one of them, who was the most prominent female shaman at the time, was somewhat critical of her protégé being converted to Christianity. Nonetheless, she did have a visionary experience which she herself regarded as divine counsel to propagate Christianity; whereas the other female shaman had a premonitory dream about the founding of a church in the village, which is still remembered by Christian converts in the village as a fortuitous event foreshadowing the righteousness of their cause. The intriguing question here is, obviously, if these female shamans were against the propagation of foreign religion, why did they have such numinous experiences which in effect would favor the mission work? It is precisely such a question that practice theory seems most capable of insightfully explaining. Certainly, the female shamans as the bearers of "traditional" religiosity were by no means intending to lend a hand in the propagation of Adventism, but they were unmistakably aware of the radically changing social environment engulfing Okinawa at the time, as clearly indicated in the revelation received by one of the female shamans that all the *sadaka* individuals must be united in upholding the "spiritual power of the era of knowledge" (*gakumun yt nu chiji*). Thus while the revelation itself might be an unpredictable numinous experience, there was somehow an element of purposeful strategizing in that the receivers of the revelation intended to hold steadfast to the will of the deities while at the same time adjusting their religion to the new era. This curious interplay between an unintentional vision and a conscious anticipation illuminates the paradoxical point made above, that while practice is accomplished without conscious deliberation for the most part, it is nevertheless not without purposeful strategizing. Bourdieu (1990: 59; cf. Jenkins 1992: 70–71, 80–81) refers to this as a significant generative mechanism of social practice, i.e. "the subjective expectation of objective probabilities," the unconscious mechanism by which agents' subjective aspirations are adjusted to what they perceive as objective probabilities.

Such an understanding of religious processes taking place in Okinawa has a further implication for the study of Okinawan religion as such. As has been pointed out earlier, while considerable research has been carried out on beliefs and practices in each major domain of Okinawan religion such as priesthood organization, shamanism, and the influx of foreign religions, the interactions of these elements at the local level have surprisingly remained unexplored. Especially untouched is the relevance of "traditional" Okinawan religiosity to the adoption of foreign religions. Due to this oversight, many outstanding works on Okinawan religion have failed to discern and appreciate probably the most dynamic aspect of contemporary Okinawan religious life, that is the religious processes involving an encounter with world religions. A concrete example may help illustrate this point.

A recent excellent study of *kaminchu* or hereditary priestesses of northern Okinawa by Kawahashi (1992) provides a convenient case in point for this discussion. My only quibble with this otherwise deeply illuminating work – and I hope my critical comments on this work will be taken as remarks made by a sympathetic colleague engaged in a common collective enterprise – is that despite her apparent intention to present a "polyphonic" discourse on religious life in northern Okinawa, as is evident in her section entitled "Multiple Voices of the Village," the voices represented in the section, and in fact throughout her study, are predominantly those of the traditionalist perspective. This in a way is understandable given that the subject matter of her study is hereditary priestesses who normally subscribe to such a perspective, but why such disproportionate weight is given to this view is entirely inexplicable given her stated research problem, and therefore it appears to have something to do with her acceptance of the modernity-traditionality dichotomy. A concrete example of her argument will serve to clarify this point.

The main issue advanced in her description of multivocality in the village is the conflict between the modernist and the traditionalist perspectives. As Kawahashi (1992: 153–54) describes correctly, the village of "Rejoice" where her fieldwork was conducted is known for its progressive political movement, which in the past had created a rather naive modernist perspective that equated modernization with secularization as well as assimilation into Japanese culture. She thus notes with an air of surprise that one of her key informants in the village, a woman in her late seventies who was an active member of a leftist political party, did not endorse such a modernist perspective and was of the opinion that "the welfare of her village is only possible when the cohesion of the community through a strong tie to their ancestors' religion is achieved" (Kawahashi 1992: 155). Because of this view, this informant was deeply concerned about the religious diversity developing in the village, where members of about fifteen households had been converted to foreign religions such as Japanese Buddhist or evangelical Christian sects. This informant told Kawahashi with exasperation, "We are having a religious war in this village!" and that "Preserving the ritual practice of the ancestors is the only way to make our place a golden village" (Kawahashi 1992: 156). This view, which I refer to in this discussion as a traditionalist perspective, is certainly a legitimate viewpoint held by many Okinawans today who are concerned about the preservation of their cultural heritage, but it is surely not the only Okinawan view which opposes or differs from the modernist perspective. In fact, as has been shown in this study, many Okinawans who have been converted to a world religion are not only against the naive modernist perspective, but also believe that they continue to uphold or even invigorate their Okinawan identity precisely by converting to a world religion. The best example that illustrates this point is the Adventist believer in Okuma who discovered after conversion that his traditional guardian spirits, *Misama nu kami* (the tripartite Okinawan gods of sea, mountain and earth) were actually equivalent to the trinity in Christianity, and that the sacred grove of the village, Amangushiku, was in fact the temple of the God the Creator. The development of this sort of religious perspective, which is opposed to both the traditionalist and the modernist perspectives, and which I call nonconventional nativism in this discussion, clearly signals the contested nature of cultural and religious identities in contemporary Okinawa that can hardly be grasped within the single axis of the traditionalist-modernist dichotomy. And yet, the case study of the Adventist movement in Okuma has shown that while such a nonconventional view is distinct from both the traditionalist and the modernist perspectives, it is nevertheless firmly anchored in the particular local concept of the gift of spiritual power, or *sadaka*.

Conclusion

The foregoing discussion of the inadequacy of the traditionalist-modernist axis for explaining the multiplicity of Okinawan cultural processes suggests that the cultural and religious identities in Okinawa today are equally inexplicable from the conventional, binary scheme juxtaposing Okinawan "traditionality" or "ethnicity" over and against the totalizing images of Japan representing "modernity" or "nationality." It is true, as Benedict Anderson (1993) puts it cogently in his discussion of Dutch colonialism in Indonesia, that the language (and by extension, culture) of the colonizer provides access to modernity and the world beyond the colony. For young Indonesian intellectuals at the turn of the century, he suggests, Dutch provided such an essential function, thereby unintentionally contributing to the nationalist cause while at the same time functioning as the language of repression. Likewise, because Okinawa was once coercively annexed by Japan, it is undeniable that the Japanese language once played such a role in Okinawa, occasioning powerful dissenting discourses around such dichotomous axes as Japanese/Okinawan, modernity/tradition, and nationality/ethnicity. And yet, for most of the Okinawans today, having voluntarily endorsed the island's reversion to Japan, there seems to be no compelling reason to define their cultural and religious identities primarily against the background of the Japanese (or American, for that matter) hegemonic presence. This short study, which seeks to describe the development of a non-conventional religious perspective that still hinges on Okinawan cultural identities, is but a small attempt to demonstrate the complexity of the interplay between local and national culture.

Notes

1 This paper is based on my Ph.D. thesis (Alam 1995a) submitted to the Department of Anthropology, Harvard University, in January 1995. An earlier paper based on this material was published in Japanese as Alam (1995b).

2 So far as I am aware of, Ikegami (1991: 13, 213–14) was the first to point out the high concentration of Christian organizations in Okinawa. The continuous increase in Christian conversion in Okinawa, however, does not seem to be the case with all the Christian sects and denominations. Anzai (1976: 65) for instance has pointed out that the number of baptisms at Catholic churches in Okinawa showed a steady increase until 1954 but has presented a downward curve since 1960.

3 It is understandable that Tokyo as the largest metropolitan center and Nagasaki as the historical venue of Catholic missionaries in Japan should have a high concentration of Christians, but why Shiga, a small prefecture in the Kansai region, ranks as the third remains an open question.

4 Samples (1990) suggests that presently one can discern at least three distinctive theological perspectives within North American Adventism, i.e. evangelical, traditional and liberal Adventism.

5 The Adventists' denial of Pentecostalism has occasioned yet another ambiguity of its doctrinal position, evident among others in Ikegami's understandable but erroneous classification of Seventh-Day Adventism as a "Pentecostal" sect (1991: 26).

6 I am grateful to Junkei Ogawa of Komazawa University, who drew my attention to the preponderance of trance experiences among the early members of the Okuma church.

7 Appropriate pseudonyms are used for all the personal names of Okuma residents mentioned in this chapter.

8 The Ryukyu government was a civilian government organized under the American military occupation.

9 According to Rev. Nakamura, a testimony (*akashi* in Japanese) relating one's readiness for Christ's second coming is fairly common in Adventist meetings; but his testimony and that of his wife during this period were especially impassioned due to their unique experiences.

References

Alam, Bachtiar. 1995a. "Diverging Spirituality: Religious Processes in A Northern Okinawan Village." Ph.D. dissertation, Department of Anthropology, Harvard University.

Alam, Bachtiar. 1995b. "Okinawa no amerikanaizêshon saikôsatsu" [The Americanization of Okinawa reconsidered], *Shisô no kagaku* 33: 19–32.

Anderson, Benedict. 1993. "Imagining East Timor," *Arena Magazine* (4).

Anzai, Shin. 1976. "Newly-adopted religions and social change on the Ryukyu Islands (Japan)," *Social Compass*, 23: 57–70.

Anzai, Shin. 1984. *Nantô ni okeru kirisutokyô no juyô* [The importance of Christianity in the Ryukyus]. Tokyo: Daiichi Shobô.

Bourdieu, Pierre. 1977. *Outline of a Theory of Practice*. Cambridge: Cambridge University Press.

Bourdieu, Pierre. 1990. *The Logic of Practice*. Stanford: Stanford University Press.

Bull, Malcolm. 1989. "The Seventh Day Adventists: heretics of American civil religion," *Sociological Analysis* 50(2): 177–188.

Bunkachô ed. 1993. *Shûkyô Nenkan Heisei 4–nen* [Yearbook of religion, 1992]. Tokyo: Bunkachô.

Butler, Jonathan M. 1991. "Prophecy, gender, and culture: Ellen Gould Harmon (White) and the roots of Seventh-day Adventism," *Religion and American Culture*, 1(1): 3–29.

Butler, Jonathan M., and Ronald L. Numbers. 1987. "Seventh-Day Adventism," pp. 179–83 in *The Encyclopedia of Religion*, 13, eds. M. Eliade, and C. J. Adams. New York: Macmillan.

Chinen, Katsuyuki ed. 1970. *Gendai no shinri* [Contemporary psychology]. Naha: International Health Institute.

Ikegami, Yoshimasa. 1991. *Akuryô to seirei no butai*. [Evil spirits and the soldiers of the Holy Ghost]. Tokyo: Dôbutsusha.

Ikegami, Yoshimasa. 1993. "Okinawan shamanism and charismatic Christianity," *Japan Christian Quarterly* 59: 69–78.

Itoh, Mikiharu. 1980. *Okinawa no shûkyô jinruigaku* [The religious anthropology of Okinawa]. Tokyo: Kôbundô.

Jenkins, Richard. 1992. *Pierre Bourdieu*. London: Routledge.

Kawahashi, Noriko. 1992. "Kaminchu: Divine Women of Okinawa." Ph.D. dissertation, Department of Religion, Princeton University.

Kelly, William W. 1991. "Directions in the anthropology of contemporary Japan," *Annual Review of Anthropology* 20: 395–431.

Kreiner, Josef. 1968. "Some problems of folk-religion in the Southwest Islands (Ryukyu)," pp. 101–18 in *Folk Religion and the World View in the Southwestern Pacific*, eds. N. Matsumoto and T. Mabuchi. Tokyo: Keio Institute of Cultural and Linguistic Studies.

Lebra, William. 1966. *Okinawan Religion: Belief, Ritual, and Social Structure*. Honolulu: University of Hawaii Press.

Lewis, Ioan M. 1977. *Ecstatic Religion*. Harmondsworth: Penguin.

Moore, Sally F. 1987. "Explaining the present: theoretical dilemmas in processual ethnography," *American Ethnologist* 14 (4): 727–36.

Ohnuki-Tierney, Emiko. 1995. "Structure, event and historical metaphor: rice and identities in Japanese history," *Journal of the Royal Anthropological Institute*, 1 (2): 227–54..

Ortner, Sherry. 1984. "Theory in anthropology since the sixties," *Comparative Studies in Society and History* 26: 126–66.

Samples, Kenneth R. 1990. "The recent truth about Seventh-Day Adventism," *Christianity Today*, 34 (2): 18–21.

Sômuchô Tôkeikyoku. 1990. *Population Census of Japan: Preliminary Counts on the Population on the Basis of the Summary Sheets*. Tokyo: Nihon Tôkei Kyôkai.

Takaishi, Toshihiro. 1984. "Minkan shinkô to seishinka iryô" [Popular belief and mental health treatment], pp. 23–44 in *Okinawa no bunka to seishin eisei* [Okinawa culture and mental health], ed. Y. Sasaki. Naha: Kôbundô.

Theobald, Robin. 1985. "From rural populism to practical Christianity: the modernisation of Seventh-Day Adventism" *Archives de Sciences Sociales des Religions* 60 (1): 109–30.

White, Ellen G. (1890) *Patriarchs and Prophets*. New York: Pacific Press.

White, Ellen G. (1911 [1888]) *The Great Controversy Between Christ and Satan*. Mountain View: Pacific Press.

Chapter 13

Ethnographies of the Vanishing? Global Images and Local Realities among the Aborigines of Taiwan, 1600–2000

J.S. EADES

Introduction: The Dancers of Hualien

The idea for this paper arose from an almost chance encounter I had with the Ami Cultural Village outside Hualien, in eastern Taiwan, in the autumn of 1996.[1] It was outside the tourist season, and the taxi driver clearly thought it was an odd place to go at that time of the year. When I got to the "village," it turned out to consist mainly of an auditorium with a closed souvenir shop attached, and with a group of teenagers in sneakers, shorts and t-shirts playing basketball outside. Luckily there was a performance about to start, even though the five daily performances advertised by the guidebook had been reduced to two because it was off-season. The audience was much smaller than the number of performers (who included the young basketball players), and nearly all the dozen or so spectators, including myself, were from Japan. The lead dancer came and chatted to us before the performance in Japanese which he spoke fluently.

The costumes, dances and music of these performances appeared to be a mixture of Pacific Rim aboriginal folk motifs, seemingly drawing on Maori, Native American and Chinese elements: as the guidebooks said, there probably was not much that was specifically Ami about them, even though the songs were in the Ami language.[2] After the performance, as the younger dancers stripped off their feathers and settled down to a game of soccer in the dance arena, I asked the lead dancer if there were any videos of the performances for sale. He said that he had some back at his house, so we set off back to the center of Hualien in his Japanese car – he did not live in the cultural "village," which was just "for work." His family apartment was on the ground floor of a modern concrete building in the commercial area of Hualien, and was extremely spacious and well appointed by Japanese standards. In front of the television watching a Japanese cartoon was an elderly woman who also spoke Japanese, together with his daughter who did not. Her main language was standard Chinese, thanks to the media and the education system, but the members of the household tended to speak to each other in Ami which was the only language they had in common. The lead dancer himself spoke Ami, standard Chinese, and Minanhua (the main Chinese dialect on Taiwan), together with Japanese and a few words of English "because of his work," his contact with the tourists.

This mélange of high speed growth, recently reinvented culture and multilingual lifestyles resembles other recent descriptions of tourism in the aboriginal areas (e.g. Hsieh 1994b), and is merely the latest in a series of different guises in which the Taiwanese aborigines have appeared to various groups of outsiders over the years, including the Dutch, Chinese, British, Americans and Japanese. There is a large but diffuse body of documentation, including early Dutch, Spanish, and Portuguese records from the sixteenth and seventeenth centuries, material in Chinese from the Qing period, later nineteenth century accounts by missionaries, a mass of ethnographic material compiled by the Japanese during the colonial period, and more recent ethnographic accounts in Japanese, Chinese and English describing the contemporary scene.[3] A significant part of this literature since the 1970s has dealt with the process of Sinicization, the cultural assimilation of the aborigines to the Han Chinese. Even though the maps produced by earlier linguists and ethnographers present an image of neatly separated ethnic groups with distinct and bounded cultures and languages, movements across these boundaries have steadily increased as relative isolation has been followed by various forms of colonialism, incorporation into contemporary Taiwan and, most recently, the pressures of globalization. Thanks to migration from the Chinese mainland, and assimilation to the Han Chinese, the aborigines have gone from being almost the sole inhabitants to a small minority, less than two percent, within the Taiwanese population. These economic, political, and demographic processes have in turn generated a sequence of images and discourses characteristic of each historical period, and these have much in common with representations of aboriginal peoples elsewhere on the Pacific rim. It is this sequence of discourses and the descriptions in which they are embodied that form the subject matter of this paper. Drawing on the history and ethnography of the Taiwanese aborigines, I sketch a model of the developmental cycle of images of the aboriginal Other during the long process of incorporation into the world system.

The Aborigines of Taiwan: A Historical Sketch

Before the arrival of the first Chinese on the island in the fifteenth century, Taiwan was inhabited by ethnic groups speaking Austronesian languages who had settled throughout the island, including the broad western plain, the narrower eastern coastal plain, and the mountains in the center of the island that lie between them. Early Chinese and Japanese traders and settlers were joined by the Dutch, who arrived in the early seventeenth century and set up their headquarters near what is now Tainan on the western plain in the southwest. The Dutch became involved in the trade in deerskins and other commodities with the aboriginal hunters and the Chinese middlemen. Their relations with the aborigines generally seem to have been good, and they rapidly converted large numbers of them to Christianity, even teaching some of them how to read and write their own language in Roman script (Davidson 1903: 9–48). Dutch relations with the growing Chinese population were more ambiguous, and at times the Dutch were only able to beat off Chinese attacks with the help of their aboriginal converts. Inevitably the balance of power gradually shifted with the influx of larger numbers of Chinese, and Dutch rule did not last very long. The Dutch were expelled from the island by Koxinga (Zhen Chengong), a Chinese warlord who refused to accept Qing rule at the end of the Ming dynasty and who decided to move to the relative safety of Taiwan. The eventual outcome of this takeover was that the island was formally incorporated into the Chinese empire, as a prefecture in 1687, and as a province in 1887 (Davidson 1903: 49–101; Dillon 1998: 306).

Massive Chinese immigration, mainly Hakka from southeastern China, followed, and the aboriginal groups on the western plains of Taiwan were eventually assimilated or displaced.[4] However, the Chinese were able to exert less control over the mountainous areas of the central and eastern parts of the island. Here the local groups of aborigines largely retained their cultural identities and their independence up to the end of the nineteenth century. Their relations with the Chinese were often hostile and there were constant local skirmishes between aboriginal raiders and the Chinese soldiers and farmers located in the areas around. Punitive expeditions into the remaining aboriginal areas by the Chinese were frequent, but they failed to establish permanent administrative control, a state of affairs which lasted until the arrival of the Japanese at the end of the nineteenth century.

The Japanese had been involved in trade in the region, along with the Chinese and Dutch back in the sixteenth century, but with the establishment of the Tokugawa shogunate at the start of the seventeenth century, Japan closed up. There was an abortive attempt organized by the first Tokugawa shogun, Iyeasu, to establish control over the island, but it failed, and the unfortunate leader of the expedition was put to death, along with the rest of his family (Davidson 1903: 7). Japan remained closed for over 250 years, until the collapse of the Tokugawa regime.

After the Meiji Restoration of 1868, Japanese merchant shipping links with Taiwan developed once again. One of the most dangerous sea routes in the region was down the eastern coast of Taiwan, where many ships were wrecked by being driven against the rocky shoreline during storms. In many cases their crews and passengers made it to the shore, only to be attacked and robbed, killed or enslaved by the local aborigines (Davidson 1903: 110–22). In 1871, a Japanese ship was attacked in this way, and the result was a full-scale punitive expedition by the Japanese, with support from the Americans and British, against the aboriginal groups they held to be responsible (Davidson 1903: 123–69).

This incident also led to a diplomatic dispute with the Chinese. For years the Chinese had disclaimed responsibility for the eastern areas of the island, over which they had had little or no control. However, by this time they claimed that the whole island and its inhabitants belonged to the Chinese empire, and they complained bitterly to the Japanese that they had not been consulted before the raid, in which they would have willingly joined. They were also worried in case the raid was the prelude to a full-scale Japanese attempt to take over the island – a justified fear, as it turned out. After the 1871 incident, the Chinese backed down and agreed to pay compensation to the families of the shipwreck victims. Only two decades later, after the Sino-Japanese war of 1895, Japan took full control of the island after a last-ditch defense by local Chinese opposed to the Sino-Japanese peace treaty and the imposition of Japanese rule.[5] This rule lasted for a period of fifty years, until the island reverted to China at the end of the Second World War.

Unlike their predecessors, the Dutch and Chinese, the Japanese did manage to establish control over the entire island, including the aboriginal areas in the mountains. This process took a long time, and involved both the construction of a vast garrisoned boundary fence and substantial military force, as will be seen below.[6] The Japanese also extended the educational system to the aboriginal areas, and their schools there became something of a showpiece for their administration. As a result of this, Japanese became the lingua franca of some of the aboriginal areas, and many of the older people there are still able to speak it today. As one of the jewels in the Japanese colonial crown, Taiwan also attracted the attention of many of the pioneers of Japanese ethnology, and a substantial body of documentation and photographs of the aboriginal groups have survived from the early colonial period (Suenari 1995: 4).

After the end of the Second World War, control of Taiwan reverted to China and control by the Kuomintang (Guomindang) regime of Chiang Kai-shek (Jiang Jie-shi). In the late 1940s, at the time of the civil war between the Communists and the Kuomintang, there was a further massive influx of mainland Chinese to Taiwan, and the aborigines came to constitute an increasingly small minority within the Taiwanese population. When the Communist revolution was completed in 1949, the Kuomintang regime moved its base to Taiwan from which it laid claim to be the legitimate government of the whole of China. After the violent repression of Taiwanese students and intellectuals by the Kuomintang in 1947, academic discussions of ethnicity in Taiwan began to focus on the relations between the "mainland" Chinese and the "Taiwanese" Chinese, rather than the Chinese and the aborigines.[7] While American and Chinese researchers concentrated on the Han Chinese, it was mainly Japanese scholars who continued to carry out research among the aboriginal groups, the main figures including Toichi Mabuchi, the leading ethnographer of the prewar generation, who returned to the field in the 1960s, and his student, Michio Suenari.[8] Japanese scholars have concentrated on two aspects in their ethnography: variations in social structure and their relationship with other variables such as language and material culture; and the process of Sinicization, the assimilation to Han Chinese culture, as, for instance, in mortuary rites and the preservation of ancestral tablets (Suenari 1995). There has been comparatively little work on these groups by Western scholars, in sharp contrast to the massive literature which they generated on the Chinese of Taiwan during a period in which fieldwork on the Chinese mainland was virtually impossible.[9] This relative neglect reflected the increasing marginality of the aborigines as a declining percentage of the Taiwanese population. Many of them became absorbed into mainstream Chinese society through intermarriage, and today they only account for less than two percent of the Taiwanese population as a whole, just under four hundred thousand people out of a population of twenty million. The neglect also reflected the technical difficulties of aboriginal research which involved a large number of local languages, in addition to a diverse and sometimes rather obscure historical literature in Dutch, Spanish, Portuguese, Japanese, Chinese, English, and French.

But despite their increasingly marginal status within the Taiwanese population, these groups are very interesting historically, especially in relation to comparative studies of colonialism and ethnicity. In most other parts of the world local peoples were only subjected to control by one group of outsiders. In the case of Taiwan there were a succession of outsiders within the context of the developing global economy: the Dutch, the Chinese, the Japanese, European missionaries, and the Kuomintang regime from the mainland. Each of these groups of intruders from outside generated their stereotypes and discourses in relation to the aboriginal population, and these can be directly related to the political and economic contexts within which interaction with these ethnic others took place. Many of these are shared with other aboriginal minority ethnic groups in the Asia Pacific region and elsewhere whose members have also been variously seen as representing primordial simplicity, a threat beyond the frontier, targets for colonial development or Christian conversion, or as a potential basis for an ethnic tourist industry – which will bring us back to the dancers of present-day Hualien.

Paradise Discovered

As mentioned above, the Dutch on their arrival found most of the island occupied by aboriginal groups, with a few Japanese and Chinese pirates and traders operating along the east coast, and a growing population of Chinese immigrant farmers from southeast China settling in the west. They were instantly struck both by the beauty of the island, and the nature of the people. Campbell, for instance, quotes the description of the island by the early Dutch pastor, George Candidius.[10]

> The country is intersected by many beautiful rivers, containing abundance of fish, and is full of deer, wild swine, wild goats, hares and rabbits, with woodcocks, partridges, doves, and other kinds of fowl. The island contains also animals of the larger kind, such as cows and horses, the former having very thick horns with several branches. The flesh of these animals is considered very delicious ... The land is exceedingly rich and fertile, though very little cultivated ...
>
> The inhabitants are very barbarous and savage, the men being generally very tall and exceedingly robust, in fact almost giants. Their colour is between black and brown, like most Indians, but not so black as the Caffirs. In summer they go about perfectly nude, without any feeling of shame. On the contrary, the women are very small and short, but very fat and strong, their colour being between brown and yellow. They wear some clothes, and possess a certain degree of shame except when they wash themselves, which they do twice a day with warm water. At such times, if a man passes by and sees them, they do not mind it very much, if at all.
>
> On the whole, the people of Formosa are very friendly, faithful and good natured. They are also very hospitable to foreigners, offering them food and drink in their kindest manner and according to their means. (Campbell 1987: 9–10)

Although Candidius' account went on to give a detailed account of Formosan warfare and headhunting – on which many later writers were also to remark – the picture that he presents is generally one of simple nobility, unsullied by civilization. Later generations of European writers of course simply described the aborigines as "savage," but in Candidius' account it appears that the comparative simplicity of these peoples in comparison with the much more sophisticated (and therefore unpredictable) Chinese made a deep impression on the Dutch. Relations between the Dutch and the aborigines were to remain generally good through the brief period of Dutch colonial rule. Within the space of a few years, Candidius, his assistant Robert Junius and their colleagues were able to create a writing system for the local language. They were also able to create a sufficiently large body of aboriginal converts to help them ward off Chinese attacks for a while, before their final expulsion.

Dangerous Mountains

With the establishment of Chinese rule, the histories of the various groups of aborigines in Taiwan began to diverge markedly. The main recent synthesis of information on the plains aborigines during the Chinese period is the lengthy monograph by Shepherd (1993), which describes the various kinds of economic accommodation they made with the growing Chinese population. At first during the Dutch period, deer hunting formed the basis of the economy, with the Chinese acting as intermediaries both in the trade in deerskins and in tax collection. Chinese agriculture developed gradually, and the illegal acquisition of aboriginal land by the Chinese led to the Chinese government enacting legislation to protect aboriginal rights. As the deer disappeared, the aboriginal men were gradually reduced to subsistence farming, previously regarded as a women's occupation, while intermarriage and sinicization continued apace.

The groups in the mountains however were gradually seen in more and more negative terms. They were able to resist the advance of the Chinese until a de facto frontier developed between the two groups, marked by skirmishes, atrocities, and ferocious reprisals on both sides. Many new bones of contention arose along this frontier, in addition to long-remembered grievances. Davidson, for instance, recounts stories of early Chinese massacres of aborigines during their early searches for gold on the island. The image of "innocent aborigines" versus "perfidious Chinese" which he presents is a recurring one in the European literature:

Father de Mailla, one of the Jesuit priests who visited Formosa in 1715, and who gave the world much reliable information on the condition of the island in his days tells us that the Chinese lost no time, after the subjection of the plain savages, in searching for the treasures which had been so frequently reported as existent in the savage districts on the east coast. They equipped a small vessel that they might make the voyage by sea, rather than attempt the dangerous journey over the mountains. Hospitality was then considered a virtue by the savages; and on the arrival of the strangers they were given a generous and friendly welcome. Houses were placed at their disposal, food provided, and every assistance rendered them during the week they remained. Diligent search and persistent questioning did not reveal to the Chinese the location of the Gold deposits. They did, however, unfortunately find in one of the huts of the savages a few ingots of Gold, which the aborigines regarded as of little value. The Chinese .. invited the hospitable and unsuspecting savages to a grand feast ... The unfortunate guests on arriving were plied plentifully with intoxicating liquor, and, when in a state of semi-consciousness, were massacred to a man, and the Chinese, quickly possessing themselves of the Gold, set sail and returned to the west coast. (Davidson 1903: 462–63)

But it was not only Chinese who carried out these kinds of raids, as is reflected in the negotiations in 1867 between the American Consul at Amoy, General Le Gendre, and Tokitok, the chief of one of the local groups accused by the Europeans of killing shipwreck victims. Tokitok is reported as saying that "a long time ago white people had all but exterminated the Koolut tribe, leaving only three who survived, to hand down to their posterity the desire for revenge. Having no ships to pursue foreigners they had taken their revenge as best they could" (Davidson 1903: 120).

The European attitudes to the mountain aborigines during this period were therefore ambiguous. It is clear on the one hand that they had considerable sympathy for them because of their own dislike of the Chinese (who were also accused of a number of atrocities against European shipwreck victims). This comes out clearly in the accounts by George Mackay, a missionary who spent many years in the island, from 1872–1901 He visited aboriginal villages in the mountains and seems to have established some rapport with them – they were soon singing hymns together. He discusses both the intense hatred the aborigines felt for the Chinese, and particularly the camphor and rattan traders who were encroaching on their terrain, and he also describes (in grisly detail) the savage reprisals meted out by the Chinese on any aborigines unlucky enough to have been caught by them (Mackay, 1896: 251–77).

It is not surprising therefore that at the time of the Japanese takeover, the Japanese too should have seen the aborigines as a threat, though they did apparently try to contain it with much greater efficiency.[11] In the early years of the Japanese occupation, the government was mainly concerned with extending control over the plains in the east of the island with their mainly Chinese populations. In 1910-15 the governor-general, Samata Sakuma, conducted a pacification campaign in the mountains, "followed by land expropriation, forced relocation, and the establishment of permanent reservations" (Ching 2001: 135). The Japanese aim was to settle the ab-origines in administrative units, restrict hunting, and encourage rice culti-vation, leaving the forests free for exploitation (ibid: 135-36). A huge num-ber of police were drafted into the area, and they were responsible not only for law and order, but also teaching, medical care, general administration and forest management. Many of them apparently married local women.

Both the efficiency of the Japanese occupation and some of the prob-lems encountered are clear from an account by Owen Rutter, a British ad-ministrator from Borneo who passed through Taiwan in 1921. It is worth quoting his account in some detail as it describes well the methodical way in which the Japanese advanced the colonial frontier:

> Once the Japanese had established law and order in the territory which had been under the influence of the Chinese Government, they turned their attention to the aborigines. A committee for exploring the savage area was formed and a department for dealing with native affairs estab-lished. No unauthorized persons were allowed to enter the savage area without special permission, and an ordinance was promulgated forbid-ding anyone to occupy or lay claim to any land within the native terri-tory without special authority ...
>
> They soon found it necessary, however, to establish guards along the frontier to protect the camphor workers, and they revived the old institu-tion of the Chinese, which had fallen into disuse. The guard-line, or *aiyu*, as reorganized by the Japanese, consisted of outposts of military police; in 1895 it stretched for 80 miles and was extended later to 300. The line was advanced into the native territory when an opportunity arose, and the inhabitants who had been "suppressed" were then "tamed" ... Agricultural implements were given them; they were taught to plant rice instead of the millet which had hitherto formed their staple food; their sick were attended and supplied with medicine; salt and other nec-essaries were exchanged for the game and forest products they brought in.
>
> The guard-line was made by cutting a track through the forest, called the guard-road. It usually followed the summit of a range of hills, the

trees being felled for some distance on the native side, to make it possible to give warning of the approach of any aborigines and to afford a field of fire. At strategic points guard-houses, of which there are now over 800, were established and garrisoned, the average distance between each being a quarter of a mile ... In the *Report on the Control of the Aborigines in Formosa*, published by the Formosan Government, it is stated: "Where it becomes necessary to perfect the defensive arrangements, wire entanglements, *charged with electricity*, are used or mines are run. These have great effect in giving an alarm of the invading savages. *Grenades are very often used in the course of fighting.* Telephone lines are constructed along the guard-road, and in certain important places *mountain and field guns are placed.* One gun is sufficient to withstand the attack of several tribes." ... Beyond the outposts stretches what is looked upon as enemy country. ... Neither natives nor Formosans are allowed to pass the line without special permits ...

From time to time, as I have mentioned, the guard-line is advanced, and the territory so occupied is then available for development once it has been settled. In some cases the natives have themselves realized the advantages of living under settled Government, and then the occupation presents no difficulties. At other times every possible obstacle is put in the way of the advance, and a guerrilla warfare ensues in which the natives usually have the best of it, in spite of the troops equipped with the devices of modern warfare sent against them ...

As a rule the punitive expeditions, which have been frequent, achieved their objects, inasmuch as a certain number of natives were killed and a certain number of villages were burnt ... In some cases the failure of an expedition did more harm than good, for it left the natives defiant and with even less respect for the Government than they had had before ... And the fact remains, as even the Formosan Government must itself admit, that in spite of all these efforts and operations, in spite of these expensive expeditions and desultory campaigns extending for nearly thirty years, the natives of the Formosan hills, numbering less than 100,000, are still able to keep the Japanese out of half their colony and prevent them from developing what may yet prove to be the most valuable part of the island. (Rutter 1923: 226–32, emphasis in original)

The scale of the fighting can be gauged from the official figures for casualties during this period. According to the Taiwan administration, 7,100 Japanese and Taiwanese were killed, and 4,100 were injured between 1900 and 1930 in action against the aborigines. These figures do not include aboriginal losses which were not recorded.

Rutter's self-confident pronouncements on the failings of Japanese colonial rule, which he discusses at great length and compares with his own experience with hill peoples in Borneo, are also illuminating from the point of view of the comparative study of imperialism (Rutter 1923: 234–61). Japanese administrators appeared to him to suffer from two drawbacks in comparison with their British counterparts: they were lower class, and they were not English, as a consequence of which they lacked the sympathy of the local people. The solution to the Japanese administrative problems was therefore obvious:

> It seems clear that the Formosan aborigines are amenable to right treatment even when administered by an Asiatic. It is even clearer that they are prejudiced in favour of the white races. If the Formosan Government asked tomorrow for twenty young Englishmen with experience of administering native races, they would get the men to send into the Formosan hills. They would probably have thousands to choose from, and I believe that in this way the whole of the "savage" area could be settled in five years. (1923: 256–57)

Rutter also commented at length of Japanese education policy:

> We went on to the school for the children of the "tamed aborigines." The schoolmaster was one of the police. The children, who were out working in the fields on our arrival, were summoned by bell, and they came dashing back. They were all dressed in uniform grey kimonos and peaked caps, and they proceeded to give us an exhibition of musical drill with flags, the singing being in Japanese. In Japanese fashion, they bowed profoundly when the parade was over. ... The Japanese are very proud of these schools, of which there are over thirty in the island. They point to them as a sign of progress, as a testimony of their benevolent influence over the "savages." To me, however, it seemed pathetic to see these children of nature being, to coin a word, Japanized. ... The conditions under which they live are undoubtedly improved, but whether by the process of assimilation (which is admittedly the object of the administration) they do not lose more than they gain is a moot point. ... [T]hey forget their customs. They leave the villages simply upcountry native children, and in five years they return Japanese citizens. (Rutter 1923: 227–29)

Whether a British or French colonial school during the same period would have been much different in its aims, apart from the obvious differences in clothes, language, and flags, is of course a moot point.

Rebels, Collaborators and Converts

Despite these efforts, the fragility of Japanese rule is shown well by the so-called "Musha Incident," which took place at a local sports day in the Taiyal (Atayal) region of central Taiwan in October, 1930 (Ching 2001: 137-40). This brought together aboriginal, Chinese and Japanese children from local schools, the provincial governor, police officials and other guests. Suddenly the crowd was set upon by three or four hundred aboriginal men in traditional dress who killed 134 Japanese. This caused considerable shock because it took place in one of the most "enlightened" aboriginal regions, and because of the complicity of two distinguished aboriginal police officers who committed suicide rather than warn the authorities. The Japanese response was predictably massive, with around 3,000 soldiers and police brought in against the rebels (Ching 2001: 139). A number of official enquiries into the incident were carried out, which highlighed a number of problems including lax police discipline, and resentment at the government's use of forced local labor in construction projects such as the building of a local primary school (Ching 2001: 141-43).

Ching prefers to locate the causes of the rebellion at a deeper level: "aboriginal issues ... entail not only questions of colonial administration and aboriginal rule, but also the fundamental contradiction of Japanese colonial modernity itself ... the savagery displayed by the supposedly civilized Japanese nation and its civilizing colonial mission" (Ching 2001: 151). After the Musha Incident, "Japanese colonial attitudes towards the aborigines underwent a conspicuous shift ... The aborigines were no longer the savage heathen waiting to be assimilated: they were now imperial subjects acculturated within the Japanese national polity" (Ching 2001: 151-52). The new aim was to "enlighten and educate" the aborigines, and turn them into loyal citizens of the emperor. The colonial government stopped using the term *seiban* ("raw savages"), and substituted the more neutral *takasagozoku*, glossed by Ching as "tribal peoples of Taiwan" (Ching 2001: 153). During the Pacific War, many aborigines volunteered to fight for the Japanese. Years later, when they returned to Japan years later to demand compensation from Japan and the return of the spirits of their dead, they stated that "We Takasago people were Japanese during the war" (Ching 2001: 2).

Part of the reason for this transformation from might have been the massive expansion of education that took place during the 1930s. Mendel (1970: 21) notes that elementary schools had been established in all towns and cities by 1920, but that even by 1932 only one-half of the boys and one-fifth of the girls were attending grade school. Ten years later 90 percent of children were in school, including 75 percent of the aboriginal children, and by the end of the Second World War, 70 percent of Formosans were literate in Japanese. Ten thousand aboriginal children attended the special schools in the mountains.

Christians and Compatriots

The Christian missions also had considerable interest in the aboriginal areas as a possible sphere of influence. It is clear that during the early years of Japanese rule they had been very optimistic about making progress there – in part because they too had been on bad terms with the Chinese authorities before the Japanese takeover. In the event, however, they were banned from working in the aboriginal areas during the Japanese colonial period. It was not until the Pacific War that Christianity started to spread there, and that was the result not of mission influence but of a locally led revival movement similar to those in other parts of the colonial world, such as Africa or Melanesia. Freytag, himself a missionary, describes it as follows:

> Before the Second World War only those tribes living near the plains had any contact with Christianity. Very few tribesmen became Christians. They had little influence in their tribes and were regarded as traitors of the tribal way of life. The Japanese Government did not allow missionaries to enter the tribal areas. During the Second World War a movement toward Christianity started in the eastern part of the Atayal and among the Ami. The leaders of the movement were tribal people themselves. The first Christian groups came from tribal communities which had been transferred from the mountains into the plains and were already uprooted. The Japanese persecuted the first congregations. However the movement spread quickly along kinship lines and among the community of the tribes. The witness of the tribal people to their families and fellow tribesmen, but also the longing for modernization among the isolated tribal groups and a resistance against the Japanese motivated this break-up. In the persecution, the power of Christ was a vivid experience, and the tribal people identified with Christianity, the image of a new community – life based on mutual trust, truth, fidelity and love and the expectation of a higher standard of living. In the changing times they felt that their old religion had proved to be inadequate. Moreover, Christianity liberated them from the fear of animistic spirits and powers. Chinese religion, like Christianity, could not proselytize among the tribal people under Japanese rule. But it was an alternative for the tribal people. Until today few tribal families among the Ami and the western

Atayal have turned to Chinese religion. On the whole, the tribal people looked for a new start from their own. (Freytag, 1968: 18–19)

With the end of the war and the lifting of the ban on mission work by the Kuomintang regime, the missions, and particularly the Presbyterians, took the new converts under their wing. By 1965 the Presbyterian Church claimed 67,000 aboriginal members – approximately one-third of the total tribal population. Freytag estimated that Christianity had influenced about 70 percent of the tribal population and that the tribal Christians made up 30 percent of the total Christian community in Taiwan.

The economic processes which underlay this change can also be seen in Freytag's account. One of the results of the reversion to China was a change in the status of the aborigines, who were now given equal rights with the rest of the population. The new term used to refer to them officially was *shanbao*, "mountain compatriots." A large part of the mountains still formed a separate administrative region, but this separation was now based on special economic arrangements rather than a guarded boundary fence. Within this area, land was owned by the state, and Chinese could only use it with government approval. There were also restrictions on Chinese trade. The government also attempted to enforce agricultural development and reforestation programs. A process of land surveying, land registration and the allocation of non-forest land to the local people began in 1958, with the aim that it would gradually become private land and be absorbed into the national land market. At the same time, the exemption on the land tax, which the aboriginal peoples had enjoyed, also ended. With the collapse of the hunting economy and the end of shifting cultivation, the population was resettled in larger settlements to make service provision easier, a process that had begun during the Japanese colonial period.

Along with these changes went others. The local farmers who were successful were able to extend their holdings by acquiring land from those who were not, and Chinese farmers were also able to move into the area. Post-primary educational provision was also patchy. A large proportion of the population had started to go to primary school during the Japanese colonial period, and rates of primary school attendance were much higher in the tribal areas than in the population in general. However, even by the 1960s, only 6 percent of the tribal children were moving on to secondary school and beyond. Reasons for this included the poor quality of the teachers, who regarded working in aboriginal areas as a hardship post, and the small size of the schools. Efforts at positive discrimination simply gave the tribal children a feeling of being inferior students. Economic factors also played a part, as children from poorer tribal families had to drop out of school to help with agriculture either temporarily or permanently. Many families also doubted whether education was of any benefit in getting jobs, given the range of low status occupations generally open to them. The aboriginal population was still predominantly agricultural, the major exception being those that had sold their land, often to Chinese with better agricultural skills and more capital. Agricultural wage labor had become the most important occupation, and there was also a gradual drift of the aboriginal population into the cities.

The Other as Tourist Attraction

The end of Freytag's book touches on a point also made by Shepherd and others: the extent to which the processes of acculturation and Sinicization were resulting in the loss of ethnic identity, even though in some cases it was possible for ethnic identity to be "reinvented." Sinicization was proceeding fast, even in the mountain aboriginal areas, and was virtually complete throughout most of the plains. Even among the Pazeh, one of the aboriginal groups of the western plains which had held on to its own cultural distinctiveness the longest, the local language had virtually disappeared by the mid-twentieth century. Shimizu's more recent work on the Kvalan, an aboriginal group in the northeast, shows well the process of the erosion of ethnic distinctiveness there as well (Shimizu 1991; 1995). The Ami, on the eastern plains, on the other hand, still see themselves as a distinct ethnic group, and, as in the case the dancers of Hualien, it is the tourist trade which has been one of the major factors in the perpetuation or reinvention, of cultural tradition. Even in the 1960s, Freytag could see this point very clearly:

> However to become like the Chinese does not mean for the tribal people to deny their own cultural heritage. The economic problems have priority, but when people have reached a similar level as the Chinese they face again the question of their own distinct cultural tradition in the context of the wider society. Now they need no longer to approach this question from the aspects of self-defense. Rather it is possible to consider, what parts of the tradition could be mobilized to determine the way into the future not only that of the own group, but also that of the whole society. Such rethinking has already started where a fresh access to the cultural tradition has been gained. The popularity of tribal dances and songs is only a small, however very obvious part of this redefinition. The skills in wood-carving and weaving are becoming known ... Tribal people, who have learnt to see themselves on the same level as the Chinese and as a cultural minority in the wider country raise these ques-

tions. The way for them to keep their identity as tribal people is not a rigid conservatism but the openness to rediscover their own cultural traditions as a ferment for the wider community. For the present the process of continuing and popularizing tribal culture relies still heavily on commercial interests of dancing groups, mass-communication medias and shops. Besides this there is the small circle of cultural anthropologists at the National Taiwan University and the Academia Sinica which has conducted many anthropological field studies among the different tribes. But their findings are known only among a small group of experts with special interest in anthropology. Further local committees for the annual community festivals in the villages promote again tribal customs and traditions. Missionaries work on different translation programs into the tribal languages. It could be of great importance for the tribal people and the whole society to give these efforts a stronger institutional base in a center for tribal culture. (Freytag 1968: 44)

Freytag therefore concluded that the establishment of cultural centers was the way forward: to coordinate efforts, to promote information and exchange of ideas between the different interest groups; and to introduce a wider public to the cultural traditions of the tribal people. The centers, he suggested, should be related to an institution of training or higher learning serving the tribal groups. In fact, tourism was becoming established in some aboriginal areas soon after the end of the Second World War. Sun Moon Lake became especially popular, with the aborigines operating boats across the lake and posing for photographs in traditional costume.

Amongst the Taiwanese academics concerned with these issues, one of the most influential figures was Chen Chi-lu, a Japanese-trained anthropologist, and author of a detailed monograph on the material culture of the Taiwan Aborigines (Chen, 1968). In a later book, Chen also advocated the establishment of cultural villages as cultural centers. He was particularly concerned with what he saw as a decline in Taiwan art, with the collapse of the old stratification and chiefship systems which produced it, with changes in technique and design motifs, and with the flooding of the market with "fake" rather than authentic pieces as prices had risen. To him, the most important thing about ethnic art was that the "spiritual content find suitable expression" and it was this that would enable it to continue to develop. The processes could be assisted by a government organization for training in traditional arts, which could itself be located near other tourist attractions, as had happened at a Maori arts center established near a hot spring resort in New Zealand which he had visited. The result there was the establishment of a model Maori village combined with an institute for the study of

241

traditional art, which became famous throughout the country for its Maori-style buildings and woodcarving. Chen saw this, together with similar examples elsewhere, such as the Korean Folk Village near Seoul, as a possible model for aboriginal arts centers in Taiwan. He therefore proposed the establishment of cultural villages in Taiwan as training institutes, centers for the revival and presentation of the "immaterial culture" of crafts and performing arts, and as tourist attractions (Chen 1987: 75–78).

It is not clear to what extent Chen's wish that the "spiritual" dimension of traditional culture has been maintained and developed by these institutions, but certainly they have been established and have flourished to a lesser or greater degree as commercial enterprises. The fullest description of such a place in Taiwan is that by Hsieh Shih-chung (1994b). Interestingly, he discusses the Atayal of Wulai as an example of an indigenous people "who have lost all their own traditional artifacts, clothing and other attributes, and who ... have, in spite of no longer being culturally exotic, nevertheless devised a strategy for making a living from ethnic tourism." This recalls the seminal work on ethnicity by Abner Cohen who suggested in a series of studies that an ethnic group may display its unity using what are in effect completely new ethnic symbols and boundary markers (cf. Cohen 1974). It also recalls the insight of Eric Hobsbawm (1983), that many cultural "traditions" are in fact recent inventions. Hsieh argues that the creation of the "Atayal" as an ethnic group was actually a result of the work of Japanese ethnographers who based their findings mainly on linguistic evidence, rather than a common cultural core. Wulai itself, in which the Atayal are actually a minority, is well known for its beautiful scenery and hot springs, as well as its ethnic tourism. (Along with Sun Moon Lake in Nan-t'ou county, it became one of the best-known sites in the country, with around three thousand visitors a day.) The activities included dancing and the sale of ethnic crafts, as in Hualien, and the area attracted migrants from outside, both Atayal and Han Chinese, looking for economic opportunities. Despite this, Hsieh argues, there was little new development in the attractions on offer, and the tourist trade therefore continued to rely largely on foreign visitors and links with travel agents. Few of the commercial establishments belonged to the Atayal, though in some of them the Atayal worked for Han Chinese. The Atayal were also shareholders in two of the main enterprises in the Wulai Aboriginal Cultural Village, namely the performance area and the restaurant. The Naluwan Culture Plaza, a third enterprise which was privately owned, was in effect in competition with the Wulai Cultural Village. Generally therefore the Atayal seemed to be in a subordinate position within the economy of the area and its cultural facilities, and to lack the initiative and the capital to expand their role.

As for cultural identity in general, Hsieh also points out that the Atayal had lost their religion (by becoming Christians), their language (because of the educational system), their traditional organization (which had been replaced by the modern bureaucracy), and even their traditional dress. Even a local ethnographer doing research on Atayal culture was forced to gather most his material from older published sources and collections of artifacts rather than the people themselves. However, Hsieh continues:

> Nevertheless, it is interesting for us to note that Wulai's Atayal – who speak Mandarin Chinese, wear the same clothes as the Han people, live in modern concrete multi-storied houses, and believe in the social values of the Han Taiwanese/Chinese still distinguish themselves from the Han. The Atayal in Wulai call themselves "Daiyan" in opposition to "Mugan" (Taiwanese), "Kelu" (Mainlanders), and "Kelang" (Hakka). ... Regardless of different interpretations of the term Daiyan, the Wulai Atayal do identify themselves as Daiyan. (Hsieh 1994b: 193–94)

So how is this boundary maintained in the absence of traditional ethnic markers? It is partly a function of space, given that the Han Chinese and Atayal are located generally on opposite sides of the river. It is also partly a function of religion: the Atayal and other mountain peoples are mainly Christians. Neither of these, however, are traditional ethnic symbolic markers. Hsieh's conclusion stresses the important role of tourism:

> Activities related to the dance performances in Wulai form a contemporary Daiyan or Atayal cultural attribute ... When an independent people or ethnic group is identified or accepted, the most important thing for its members to grasp is what their culture or tradition is. Something must be counted as tradition, because a distinct people should possess its own particular culture. ... The Daiyan, faced with losing their original traditions, identify the dance performances for tourists as representative of contemporary Daiyan culture, even though the nature of the dance group combines traditions from all Taiwan aborigine groups. (Hsieh 1994b: 199–200)

Everybody seems to gain, therefore. The Korean and Japanese tourists are happy with the "authentic local culture" which they are paying for, and the local residents gain from it a comforting sense of identity and social solidarity, as well as an important source of income.

The Politics of Otherness

This brings us back full circle to the dancers of Hualien, the origins of whose costumes and performances are no doubt very similar to those of the Atayal of Wulai. For these dancers, staging Ami culture is "only work," a job which provides a reasonable standard of living. The lifestyles and housing of the Ami people of Hualien, based largely on the tourist trade, have improved along with the economic situation of Taiwan as a whole, speeding up the process of acculturation to the Han Chinese. But will the Ami themselves ever see this assimilation as complete and regard themselves as Han Chinese?

In part this is probably a political question which is discussed in another of Hsieh's papers (1994a). Here he is again concerned with the construction and maintenance of identity, but this time in relation to local and national politics. By the 1980s, he argues, the aborigines were on the point of disappearing as a separate group for a number of reasons: government policies of "amalgamation," i.e. assimilation; the belief on the part of the Han Chinese that Sinicization is inevitable; and economic threats by the government to open up the mountain reservations to development, ultimately destroying the aboriginal groups living there as viable communities. The aboriginal students interviewed by Hsieh saw themselves as treated negatively by the Han, and in public they reacted to this by trying to "pass" as Han. But an alternative reaction which developed during the 1980s was political mobilization to protect their ancestral heritage. The most important of the movements he describes was the Alliance of Taiwan Aborigines (ATA), which adopted a high public profile in publicizing its demands. Most of the members were graduates of Christian schools and seminaries. At first they were concerned with better services for aborigines, but gradually they became more and more concerned with the territorial issue, the control of the mountain reservations, and the "Han invasion" of aboriginal land. Clearly given the small size of the individual aboriginal groups, a united front was essential, and so the movement adopted the term *yuanzhumin* (aborigines) to refer to itself, rather than traditional terms such as *gaoshanzu* ("highland people"). The movement achieved a degree of unity and popularity, and some successes such as the decision by the government to change the status of the mountain reserve administration, even though these were regarded largely as cosmetic by many members. But by the late 1980s, membership had reached a plateau, and the movement's candidate was heavily defeated in the 1989 elections, a crushing blow to the membership.

Hsieh's conclusion is that even though the movement became popular among the young urbanized aborigines as Taiwanese politics were liberal-ized, it had failed to develop a local power base in the home area. This was because of three factors: the power of the state and the ruling party, the fact that the aboriginal peoples are scattered all over Taiwan, and the fact that they are divided into so many cultural and linguistic groups. Given the growing strength of local ethnic political movements in other parts of the world, greater influence in the future cannot be ruled out. Perhaps the most positive scenario is that of a small group of aboriginal representatives in the national parliament elected on the basis of proportional representation or reserved seats, collaborating with other parties on issues that concern them, in relation to minority rights, and environmental and welfare issues. A less attractive scenario also suggested by Hsieh is that of economic recession giving rise to local resistance and nihilism, and forms of mountain-based resistance and terrorism. The old sinister image of the mountains of Taiwan as being dangerous places beyond the frontier would then take on a new lease of life.

Currently, it could be argued, this is unlikely to happen. In addition to the continuing economic miracle, other forces in the 1990s seemed to be working to the advantage of the aborigines. Some of these stem from Taiwan's continuing dispute over sovereignty with China. As Ku's recent doctoral dissertation on the Paiwan shows well (Ku 2000), events at the national and international levels are having an effect on political movements and the political opportunities available at the local level. The end of of the KMT monopoly on power and the rise of the Democratic People's Party (DPP) has raised the debate about Taiwan's links with China and, by implication, its own distinctive identity, of which the aborigines form a part. Political competition has also increased the importance of the small group of aboriginal politicians with reserved seats in the legislature. A balance between competing major parties can create opportunities for smaller groupings which can lend their support in return for political concessions. If these kinds of conditions hold over time, it could be that the aborigines of Taiwan will continue to resist complete assimilation for some time to come, even if they rely on newly adopted symbols to do so. And these symbols may range from those which are clearly imported, such as Chrisianity, to cultural performances that appear, at least on the surface, more authentic and home-grown, such as the dances of Hualien.

Conclusion

In this paper I have discussed a sequence of stages of contact and acculturation, each accompanied by particular set of stereotypes and discourses in the accounts of contemporary observers. To the Dutch the aborigines suggested primordial nobility, while to the Chinese they represented a menace lurking beyond the frontier. The Japanese attempted policies of systematic pacification and educational assimilation, while the Christian missionaries saw the aborigines as a more attractive field for conversion than were the Chinese. Anthropologists saw the potential for a cultural revival and the development of a tourist industry, while contemporary scholars like Hsieh and Ku concentrate their attention on political mobilization. Clearly this sequence of discourses and issues has much in common with those used to discuss aboriginal minorities elsewhere on the Pacific rim, and they result from similar economic and political processes: colonization, competition and confrontation, domination and subordination, and the growth of a regional and global tourist industry. The outlines of a simple general model summarizing these processes might be traced as follows.

1. In the beginning aboriginal groups have the places where they live pretty much to themselves, developing societies based on either hunting and gathering, shifting agriculture, or, as in the case of Taiwan, both. Like various other groups on the Pacific Rim, the sheer wealth of the Taiwanese environment also gave rise to a rich local material culture, well represented in the collection of the Shung Ye Museum and the photographs in the monograph by Chen Chi-lu (1968).

2. Increasingly, as more advanced international economic and communications systems develop, the aborigines find themselves under pressure from more numerous, better organized and technologically more advanced settlers from outside in competition for land. In the Taiwanese case, the plains aborigines assimilated with the Chinese settlers. The groups in the mountains resisted, became increasingly hostile towards the newcomers, and established a de facto frontier based on a balance of terror. With the arrival of the Japanese, the balance of power shifted decisively against the aborigines. Like the Native Americans and other aboriginal minorities before them, the mountain aborigines of Taiwan found themselves up against overwhelming military and demographic pressures to assimilate and, in this instance, "become Japanese."

3. Pacfication eventually gives rise to a new set of parameters, and a new set of dominant groups with their own interests and agendas with regard to the aboriginal populations. In Taiwan, the picture was complicated by Japan's defeat in the Pacific War and the reversion of the island to Chinese rule. Christian missionaries now saw the aborigines as suitable candidates for conversion, and some aborigines on their part saw con-

version as a viable alternative to assimilation by the Chinese. Meanwhile the postwar Kuomintang regime gradually dismantled the mountain reservation system, making it possible for the Han to move in and the aborigines to move out. This left the aborigines as a generally disadvantaged group within the national labor market. Even though they were not dispossessed of their land by force, they had few other assets and in many cases they soon sold out. The result was a drift to the towns and cities, where the migrants often experienced disadvantage in the competition for jobs owing to a comparative lack of skills and educational qualifications.

4. With globalization and the rise of the tourist industry based on exotic regions and cultures, a new form of income becomes available for marginal minorities. The development of a tourist industry also fits well with the interests of local entrepreneurs, as well as with those of academics with a scholarly interest in material culture and performing arts such as anthropologists and museologists. The results of the tourist industry can hardly be said to be historically "authentic" and many of the cultural forms which the tourists enjoy are "invented traditions" based on motifs drawn from the aboriginal population of Taiwan as a whole, as well as from aboriginal groups further afield. But as Hsieh argues, they have provided a new set of ethnic markers as well as a sense of cultural unity for these peoples, as groups of aborigines in different areas of the island increasingly make use of a common pool of ideas in their cultural performances. How far these new-found sources of income will be able to help the aborigines overcome the economic disadvantage from which many of them have long suffered remains an open question.

5. Finally, there is a possible fifth stage, with the appropriation of aboriginal culture as a national icon in the debate over the island's future and its relations with the regime on the mainland. This is a process which is already well-established elsewhere in the Pacific Rim. Visitors to Vancouver Airport are greeted not by displays of British and French culture, but by exhibitions of Inuit and Northwest Coast art. Canadians, Australians, and New Zealanders make free use of minority aboriginal cultures to stress their differences from the rest of the Anglophone world. In the same way, a resurgent nationalism in Taiwan could result in the use of its aboriginal cultures to symbolize Taiwan's otherness in relation to mainland China, as well as its ancient links with Southeast Asia and the Pacific.[12] A typical result of this appropriation is that the aboriginal groups become politically and culturally more visible, and are able to

renegotiate some aspects of their position in relation to the dominant groups and political parties within the state as a whole. At the level of individual identity, multilingualism, social mobility and intermarriage mean that an increasing number of people can claim membership of multiple ethnic groups, together with access to the resources which these groups control. Thus, in a postmodern and globalized world, aboriginal culture seems destined to become increasingly commoditized and appropriated in forms increasingly separate from people's daily lives, like the dances of Hualien. Meanwhile, aboriginal identity will increasingly become a question of lifestyle choice and personal advantage in the increasingly homogenized consumer culture to be found in present-day Taiwan and the other high-speed growth regions of East and Southeast Asia.

Notes

1   This paper is largely based on material collected during a brief field trip to Taiwan in September 1996 as part of the research activities of the Shung Ye Taiwan Aborigines Research Group in Japan. I am grateful to Michio Suenari and the other members of the group in Japan, to the Shung Ye Museum of Formosan Aborigines in Taipei who made funding available, and the staff of the Academia Sinica for providing excellent accommodation and library facilities. An earlier version of the paper was presented at the International Congress of Anthropological and Ethnological Sciences held in Williamsburg, VA, July 1998. This was before the earthquake of 1999 which devastated much of the aboriginal tourist industry.

2   The Ami on the east coast of the island are the largest of the surviving Taiwan aboriginal ethnic groups. Others include the Saisyat, Atayal, Sedeeq, Bunun, Rukai and Paiwan, extending from north to south in the center of the island, the Puyuma on the east coast, to the south of the Ami, and the Yami who live on an island off the coast. Variant spellings of the names of all these groups are common. See Chen (1968: 8–14) for a discussion of the classification of the aboriginal groups and its problems. Most of the "plains" aboriginal groups to the north and west of the island have been assimilated to the Chinese population, and their distinctive languages and cultures have been lost, while others like the Kvalan (Shimizu 1991) are in rapid decline.

3   Much of the earlier material was collected together in Davidson's monumental history (1903). See also the bibliography on English languages sources on Taiwan compiled by Chen (Zhen) Ruo-shui (1994). For a

useful recent review of the Japanese literature on the Taiwanese aborigines, see Suenari (1998). Much of the most recent Japanese research on these groups is published in the Japanese language journal, *Taiwan Genshumin Kenkyû* (Studies of Taiwan Aborigines), edited annually by the Shung Ye Taiwan Aborigines Research Group from 1996 on. A detailed bibliography of postwar Japanese research on Taiwanese Aborigines by Kasahara (1997) has also been published by this group, along with a general introductory monograph (Shung Ye Taiwan Aborigines Research Group 1998).

4   The most detailed account of this process is that of Shepherd (1993). See also the paper by Chen Chiu-kun (1994) and the brief references in Ka (1994: 27–30).

5   For an extended account of these events, see chapters 18–22 of Davidson (1903: 257–370).

6   For an account of Japanese colonial rule in action, see the quotations by Rutter below (Rutter 1923).

7   See for instance the volumes edited by Chen et al. (1994), Harrell and Huang (1994) and Rubenstein (1994), which include papers on the aborigines by Chen Chiu-kun (1994), Martin (1994), and Hsieh (1994a, 1994b). Otherwise they concentrate on the Han Chinese, as does the full-length study by Wachman (1994).

8   Much of the work of these authors is listed in the bibliography prepared by Suenari (Suenari, Eades and Daniels eds. 1995: 292–326).

9   The major recent exception is the historical study by Shepherd (1993), already mentioned, together with earlier work such as that of Raleigh Ferrell (e.g. 1966).

10   The Dutch accounts of the island dating from the brief period of Dutch colonial rule in the early seventeenth century are extremely rich, particularly those of George Candidius and Frederic Coyett. For English translations, see the works by Campbell (1903), and de Beauclair (1975). A useful bibliography of early work is contained in Imbault-Huart (1968).

11   The main recent account in English of the Japanese colonial period in Taiwan is that of Ka (1995), and though he has little to say about the position of the aborigines, apart from a few historical comments on their relations to the Chinese during the Qing period. Ching (2001) deals with Taiwanese identity formation and colonialism, including a valuable chapter on the aborigines (2001: 133-73) which I draw on here.

12   The transnational approporiation of aboriginal culture is already a fact of life, as was shown in the mid-1990s furore over the inclusion of the voice of an Ami farmer, Gwo Li Feng (Kuo Di-fang) by the German pop group, Enigma, in their song "Return to Innocence." Gwo's singing had

been recorded by the French cultural ministry, which then sold the material to Enigma without the knowledge of the Taiwanese, raising complex issues of intellectual property and its ownership. Though he was never apparently given credit for his singing in the Enigma record notes, Gwo/Kuo did become a minor celebrity on the ethnic music scene. See "Pop group Enigma's use of Taiwan folk song stirs debate," National Public Radio, 11 June 1996, and "World music singer Difang of Taiwan's Ami tribe dies at 81," Kyodo World News Service, March 29, 2002. Both of these are available through the Electric Library Internet site (www.elibrary.com).

References

Campbell, William. 1903. *Formosa under the Dutch: Described from Contemporary Sources with explanatory notes and a bibliography of the island.* London: Kegan Paul, Trench, Trubner & Co.

Chen, Chi-lu. 1968. *The Material Culture of the Formosan Aborigines.* Taipei: Southern Materials Center Inc.

Chen, Chi-lu. 1987. *People and Culture.* Taipei: Southern Materials Center Inc.

Chen, Chiu-kun. 1994. "State, propriety rights, and ethnic relations in Ch'ing Taiwan, 1680–1840," pp. 25–39 in *Ethnicity in Taiwan: Social, Historial and Cultural Perspectives*, eds. Chen Chung-min, Chuang Ying-chang and Huang Shu-min. Taipei: Institute of Ethnology, Academia Sinica.

Chen, Chung-min, Chuang Ying-chang and Huang Shu-min eds. 1994. *Ethnicity in Taiwan: Social, Historial and Cultural Perspectives.* Taipei: Institute of Ethnology, Academia Sinica.

Chen (Zhen), Ruo-shui. 1994. *A Bibliography of English-Language Sources for Taiwan History.* Taipei: Lin Ben-Yuan Foundation for Chinese Education and Culture.

Ching, Leo T.S. 2001. *Becoming Japanese: Colonial Taiwan and the Politics of Identity Formation.* Berkeley: University of California Press.

Cohen, Abner. 1974. "Introduction," in *Urban Ethnicity*, ed. Abner Cohen. London: Tavistock.

Davidson, James W. 1903. *The Island of Formosa, Historical View from 1430–1900.* New York: Macmillan.

De Beauclair, Inez ed. 1975. *Neglected Formosa: A Translation from the Dutch of Frederic Coyett's "'t Verwaerloosde Formosa."* San Francisco: Chinese Materials Center Inc.

Ferrell, Raleigh. 1966. "The Formosan tribes: a preliminary linguistic, archaeological and cultural synthesis," *Bulletin of the Institute of Ethnol-*

ogy, Academia Sinica 21: 97–126.

Freytag, Justus. 1968. *A New Day in the Mountains. Problems of Social Integration and Modernization Confronting the Tribal People in Taiwan.* Tainan: Tainan Theological College Research Center.

Harrell, Stevan and Huang Chun-chieh eds. *Cultural Change in Postwar Taiwan.* Boulder, Colorado: Westview Press.

Hobsbawm, Eric. 1983. "Introduction," pp. 1–14 in *The Invention of Tradition,* eds. E. Hobsbawm and T. Ranger. Cambridge: Cambridge University Press.

Hsieh, Shih-chung. 1994a. "From *Shenbao* to *Yuanzhumin*: Taiwanese aborigines in transition," pp. 404–19 in *The Other Taiwan: 1945 to the Present,* ed. Murray A. Rubenstein. Armonck, NY: M.E. Sharpe.

Hsieh, Shih-chung. 1994b. "Tourism, formulation of cultural tradition, and ethnicity: a study of the Daiyan identity of the Wulai Atayal," pp. 184–201 in *Cultural Change in Postwar* Taiwan, eds. Stevan Harrell and Huang Chun-chieh. Boulder, Colorado: Westview Press.

Imbault-Huart, C. 1968. *L'Ile Formose: Histoire et Description.* Taipei: Ch'eng-Wen Publishing Co.

Ka, Chih-ming. 1995. *Japanese Colonialism in Taiwan; Land Tenure, Development and Dependency,* 1895–1945. Boulder, Colorado: Westview Press.

Kasahara Masaharu. 1997. *Nihon no Taiwan Genjumin Kenkyu Bunken Mokuroku* [1945–1966]. Tokyo: Fukyosha.

Ku, Kun-Hui. 2000. "Church, State and the Aboriginal Rights Movement in Taiwan: A Case Study of the Paiwan." PhD dissertation, Department of Social Anthropology, University of Cambridge.

Mackay, George Leslie. 1896. *From Far Formosa: The Island, Its People and Missions.* New York: Fleming H. Revell.

Martin, Howard. 1994. "A cultural account of Chinese-Aborigine relations in Ch'ing dynasty Taiwan," pp. 41–73 in *Ethnicity in Taiwan: Social, Historical and Cultural Perspectives,* eds. Chen Chung-min, Chuang Ying-chang, and Huang Shu-min. Taipei: Institute of Ethnology, Academia Sinica.

Mendel, Douglas H. 1970. *The Politics of Formosan Nationalism.* Berkeley and Los Angeles: University of California Press.

Rubenstein, Murray. A. 1994. *The Other Taiwan: 1945 to the Present.* Armonck, NY: M.E. Sharpe.

Rutter, Owen. 1923. *Through Formosa: An Account of Japan's Island Colony.* London: T. Fisher Unwin.

Shepherd, John R. 1993. *Statecraft and Political Economy on the Taiwan Frontier, 1600–1800.* Stanford, California: Stanford University Press.

Shimizu Jun 1991. *Kuvaranzoku: Kawariyuku Taiwan Heichi no Hitobito.* Kyoto: Akademia Shuppankai.

Shimizu, Jun 1995. "Worshipping plural ancestors: mechanisms of change among the Sinicized Kvalan," pp. 225–47 in *Perspectives on Chinese Society: Anthropological Views from Japan*, eds. M. Suenari, J.S. Eades and C. Daniels. Canterbury; University of Kent.

Shung-Ye Taiwan Aborigines Research Group. 1998. *Taiwan Genjumin Kenkyû e no Shôtai* [Introduction to the Aborigines of Taiwan] Tokyo: Fûkyôsha.

Shung-Ye Taiwan Aborigines Research Group. 1996–1999. *Taiwan Genjumin Kenkyû* [Research on the Aborigines of Taiwan], vols. 1–4. Tokyo: Fûkyôsha.

Suenari, Michio. 1995. "Becoming Chinese? Ethnic transformation and ancestral tablets among the Puyuma of Taiwan," pp. 204–24 in *Perspectives on Chinese Society: Anthropological Views from Japan*, eds. M. Suenari, J.S. Eades and C. Daniels. Canterbury: University of Kent, Center for Social Anthropology and Computing.

Suenari, Michio. 1998. "Exodus from Shangri-La? Anthropological studies in Japan of the Aborigines of Taiwan after 1945," *Japanese Review of Cutural Anthropology* 1: 33–66.

Suenari, Michio, J.S. Eades and C. Daniels (eds) (1995). *Perspectives on Chinese Society: Anthropological Views from Japan*. Canterbury; University of Kent, Centre for Social Anthropology and Computing.

Wachman, Alan. M. 1994. *Taiwan: National Identity and Democratization.* Armonck, NY: M.E. Sharpe.

Index

253

Index

Index

Index

Index

www.ingramcontent.com/pod-product-compliance
Lightning Source LLC
Chambersburg PA
CBHW060031030426
42334CB00019B/2275